D1760330

TWICE BORN

HEALING THE PAST-CREATING A NEW FUTURE

written by Premartha and Svarup
produced and published by
Books On Demand GmbH, Norderstedt
ISBN : 978-3-8334-6602-1

ACKNOWLEDGEMENTS

To write this book has been a real adventure. With it, we have been traveling through the peaks and valleys of creation. We feel blessed to have met on our way so many friends.

We would like to mention those that have contributed in creating this book.

All the friends who participated in our groups and trainings. Their innocence, trust and courage have been a great inspiration. It has been a real gift to see through them the childlike essence of existence being reborn.

All the friends that supported us in offering our work, the Center and Commune members. The organisers. The incredible support from "lo staff", with each group a different combination, a unique international melting pot of lovers and friends.

The friends of the Osho resort in Pune, who gave us the opportunity to develop our work and to do research in Osho's discourses on childhood.

Special thanks to our parents. Even though the journey of Deconditioning has led us through deep valleys with them, we again found them back, transformed, as part of the sunlit peaks. We bow down to them.

An intimate and sweet thank you to each other for this never ending adventure we are on.

And, finally, in Grace, thank you Osho.

With love,
Premartha and Svarup

TABLE OF CONTENTS

TWICE BORN

HEALING THE PAST-CREATING A NEW FUTURE

DWIJA,

THE TWICE BORN.

ONE BIRTH HAS BEEN GIVEN TO YOU

BY YOUR PARENTS, THE OTHER BIRTH IS WAITING.

IT HAS TO BE GIVEN TO YOU BY YOURSELF.

YOU HAVE TO FATHER AND MOTHER YOURSELF.

THEN YOUR WHOLE ENERGY IS TURNING IN —

IT BECOMES AN INNER CIRCLE.

(Osho, The Beloved, Vol. 1)

PROLOGUE

Beloved.
Welcome to our book.
We are happy to meet each other in this way.

This book is the sum of what we have gathered by working as spiritual therapists in the field of childhood issues for the last twenty-five years.

We both specialize in Primal (childhood deconditioning) and Tantra (sexual deconditioning) therapy. We offer them in the form of therapy and growth groups and in the form of individual work.

Our work takes place in the West as well as in the East. In the West, we travel all over Europe and in the East we are located in India.

There are many sources which have contributed to the creation of this book. Several of them you will find mentioned in our bibliography and quotes. We thank each one for enriching our work immensely.

Our main source of learning and inspiration has been the enlightened master Osho and our participation in the life and work of the commune around him. As early as in the nineteen sixties, Osho emphasized the importance of integrating Western therapy methods with the Eastern meditative approach. We both came to his commune with backgrounds in psychology and philosophy. We benefited personally as well as professionally from the multitude of new methods introduced into the field of spiritual therapy that arose around him. We learned that spirituality and therapy do not need to be in opposition to each other. Rather, both can support each other and, through that, create new levels of understanding and meditation. As we got involved in sharing and teaching the work we love, we started adding those new insights and methods to the skills we brought with us.

Over the years, this has grown into our own style of work. The work is focused on childhood and sexuality issues. Our expression and understanding of it remain constantly evolving and growing.

Our vision is that by working on these issues, people make space to create a joyful and total life style for themselves, unencumbered by the past. Furthermore, they will be able to enter more easily into the adventure of meditation.

Group work is a very powerful form of therapy. In the groups we offer, the participants are given the opportunity to work together on their issues. This allows people to help and support each other in the "original pain" work we do. Also, they can share the joy and pleasure that comes in being like children again.

THE CHILDHOOD DECONDITIONING WORK

In this work, we are offering group therapy, under the name Twice Born Primal, and single sessions exploring the same theme. Next to that, we offer an individual childhood process called Twice Born Childhood Deconditioning. This process works over an extended period. It is designed as a series of ten sessions in which we gradually move through a healing journey, that from school time moves all the way back to conception.

"Healing the past - creating a new future" is not only a journey through memories and facts. It is a "reliving" of our past experiences, in which our body, our feelings, and our mind are engaged in their totality. We become the child again, and experience past events with all our senses. At the same time, we learn to take distance as adults to review these events with the compassion and understanding that comes with our maturity.

As we move back in time, from early school-age years to conception, we explore the developmental stages that we go through as children. In this way, the specific issues associated with each different period can be addressed, like the peeling of an onion layer by layer toward the core.

At each stage of this journey, we meet that child that we were at that age. Some of us might think that it is difficult to have access to our childhood experiences. We can't recall anything consciously anymore. Forgetting it all might have been the protection we found as children to deal with the pain of these past experiences. We don't intend to invalidate this protection. Rather, we will slowly work on regaining our trust, so that whatever is held inside can surface.

As we reach the earlier period of our lives, say from age three back, visual memories become less available. The world of that time is less defined, and yet it has left a very deep imprint close to our core. For that period, we will need to trust what we feel. This might contradict what we have been told about ourselves, but the child inside us needs to feel validated in its experience, no matter what its environment, family, and parents present as the facts of that time.

From there, we move even further back than birth, into the womb and to the moment of conception. We touch a space (from the third month back) which is on the border of becoming an individual, and on the edge of the mysterious. The Tibetan Buddhists have widely experimented with this dimension, which includes the experience of choosing the parents and the womb through which we take birth once again.

This part of our process becomes a shared experience into the realm of the unknown. It is like getting a glimpse of the discontinuity, from formlessness to body, from light to matter. It is a metaphor to get a taste of the spark, the impulse which brought us into this life.

What we offer for each stage of development is a process of reliving, expressing, healing and understanding. We describe what happens at each stage by focusing on which emotions are blocked or disowned during that time, what effect their repression has on our bodies and mind, and which inborn essential qualities are lost through that. This opens up the possibility for each one of us to rediscover and support the unpolluted forms of our energy. We start off on a journey of retrieval of different aspects of our lost essence: courage, love, trust, being, among others.

To facilitate the entry into each issue, we decided to create one method for each stage that differs in its approach from the others. The techniques vary from guided regression, Gestalt, Reichian Pulsation, Family Constellation, and emotional release work to rebirthing. They apply to different stages of the journey back in time. They also open different channels of perception, so that through our different senses, we can regain access to memories which are stored in our bodies.

With this understanding, we can set off on our journey without worrying at all whether or not we have conscious memories of our past. We will rediscover them anyway, stored in our bodies and in our present patterns of relating and moving in the world.

So, when in the theoretical section we refer to a certain age (for instance three to five years old for the issue of sexual identity), there is no need to struggle to recall memories of that time if they are not available. The influence of that time will be revealed and visible through other events in a later period of life, in our bodies, in the feelings we still carry inside from that time.

What we offer through this book is a "map" for traveling through your childhood. The journey itself brings different experiences for each individual. By following the guidelines we offer, you can start exploring the territory yourself. But, as in any travel though an unknown or forgotten territory, it is good to have a guide who has covered the ground already, who can notice things along the path which your eyes might not be attuned to seeing.

In this way, reading and experimenting with the methods offered in this book is a good beginning for getting acquainted with the issues of childhood. Nevertheless, what actually happens in sessions or groups with a trained facilitator is different: in the sessions, we will ask you questions, suggest that you stop wherever you meet difficult passages "on the road" and feel what is going on, or we point out where on your journey you are taking a turn that prevents you from continuing.

In the groups, there is the extra support from the other group participants. Their commitment to the exploration of their childhood becomes a great inspiration. Their tears and laughter activate new sources of energy inside of us. Their trust and opening up act like an invitation for our own inner child to surface again, so that we can heal its wounds.

Some of us might explore the map of this journey alone before, to prepare ourselves well for the adventure we are setting off on. This book will be of help for them also, like a good friend on the road.

TWICE BORN, A SHARING OF OUR EXPERIENCE

When we felt the inspiration to write a book on the Childhood Deconditioning process, the first thing that became clear was that we would like to bring in our own personal experience of returning to our childhood, and how we learned to support and heal the child inside of us.

This is in contrast to the classical view on therapy, in which the therapist has to remain neutral to be able to facilitate his or her client.

Around Osho, we have been carefully taught to not trespass and invade the client's boundaries, be it physically, emotionally, or sexually. At the same time, we have been invited to be honest about ourselves, to admit the limitation of our own perspective, and to share only that which we have experienced ourselves.

To a question from one of his therapists on this subject, Osho answered:

> The therapist is in the service of life. He has to create life-affirmative values by living them himself, by going to the silences of his heart.
>
> The deeper you are within yourself, the deeper you can reach into the heart of the other. It is exactly the same... Because your heart or the other's heart are not very different things. If you understand your being, you understand

everybody's being. And then you understand you have also been foolish, you have also been ignorant, you have also fallen many times, you have also committed crimes against yourself and against others, and if other people are still doing it there is no need of condemnation. They have to be made aware and left to themselves; you are not to mold them in a certain framework.

Then it is a joy to be a therapist, because you come to know the interiority of human beings -- which is one of the most secret hiding places of life. And by knowing others you know yourself more. It is a vicious circle; there is no other word -- otherwise I will not use the word "vicious."

Allow me to coin a word: it is a virtuous circle. You open to your patients, participants, and they open themselves to you. That helps you to open more, and that helps them to open more. Soon there is no therapist and there is no patient, but simply a loving group helping each other. (1)

So, on our yearly retreat to India when we stopped over in Goa, we decided to write about our own childhood, following the methods we use in our sessions and groups. We did most of it on the beach at the seaside, our inner exploration accompanied by the sound of waves lapping the shore.

Each person's exploration of their childhood is unique. Because of this, the account you find can be different from the one you will experience when you do the work yourself. Going back in time, we write about our experiences, describing our inner process as it unfolds.

Neither do we want to offer it as a model outcome of the work, nor do we want to offer it as a literal application of the methods we offer in each session. Rather, the way we would like you to use it is as an evocation, a support for bringing up memories of your own past, and discovering the child inside you.

This book is structured on three different levels:

• We start each chapter with a theoretical section. It gives you an in-depth understanding of what happened to the child in each part of its individual development. In this section, we are happy to quote from the many sources that are so precious to us. In addition, we share our experience in the work through "case histories," giving you examples of what can happen, and a taste of the interaction that becomes possible when a trained "guide" is available.

• In the middle, is our personal story; we call it the "evocation."

• At the end, you will find a short "Recipe". This Recipe can support you to connect with your own childhood. In a simple way, it leads you back in time, and helps you to discover what issues coming from there need healing.

If the understanding arises that you need to do the childood work under guidance, contact us or our students. we will be able to direct you towards the sessions or groups, that are available in your vicinity.

BE AWARE: The methods described in this book are not meant to replace any therapy or therapy group you might be already involved in. If you have been diagnosed as mentally ill, or are undergoing pharmaceutical treatment, professional help is essential for you.

If while reading these methods you start to experience emotions that are beyond your capacity to contain, you need to take a break from reading, and look for the help of a trained therapist with whom you can exlpore the issues that surface.

WHERE DO THESE NAMES COME FROM?

You might have already felt surprised when you read both our names, Premartha and Svarup. You might have asked yourself, "Where do they come from? And who is who?" These are the names we received when we decided to take initiation and become sannyasins, disciples of Osho. They have beautiful meanings and indicate in their own way the direction of our personal spiritual search. Sannyas names are unisex: both men and women can have the same names. Here, Premartha is the name for the man. You will meet his inner child by the name Wimke. Svarup is the name for the woman. Her inner child is called Manú.

We are aware that just changing one's name is not sufficient forchanging the old patterns, habits, and beliefs we carry inside. But when we reach the point in our life in which we feel ready for a second birth, the birth to ourselves, for some of us it feels right to demonstrate this with a change of name. It becomes a symbol for the next stage of the journey. The only thing that we can truthfully share about it, is that it has been very helpful for us, and that we both enjoyed the new sound and the new meaning of it.

Because of the large interest in this process, we offer trainings for people to learn it. In these trainings, we teach the theory as well as allow people to experiment with each technique for themselves. The participants work on the issues with co-participants or with us, the training leaders. These trainings are conducted in several countries in Europe and America. Some of the participants join because they like to undergo an in-depth experiential process on childhood issues, others join in because they want to learn how to apply this method in their work as therapists. For those who are interested in offering the Childhood Deconditioning series of sessions in its official format we offer further apprenticeship and specialized training. When they complete this successfully, they are allowed to use the name and to offer the work in its original format.

After offering these trainings for many years, we have gathered from them an international, beautiful, and talented group of students. Several of them are now successfully offering the series of sessions in their own countries. Few of them, have graduated and are now starting to offer weekned groups in Childhood Decodnitioning work. We are proud to introduce them to you. For more detailed information, please visit our website:

www.primaltantra.com

With love,
    Svarup and Premartha
    svaprem@yahoo.com

INTRODUCTION

> The child never dies...nothing ever dies. The child is there, always is there, wrapped by other experiences...Wrapped by adolescence, then by youth, then by middle age, then by old age...but the child is always there.
> You are just like an onion, layers upon layers, but if you peel the onion, soon you will find fresher layers inside. Go on deeper and you find more and more, fresher layers. The same is true about man: if you go deep into him you will always find the innocent child...And to contact that innocent child is therapeutic.
> (Osho, *The Wild Geese and the Water*)

THE CHILD IN US IS STILL ALIVE

The child in us is still alive.

In the Western psychological tradition, from Freud onward, this means that all the unresolved issues of our early childhood play an essential part in the way we behave, feel, and relate today.

In the Eastern spiritual tradition, from Buddha onward, this means that we were already born with the qualities of being, presence, individuality that are essential for the search. These qualities are still in us, waiting to be rediscovered and flower into a second birth.

What we would like to offer with this book is a synthesis of these two approaches, based on many years' experience working with people on childhood issues, on our interest in psychology, and on our love for meditation.

THE WESTERN APPROACH: HEALING OF THE WOUNDS OF CHILDHOOD

The Western psychological approach has brought great understanding and insight into the conditioning process that is at the root of our personality. Starting with Freud and Jung, all the way through Wilhelm Reich, Margaret Mahler, R. D. Laing, and a vast number of other authors and researchers, we now possess valuable information about the effects past wounds have on our present behavior and life.

Each child is born as an already sentient and perceptive being. A small child is entirely dependent on its parents' protection and love.

Parental conditioning has a great impact on each child. From the very beginning, the child needs to have an incredible natural intelligence to be able to adjust its responses to expectations.

In a simple way, "conditioning" means: what the conditions are that I need to fulfill so that I can receive the love and attention I need so badly in order to grow, feel seen, be nourished, appreciated, and welcomed.

Some of these conditions are passed down by parental rules and beliefs. Other conditions, especially those imparted at the earliest stages of childhood, are not overtly expressed by the parents or caretakers. The child is affected by moods, behaviors, and attitudes of which the parents themselves are not necessarily conscious. Some of us might be able to remember stopping ourselves from expressing or doing something just by the look in mother's or father's eyes, or by sensing their disapproval or fear. The rules and beliefs, as well as the energetic exchanges, become internalized later. They become part of us when we grow up. Our vision of ourselves, of love, and of the world around us is conditioned by them.

For instance, as adults, we might really want to say no to something or someone, but the early impression of the way our "no" was punished or not respected, prevents us from saying it without guilt or self-doubt. Or we feel a true need for closeness, a longing for intimacy, but the early experience of mother's hostility or rejection has left us with the belief that we are not worth being loved, or that trusting is dangerous.

At each stage of our childhood, the body, the feelings, and later the mind, register these conditionings. Layer by layer, our "ego" solidifies around them, with all its beliefs and fixed responses. What initially was an intelligently developed survival strategy in response to circumstances which we couldn't change, becomes an automatic way of acting, feeling, and thinking. We end up anticipating and recreating the same patterns again and again. Our personality is born: the "persona," our social mask.

Our soul carries a true need for an identity as part of its unfolding in the world. If we as children are not seen and mirrored for our true nature, then we learn to identify with what others mirror as our image. At the level of personality, we all carry the mostly unconscious belief that we can only belong, that we only have a place in life and an identity, by having an image of ourselves. An image that we can present to others.

Questioning our personality, our social image, brings up fear. Because underneath this image lies our original pain. It is an accumulation of unresolved feelings that cannot be expressed as part of the image we have of ourselves. We have repressed and hidden them. Most often, we do not even experience them any more. But these feelings persist in influencing and contaminating our adult life.

Even when our personality succeeds and achieves good results, if we have not worked on our original pain, our anger, sadness, and grief, it will just be a mask that hides the wounds of our childhood. At any moment, this wounded child can burst through our adult behavior and, in its feelings of being rejected and repressed, sabotage our adult life.

In working on this original pain, in helping it to come to our consciousness, to release and to heal, the effort to hold our personality together can relax.

As R. D. Laing says:

> Our capacity to think…is pitifully limited: our capacity to even see, hear, touch, taste and smell is so shrouded in veils of mystification that an intensive discipline of un-learning is necessary for anyone before one can begin to experience the world afresh, with innocence, truth and love. (1)

Underneath the layers of conditioning there is something else, very palpable and authentic. There is a child born already sentient, perceptive, and present in all its potential, a child with its own individuality.

THE EASTERN APPROACH: REGAINING INNOCENCE

From the East, came the inspiration to look at the child as a metaphor for our transformation. "Become a child again" is a sentence which weaves itself through most spiritual traditions.

It is an invitation to return to the original source, the innocence of a child. In the restfulness and inspiration of this inner space, actions arise as a response to the present rather than a reaction to the past.

In the world of spirituality, the conditioned child has no real substance: It feels very real to us only because, as long as we don't acknowledge and release the hurts of our childhood, we unconsciously behave like the wounded child we once were.

The child of Buddha and Jesus reflects the potential with which each and every one of us is born.

As babies, we all start off with a pure sense of being. There is no separation from the world, no division of good and bad, no anticipation of what could or should happen. This innocence allows an openness and an availability that has enormous potential.

On the Eastern path, this innocence carries great value. As children we have to lose it in order to learn the ways of the world. In the course of this process, we forget ourselves. However, when we regain it later with awareness, through exploring different spiritual techniques, this innocence leads us back to a space of individuality, self-remembrance. This dimension is not a product of the mind, it is neither conceptual nor analytical. It is a state of being, a sense of presence and spaciousness in which all effort or tension drops. We can still act in and exchange with the outer world. This actually has more truth and substance to it. But, at the deepest core, we remain unattached and disidentified in just being a watcher, the way newborn children are spontaneously.

In the Sufi tradition, as reintroduced and updated with psychological insight by A. H. Almaas and Faisal Muqqadam, the original wholeness and fullness we were born with is called "essence." In a multicolored and poetic way, they illustrate how different aspects of essence leak out and are lost throughout the stages of child development. They explain that this is mainly because our parents don't value or recognize these aspects, even in themselves. In this way, original trust is substituted with calculation or hostility, original strength is replaced with effort.

We are left with holes in the texture of our being. We try to fill them up with a self-image through our compensations, hopes, and dreams. On the spiritual path, we are confronted with these holes. Acknowledging them, allowing ourselves to experience the falsity of what we filled them with, and our lack of feeling them opens up the possibility for us to become receptive for essence to flow back in, and for our original fullness to return. As Lao Tzu says:

> When man is born, he is tender and weak; at death, he is hard and stiff. When things and plants are alive, they are soft and supple; when they are dead, they are brittle and dry. Therefore hardness and stiffness are the companions of death, and softness and gentleness are the companions of life. (2)

THE SYNTHESIS BETWEEN EAST AND WEST: OSHO

During these last 20-30 years, the age-old division between East and West has begun to dissolve. Maybe it is happening because of the boredom and depression that have infiltrated the wealthy West, or because the East is no longer contented with its fatalism. Or, because there is greater access now to information on both sides. Or it may have been caused by some more mysterious development in human consciousness. Whatever the reason, the separation is no longer clear.

The experiment in therapy and meditation that has grown around the enlightened master Osho, flowered precisely in that new spirit of synthesis between East and West.

From our involvement in this experiment and sitting in meditation with Osho, we received an alive transmission of what the books we had read and the therapies we had participated in had pointed out, and something more which no words could describe.

This experiment originated with the practical insight that the Western mind, with all its conditionings, ambition, compensations, is--a hard nut to crack: it is not so easy to sit and watch while being guarded, tense, fearful, and mistrusting. Behind these defensive strategies, there must be some original pain, rage, or wound that needs to come to the surface, to be acknowledged, expressed, and dissolved. Again and again, the cathartic methods in the active meditations created by Osho, and the emotional release techniques applied in therapy groups which take place in his communes prove to be followed by a sense of lightness and a spaciousness which make disidentification easier. "Sitting and watching" becomes associated with a state of relaxation rather than with renunciation or suppression.

Throughout the years of experimenting with many different therapy methods, there has come, along with the initial expression of raw "negative feelings," a greater understanding of how conditioning occurs. More refined methods are used to support the process of disidentification from the personality, on a physical, emotional, and mental level. This has developed into what is known today as "Osho Spiritual Therapy."

Meanwhile, as the practice of meditation has deepened around the Master, "the child" has also become a conscious metaphor for the innocent, unpolluted presence which arises in the moments when we lose our identification with the mind.

In this way, the work in field of child development becomes a living bridge to meditation: as the ground is cleared from the misunderstandings and hurts of our past, a space of love and appreciation of our original nature can support us on our search.

Just before leaving his body, Osho created a "meditative therapy" process called "Born Again." For seven days, for one hour each day, the participants can "do whatever they could not do as children." For the second hour, after having experienced their original child energy, the participants sit and watch what comes to their consciousness. This is a direct transformation of the energy released by playing, regressing into a child's body, and just being like a baby, into silence and watchfulness.

FROM CONDITIONING TO BEING

Regaining connection with the child, which is both our past and future, is the theme of this book. The child of the past needs to be healed in its original pain, and the child of the future needs to reclaim its individuality.

What we offer here is not exclusive or esoteric knowledge. Nor do we claim that we have reached more than a sincere longing and a deep commitment to come back home to ourselves.

We simply love to share our experience in working with people, and in this way, to contribute to the synthesis of therapy and meditation happening all over the world.

Our work contains an invitation to grow up, rather than to grow old and fade away into resignation or respectability. Through the work we do, we reclaim the child in us. We can learn to support ourselves to be there and take responsibility for the child, thus discontinuing the patterns that create separation and pain.

Looking at oneself as "still a child at the core" is a very juicy, rich, and colorful approach. No renunciation of the pleasures of the world is required for this. Just a growing awareness of when our real joy in life is prevented by the compensations and dreams with which we cover our old wounds.

We want to wipe away the dust in our "house" so that more light can enter, enabling us to live a life that is authentic in both being and action.

It is not our intention to present any ideal life style or specific behavior as the door to "real transformation." What we like to share is the joy that comes with rediscovering our inner sense of being here, responding to whatever comes to us with maturity and openness, and with having the courage to be an individual, whatever the expression of it is.

This sense of being here as an individual is something we all have experienced. When we are in love, or in meditation, or in an outburst of creativity, we have a taste of the fragrance of our inner world.

Those moments in our lives when we experience ourselves in our original nature are what makes life worth living, and move us on the search for more.

On our search for "more," we are all confronted with our conditioning. And to be able to move forward, we need to free ourselves from the unnecessary weight of the past. In this way, we can live our life in a light, joyful, and authentic way, entering into meditation unburdened.

The Childhood Deconditioning method helps us become aware of the image, ideas, and feelings about ourselves and others that don't originate from our experience in this moment, but are the result of conditioning. It will help us to remove those beliefs that prevent us from being present to what life offers us now.

We become more real

In the Childhood Deconditioning work that we do, we focus on the subjective truth of the client. This does not deny the objective truth of their past. For example, if somebody relates the facts of their childhood to us, such as the date they were born, or the year they started kindergarten, we leave these facts simply for what they are: objective recordings of that time.

When we come to the area of subjective truth, we make the choice to emphasize the importance of the client's own emotional reality. This sometimes contradicts what others around him or her felt in that same situation.

This choice is based on a very simple consideration: the material necessary for our own transformation will never be provided by the subjective truth of others. We cannot transform the feelings that others tell us we had, but we can transform our own feelings. In this way, we become more real.

In the "evocation" part of this book, we, as therapists, also expose the subjective truth of our past. If we were to ask our parents about it, we could agree with them on dates and facts, but if they were to share what they experienced within a certain moment in their life with us, it might be very different, even the opposite, from what we ourselves experienced in that moment. So, the parents you meet in the evocation are our parents of the past who we have internalized and, in this way, still carry around inside us. For all of us, it is those internalized parents that we have to let go of. This will make it possible for us to meet our parents for who they are now.

When we go deeply into our subjective truth, we come to an area where the level of collective truth is touched. Within this area, it is no longer our personal parents that we meet, but the archetypes they represent. Deep down, at the core of our connection to our individual parents, lies the connection of each child to its parents. In the same way that we learn through therapy to let go of our personal internalized parents, we learn through stories and myths on the collective level, to let go of the parental principle. There, lies the understanding that separating from the parents is and has always been a necessary step in the growth of each individual.

When we work with the subjective truth of the client, we do not involve our own subjective truth of our past. It is the art and skill of a good therapist to be able to leave his or her personal story out of the session room while the work is happening. Yet, it can help immensely to understand that at the core of all our experiences, therapists and clients alike, lie collective truths.

A RELATIONSHIP BASED ON FRIENDLINESS

At the beginning of psychoanalytical thinking, therapists were taught to keep a safe distance from their own issues while being involved with the client. Regrettably, much of this attitude was based on the patriarchal model of the world of that time, in which the parents kept that same safe distance from their children, making sure that they would never expose themselves. At that time, the therapist-client relationship became a copy of the parent-child relationship.

Therapists were also taught to be extremely aware of the transference coming from the client. The client might project on them an authority of the past, be it the ideal father or mother, or also the "bad" father or mother. Therapists would mirror this projection, and keep themselves invisible and aloof.

Our understanding, based on a time in which the patriarchal model of the world is slowly losing its hold, is that the relationship between therapist and client can be one of friendliness.

Therapists do not have to present an ideal image of the unreachable person. They can be there with all their skills and talents, and yet make it clear that their experience has its limitations too, that what is being worked on is between two equals.

This does not eliminate the transference described earlier. It does, however, create a more relaxed context in which the client can be made aware that he or she is projecting the "good" or "bad" parent or authority of the past on the therapist, and the therapist need not be so extremely wary of fulfilling that projection. The client needs to go through this stage because of his or her narcissistic wounds around being acknowledged and loved, but the therapist can handle this with compassion, humor, and a sense of his or her own limitations. After all, the same might be true for the therapist who tries to fulfill his or her narcissistic needs through the client

This does not mean, however, that the therapist can invade the client with his or her own unresolved issues. It is important to stay aware of not replacing the patriarchal attitude with a dropping of all boundaries.

By letting the client know that we are human too, and that we are also healing our own wounded child inside, we give the client the full support and acknowledgment of what is happening to him or her. Instead of getting into the old fear that, as a result, the bonding between therapist and client won't function, we can enjoy that this bonding starts off from a realistic point. The client learns, by knowing all this, that the process is all about starting to take care of him or herself.

Of course, the therapist might not like this if there is a latent desire to keep taking care of clients for years. The therapist will let them return to his or her practice again and again, fostering the clients' hope of being presented with solutions, which in fact never come. But if we understand that childhood work is a necessary stage for each person who wants to grow, we can rejoice while it is happening and equally rejoice when it's done.

> *While leading groups and giving sessions in the Osho communal experiment, we had the opportunity to experience the friendliness mentioned above in its most nourishing form. After working together for the day in the roles of therapists and clients, we would all gather together in the evening and meditate. During the time of the meditations, we all stepped out of our roles, just sitting together as fellow travelers. This experience many times has generated in the clients the trust and relaxation that has made transformation possible. And, for us as therapists, the understanding that our part in the work is like planting a seed, which then needs a richer soil for it to grow and flower.*

CHAPTER 1

MEETING THE CHILD

> Go back…Just the light of consciousness heals.
> It is a healing force. Whatsoever you can make
> conscious will be healed, and then it will hurt
> no more.
> A man who goes backwards releases the past.
> Then the past is no more functioning, then the
> past has no more grip on him and the past is
> finished. The past has no place in his being.
> And when the past has no place in your being
> you are available to the present, never before
> it.
> (Osho, *Yoga the Alpha and the Omega, Vol. IV*)

WE SELECT OUR MEMORIES

How often during the day does it happen that we spontaneously touch situations of the past? Maybe the times we actually register this are far fewer than the times we don't. To use Freud's metaphor, our whole mind is like an iceberg: what we normally consider our mind is just the visible tip of an iceberg: under the dark waters, a much bigger part, called the unconscious, contains all our memories, our wounds, losses, hopes and dreams.

On a conscious level, we notice symptoms. We are aware that something feels uncomfortable or something is keeping us busy. We may leave it at that, ignore it, or try to move away from it. On an unconscious level, underneath the surface of the symptoms, lie the deep roots into the past. There we find the cause of what troubles us, created far back in time, and the ways we learnt to deal with it in that time.

According to the "time line" method of Neuro Linguistic Programming (NLP), which describes extensively how we create our own maps of reality, and act, communicate, and think according to them, we are "in time" in the moments that we are regressed into the past. In our subjective world, we are once again "in" it, as opposed to moving "through" it with conscious detachment. To be able to watch the movement through our past, we need to take on a position that is outside of it. In our book we call this position "the observer," or the "observer perspective."

As Robert B. Dilts points out:

> Our perception of "time" influences the way we give
> meaning to an experience. Most of us have had experi-
> ences in which something seems so important at a par-
> ticular moment; but when we consider it with respect to a
> larger time frame, wondered "why was I so caught up in
> that?"... Many mental and emotional symptoms are the
> result of a regression "in time," to past experience without
> having the choice of assuming the more distant "through
> time" observer perspective. As a result, a person uncon-
> sciously reacts in the present as he or she has done at an
> earlier time in his or her life. As an example, an individual
> who has a seemingly irrational fear of public speaking
> in certain circumstances may find that there was a time
> when he or she was made fun of or humiliated as a child
> in front of a class or a group of people. Even as an adult,
> similar circumstances may trigger associations back to
> the childhood situation which the person feels emotion-
> ally but is not conscious of mentally." (1)

We select our memories. According to Milton Erikson, we do
this because some of them are just too painful to be retained in the
conscious mind. In this sense, the unconscious mind functions as a
"protection," a way of making our emotional life more bearable.

We have learned to do this so early, that the mechanism of select-
ing has now gone on automatic. When certain memories come up,
they are erased immediately from the surface of our awareness. But
like weeds we want to eradicate, if we don't remove their roots, they
tend to become more entrenched. Our painful, unwanted, disturb-
ing memories, if denied their place in our waking world, grow even
deeper underground. As Freud already observed in the early days
of psychoanalysis, they might tend to claim our attention through
unexplainable physical symptoms. Or, as NLP demonstrates, they
tend to become the unconscious background of beliefs and values
for our present actions and feelings.

HEALING LIES IN REGAINING ALL OF YOUR PAST

We all have a longing to regain our past. Without it we are
uprooted. If our past remains in the dark, we cannot live fully. To
disconnect from what shaped our early life, takes much effort and
creates much anxiety . We need to regain our past. At the same time
we are afraid of this. What if the things that come up are too painful

or confusing for us? We actually put these very things away a long time ago because we couldn't handle them at that time. Our strategies to deal with what comes up from the past get quickly activated. Maybe we shrug our shoulders, and feel it as unavoidable--what has been has been. Maybe we turn on the TV, or read, or eat something, so the feelings which may be coming up are held in check or are kept at a distance.

But then there are situations which break through these delicate defense mechanisms. A friend, a lover, our husband or wife, our children, our boss, say something or do something, and before we know it, we react. And we react in ways that surprise us. "What was it exactly that made me so angry, or so sad? Was it maybe a word, or an expression, or was it the tone of voice that did it, or a certain way of looking, or touching?" Whatever it was, we suddenly fall and break through the safety net, crashing into something that we have been carefully avoiding for so long.

The way we are able to deal with it now is bound to the way we learned to deal with it in the past. The same collapse, the same fight, the same pulling back that we experienced as children suddenly can take over our adult consciousness.

Other times, what triggers these reactions is a critical life-changing event: a death, a disease, a divorce. For that moment, our sense of reality opens up into a gap, an abyss. The pain which is there might resonate into deeper layers of pain and abandonment. Even if our defense strategies are activated, we might not be able to avoid the depth that we experience in those moments.

In fact, just by allowing the pain that is triggered to surface, the balm of healing we are longing for starts becoming available to us.

Healing lies in regaining all of your past. And not just the pleasant parts. These are worthy and need to be cherished in all their sweetness and glory. But in the same way, the painful parts need to be regained, those who have wounded us, and we have closed off from. Once all this is integrated in our consciousness, all of it together it will constitute the very base of our strength and healing qualities today.

DISCOVERING THE LOVING ADULT INSIDE

When we use the word "healing," we want to add another dimension to the detached NLP perspective mentioned above. From the observer perspective, we are watching the two main parts in our work: the inner child and the inner adult.

In our way of integrating the past into our consciousness, we would like to include also love and compassion for the inner child. These feelings have to come from our inner adult. The child has a need to reveal its truth. It needs to share about the old parental beliefs and rules that have wounded and poisoned it. To be able to do this, the child needs to trust the strength and love that we have for it as an adult. It needs to trust that it really matters to us. It needs to know that we will stand up for it and protect it. Only then, will it be able to heal its wounds and relax into itself.

To be able to share with the child how much you care for it, you first need to connect with those resources from your adult experience that can help you to protect and nurture the "child-you."

The following exercise will help you with this:

> *Remember a time as an adult that you feel comfortable recalling, when you felt caring and loving. Perhaps a time when you were caring for a friend, for a plant, or an animal.*
>
> *Imagine that you can see this time, and the gentle expression of caring and loving it brings, as a picture in front of your eyes at a distance of about three feet.*
>
> *Allow your forehead to relax, and draw the energy of loving and caring into the place between your eyes. Experience it as an infinite source of loving energy flowing to this place, and from there, flooding through your whole body.*
>
> *Allow this energy to flow from the adult-you toward the child-you. To reach all the places inside the child where it got wounded, to bring love and care there.*

The same exercise, focused on strength or compassion, can help you to connect with those qualities in your adult life.

In this way, there is a growing connection between the loving adult and the child. A connection that finally will become a real love affair.

In contrast to the psychoanalytical tradition, our "child" is not just the sum of long-gone memories we continue to identify with: it is an alive presence that carries many gifts into our adult life.

Simultaneously, by experiencing the strength of standing up for the child, the adult in us gains trust and self-respect. Our adult energy starts being in the service of our child energy. By assimilating this childlike energy inside of us, our adult form starts to expand and loosen up, transforming its fixed and conditioned reactions into an alive and loving responsibility--the ability to respond to the moment as it comes.

Where this healing leads us, we cannot predict. It may bring us to a fuller, richer life; it may bring us to a deeper let-go, surrender.

Nevertheless, however it manifests, healing is bound to happen as we gather the pieces, the fragments of our lives, into a whole. We find ourselves again at the center of a unified existence.

The observer can be practiced, the witness happens

To make the difference clear between the "observer perspective" that we refer to in this chapter, and the "witness," our quality of witnessing that happens in meditation, we would like to add a part of a discourse given by Osho in which he answers a question on this subject:

> The observer means the subjective, and the observed means the objective. The observer means that which is outside the observed, and the observer also means that which is inside.
>
> The inside and the outside can't be separated; they are together, they can only be together. When this together-ness, or rather oneness, is experienced, the witness arises. You cannot practice the witness. If you practice the witness you will be practicing only the observer, and the observer is not the witness.
>
> Then what has to be done? Melting has to be done, merging has to be done. Seeing a rose flower, forget completely that there is an object seen and a subject as a seer. Let the beauty of the moment, the benediction of the moment, overwhelm you both, so the rose and you are no more separate, but you become one rhythm, one song, one ecstasy.
>
> Loving, experiencing music, looking at the sunset, let it happen again and again. The more it happens the better, because it's not an art but a knack. You have to get the knack of it; once you have got it, you can trigger it anywhere, any moment.
>
> When the witness arises, there is nobody who is witnessing, and there is nothing to be witnessed. It is a pure mirror, mirroring nothing. Even to say it is a mirror is not right; it will be better to say it is a mirroring. It is more a dynamic process of melting and merging; it's not a static phenomenon, it is a flow. The rose reaching you, you reaching into the rose: it is a sharing of being.
>
> Forget that idea that the witness is the observer; it is not. The observer can be practiced, the witness happens. (2)

The observer perspective gives you the right distance to notice the dynamic between the adult and child parts, and allows you to enter a place of non-involvement. The witnessing quality that grows out of this even lets go of this "outsider" place, moving beyond all separations into a truly existential merging. So, in its own time, this process leads us from feeling split, to observing duality inside, and finally, to experiencing unity inside and around.

BE OPEN FOR THE MYSTERY

As we go through the journey that begins in this chapter, we take you by the hand and walk the way back in time with you.

We also want to acknowledge and honor you for having the longing and the passion to go back in time and reconnect with the child that is there waiting for you.

> Deva S., a woman whom we will follow through eight sessions of the Childhood Deconditioning process, was insecure about starting her first session. She told us that she had had enough of looking into herself. And yet, she knew that something had not been cleared out about her past. In the session, she realized that only recently had she been able to imagine taking the little girl, the child she once was, into her arms, and to have loving feelings toward her. When our journey was completed, she was surprised how quickly the time had passed in the session, and how many memories had come to her.

Among other sources, our journey has been greatly inspired by the work of John Bradshaw, who imparted the technique of the adult journeying back to rescue and heal the child within:

> At first, it may seem preposterous that a little child can continue to live in an adult body. But this is exactly what I am suggesting. I believe that this neglected, wounded inner child of the past is the major source of human misery. Until we reclaim and champion that child, he will continue to act out and contaminate our adult lives. (3)

Unlike Bradshaw, who moves from infancy to school age, we move with you further and further back in time, peeling layer after layer of conditioned behaviors, toward the original nature that contains all our potential.

In the regression that we offer in the "recipe" of this chapter, we create an invitation for you as an adult to meet your younger self. The child you meet can be between the ages of four and ten. We do it in such a way that you are not only remembering and observing. In some parts of this work, you enter into your adult part, and in others you enter back into the skin of the child and relive what was there at that time. This means that, as you become that child, you feel yourself in the body of that child, you see through its eyes, you hear the sounds of your past through its ears, you smell and touch again what was there. You open up all your senses to this experience.

In some moments you are totally there again, in other moments not. Accept it as it comes.

As the adult, it is worthwhile though to notice what fully keeps your attention, and what makes you want to disconnect. It might indicate in which moments and situations in your childhood you learned to close off. Often, in these moments the only way you could handle them as a child was through spacing out, or through retreating into your dream world. This might be repeating itself in your adult life. Those are the points where ordinarily you lose attention, become disinterested, or turn around and leave. But because we are there with you, you may want to stay a bit longer and take a step further into it.

There may be a lot of surprises for you, the adult; there are things long forgotten and things that you never observed with such clarity. The journey back may also feel familiar, the feeling of having made it many times before. It can almost be shocking to realize what details of your past you have registered inside--to discover that even in very difficult or traumatic situations a part of us, or a part beyond us, remains watchful.

Some of you might notice, though, that even if you have detailed memories of the events of your past, and everything is sharply etched on the slate of your mind, you have no feelings associated with them. As the adult, you may realize now that you can remember each detail of what happened in that time, yet you cannot connect with those initial feelings.

If you report something like this to us after the regression, we ask you to breathe in and to connect with your body. We then focus on where and how in your adult body you are affected by those events of the past, and what is happening in those places. Often, by locating the place in the body (for example, belly, chest, or shoulders) and by experiencing the physical sensations in this place (for example, contraction or disconnection) it becomes more clear what feelings you learned to hold back in you childhood.

Or, as the adult, you might notice that when memories come up from the past, you easily get overwhelmed. Instead of being able to stay with the real feelings that are there, for example, sadness or anger, you find yourself reacting to them and trying to control them, resulting in an inner panic or fear. When this happens, take time to slow down. There is no use in judging yourself. Relax until the real feelings come up. It might take time, but it is worth it.

When we lead you back in time, you might feel expectations about what you should do or not do, show or not show. You have probably lost contact with your adult part and regressed into your child part, and from there you are listening to an internalized message from your past.

We will support you in recognizing this internalized voice, to disidentify from it, and to step into your adult position again. From there, you will be able to decide what is right for you, to feel your own feelings again, and be there for the child in you.

Or, it might be initially difficult to connect with the real feelings of the child because everything felt normal and uneventful in your childhood.

> *Cristina F. came from a middle-class family. No major trauma, separation, or violence had happened in her childhood. She in fact had the tendency to blame herself for her anxiety .*
>
> *As we moved back in time, she met for the first time as an adult, her younger self. To her surprise, she saw an expression of mistrust in the eyes of her little girl. When she tried to connect with her, she felt that the little girl was not as willing to open up as Cristina had remembered her. We encouraged Cristina to ask the child some questions, but there was no real answer coming. Only when Cristina started admitting to her helplessness and insecurity about what to do, did the child open up. Cristina became aware that this was exactly what had been missing in the little girl's relationship with her parents. They had never shown her any of their doubt or vulnerability. In this way, they had taught her to keep a constant check on her own feelings. The little girl now experienced for the first time an adult being openly insecure. Cristina's obsessive fear of making mistakes was exposed, and a healing process began.*

So, it is good to have a guide on your journey. A guide who has also gone down the path of his or her childhood, and knows the journey. A guide who is happy to share this journey with you, to lead you step by step backward, until you reach your own destination.

Be open for the mystery. We contain more than we often know. Yes, you are an adult now, and you move through life in an adult body. But, inside you, the child is still very alive.

Let yourself be led back in time. Reexperience the surroundings in which you grew up. And meet the people of your past again: your friends, teachers, parents, family. And meet your younger self again. As the adult, you can still reach the child you once were, back through time and space. Become that child again. Look at the world surrounding you, the world of your own childhood. And reconnect with your adult self.

It is a journey in which the adult meets the child in you. But it is also a journey in which the child meets the adult-you. From both sides there will be deep feelings coming up.

This meeting between both parts of you is the most important. It is the beginning of the work as we present it to you. Once this meeting has happened, the journey to regain your individuality has begun.

To meet inside, to look into each other's eyes, to listen to each other's messages, to feel the longing on both sides, to reach out in your own unique way creates the right base from where to begin the journey of Childhood Deconditioning.

Kabir says (4):

Friend, wake up! Why do you go on sleeping?

The night is over--do you want to lose

the day the same way?

THE EVOCATION

M<small>Y</small> <small>PERSONAL EXPERIENCE IN MEETING MY INNER CHILD</small>

S<small>VARUP</small>

Manú's home

I am going to meet manù, the little girl I once was. There is a
sweet mix of tenderness and curiosity in me, as I reach back to
the mid-fifties , entering a silent road on the outskirts of Padova.
On each side of it, there are neat one-family working class houses,
built with the sweat of honest work. Each house has a tiny garden
with dahlias, azaleas, daisies of all colors, vegetable patches with
lush zucchini and their meaty yellow flowers. I hear the rumbling
of an occasional Vespa, the shouts of children playing in a nearby
scrawny field. The whizzing of bicycles rushing past. The sound of
a radio from an open window: "Volare...." It is a modest, decent and
tidy neighborhood. It smells like polenta and goodness. It is popu-
lated by farmers turned into factory workers, shopkeepers. They
are all proud of their plastic flowers on the dinner table, their over-
sized dolls fitted in large, lacy satin dresses in pink and light blue,
languid centerpieces over their beds, and their fluorescent statues
of Mary and her Jesus child.

I turn around the corner. I enter a smaller street, newer. The
asphalt still smooth and dark. Occasionally, a Fiat ventures this
far out of the center of town. On each side of the street, there is a
crop of newer buildings, two, three stories high, clean, light-colored
little boxes, all with the same balconies, the same railings, with a
few geraniums struggling to break their inflexible geometry. There
is fruit shop at the corner: a magical world filled with smells, colors. Inside the shop, the radio blaring at full volume: a speaker is
commenting on the Tour de France. I remember the taste of a dried
carob in my mouth, that can keep you busy chewing for hours. Next
to the fruit shop, there is the grocery. I can feel again the luscious-
ness of melted surrogate chocolate on an oily paper, waiting to be
spread onto a crusty piece of white bread.

Just across the street, in a light gray apartment lock, stands the
first childhood home I can remember.

I stop in front of the main entrance door, its aluminium frame a
statement for progress in itself. I open that door, and walk up one
flight of stairs. Finally, I reach the entrance to our flat. It's identical to all the other doors, and yet I know I am at the threshold of
another world, safe and cosy, and also very very far from the sweet

neighborhood that surrounds it. I can hear the loudly-dressed, ageless Mrs. Pellegrini playing with her newly acquired mini-jukebox. I pass the door of the Malatesta children, with whom Manú plays funeral in an old trunk smelling of mothballs.

Slowly, I open the door to our flat. I smell freshly washed laundry, clean floors, a little hint of my mother's cucumber face cream. In the air, hangs a memory of much wider marble halls in a warm faraway country. I enter the kitchen: there is a table, a cream painted pantry, a few battered pots and pans shining with pride. I see the neatly stacked grocery store wrapping paper, the folded plastic bags. I move through the tiny corridor and pass by the dark room which is hardly ever entered. It has a green and black Arab blanket on the guest bed. This room is occupied once a year by relatives who bring halvah and stuffed dates from Tunis or Paris as a present.

I enter the living room. I see the proud, half-size library, the shrine of the family. It contains art books, detective novels, science fiction, and books by American writers. The little clay head made by mother smiles cheekily from the round wooden table. On the low four-legged table there are stacks of crossword puzzles. In the window corner, the oversize armchairs give the tiny room a feeling of nobility, which is far beyond the dreams of whoever planned it.

I move to the dining room, which is rarely used for this purpose. Towering in its central place, is the magic box: the television set, a wooden space-time machine. For Manú, it is like a crystal ball, a window into endless adventures and dreams.

I move to the bedroom. I can see the large double bed of my parents, with wooden carvings at the head, and clean sheets. The room emanates a feeling of twilight. On the right side, I see Manú's little bed. A faint scent of Eau de Cologne lingers in the twilight.

Mother is in the kitchen. Sometimes she sings her Edith Piaf songs, sometimes she stamps on the floor with determination. She is focused on channeling her energy onto the meal. She is a sculptor trying to be a cook, a political agitator trying to rearrange pots. The result is not too bad, a unique mix of French and Tunisian with the first hints of fast food...

Father is in the living room, listening to a cheery Benny Goodman on the phonograph. The lights are dim, and he is slouching in the armchair, finally free from his gray office suit, finally free to roam his inner world..

Both of them are maintaining dignity and purpose, even if the Communist dreams that had brought them to move here from their colonial homes in North Africa have dissolved.

Meeting Manú

Where is Manú? Where is her place in the house? I look for her in the kitchen, in the corner where her small table and chair are set. It is the place where she draws for endless hours, plays office like daddy, asks mommy a million questions while she cooks. Manú is there, sitting at her place, intent, drawing glamorous figures of music-hall dancers, ostrich feathers, net stockings, diamonds and sequins. She draws on the back of the grocery paper with a pen from daddy's office. She is wearing a gray pleated therital skirt, a dark blue pullover, and a slightly worn white-collared shirt. Her chubby hands are full of ink spots. Her curly dark hair is untidy. She is fully absorbed, as if the drawing has the magic power to carry her out of the kitchen, out of the suburbs, straight into the spotlights, dreams and sparkles.

Manú through the eyes of Svarup

Suddenly, she senses my presence. Maybe it's my different scent, a mix of sunshine and spices, maybe it's my voice, softly whispering for her attention.... She looks up and sees me, the adult woman.

At first, she is startled, then she just looks, and then she smiles. Her eyes close almost shut as her cheeks lift up, and the rosy determined mouth opens up to reveal a pearly row of teeth.

She is happy to see me; she recognizes the scent of her dreams, the soothing darkness of my appearance.. She is attracted by my long hair, flowing dress, and shiny earrings. I want to give her time to look deeper into me: there is no sense in hurrying it feels like a door is just opening. I just stand there, inviting.

She draws closer. She shows me her drawings, her eyes opening wider. I sit next to her, and together we enter her world, made of colours and visions.

Svarup through the eyes of Manú

It's time for the magic: I allow my consciousness to float out of my adult body, up and up, and to descend into the body of Manú. I experience my surroundings through her senses, and look through her eyes.

All around me is larger, everything feels more vivid and instense. In my tiny body lives a great desire to dance and move, beyond the four safe and loved walls of this apartment. In my legs and my heart, there is a great insecurity, a need for roots, for guidance.

I look at this adult woman standing there in front of me; she has something very familiar to me. She has long dark hair, is tall and stately. She smiles and she is warm. She seems courageous and soft. I know can trust her

She tells me, in a low, calm voice, that she has been searching, moving from place to place, living in many different ways. She admits that she forgot me, and then dreamed about me, and finally decided to find me again. All this gives me a sense of worth, of being important. It takes me a moment to let it in. I feel bigger, more real.

I come closer to her, I touch her hand. It is warm and steady, and a bit rough.

There is a silence, a new, relaxing feeling of silence. I put my curly head against her belly: a belly which grumbles, is alive with scars and feelings. She smells fine, of wind, faraway places, food, life juices and balm. Can I really relax? My breathing is a bit fast; I'm overwhelmed. She holds me, silently. I feel my belly, my legs, a sense of deep rest. I need so much to be touched. And she touches me in a simple way that feels like the earth. My heart is singing a soundless song..

Coming back into my adult body

I allow my consciousness to rise again and float upward, out of Manú's body, back into my adult body. I hold that small girl. She is nestled in my arms. Her body is alive and relaxed. It is a deply nourishing feeling, like holding the softest core of my being.. I feel a timelessness, a deep quiet, while I hold her. My heart is filling up with her innocence.

She looks at me. Her eyes are like stars, dark stars. Her questions start erupting, tumbling, one after the other. She wants to know all about the places I've been, the stories about what happened to me, the people I met.. Her curiosity is boundless.I talk to her, and share the richness of a lifetime, full of light and shadows, joy and pain.

Then, after the words, in a moment of silence and peace, our bellies met, and only the song of the angels can be heard. We can no longer turn away from each other.

It will take time to heal the wounds of the past, and polish the jewels of her being.

But it will be a beautiful adventure, the most real and rewarding of all myths and fairy tales that little Manù has always loved.

As I move back to the present, I treasure inside me the very alive presence of a curly, chubby, dark, starry eyed little girl.

Premartha

Nothing is going to make me abandon you

I am walking down the road to my childhood home. There is a lark singing high up in the sky. This song expresses the magnitude of everything, of fields, and forests, of houses spread far out into the distance. The pavement of the road is uneven, and I have to stay alert where to step. There are holes in this country road, and places where there is only sand left. On the side of the road are long stretches of yellow golden fields , wheat, oats and corn, there are borders full of poppies, and purple-blue cornflowers. I hear only the sound of the wind, and high up the song of a bird. Nature is very peaceful and harmonious. It emphasizes the vast expanse of the Dutch sky above it. Clouds are in constant movement, chased along by the wind. Along the road lie wealthy homesteads, hidden by oaks and elms, surrounded by fertile fields and outbuildings for the animals.

I am happy to be here. Contented that I made the decision to return to the surrounding of my childhood. Somewhere here I will find myself again, I will find the child I once was, the child that is still alive in me.

While walking along the road of my childhood, I remember all the support I received in making this journey. How friends have shared about their experience, returning in time to meet themselves, how my beloved has been excited for me to go on this adventure, how I can feel the love from existence through the channel of wise teachers, and how all along I have been guided by the Master to heal the child of the past and retrieve its essence for my adult life.

Slowly, I am approaching my childhood home. It is a large house with stables all along. Surrounding it, is the garden and the orchard. Beyond that, lies the endless expanse of land that belongs to my family. Both my parents' families own a lot of land, and in their marriage they have brought it all together. As I look around through my adult eyes, I realize that I never understood how much of the land in the neighborhood belonged to us.

Even though my parents had the financial means to employ enough workers, they decided to do only with a few. This was completely in accordance with all the other owners of land in the south of Holland. Everyone gave himself completely to his property, sacrificing comfort and wellbeing for keeping the land together.

Passing by the orchard, I come to our large home, shaded by three huge aspens. It has an austere beauty, with a simple but appealing design. Bordering it, are the flower gardens, full of flowers in all colours.

It is quiet all around. The silence of a summer afternoon. I walk around the back of the house, where the entrance is to the stables. On this summer day, they are empty, scrubbed cleand and freshly repainted. The animals are in the fields. Dust floats in the beams of sunlight streaming in through the windows. The walls are chalked white with a shiny black tar border that reaches the middle. It is the playground of my childhood. A huge but safe ground on which to jump and run, to build and play.

In the winter the cows and horses are kept here. As a child, I was drawn to the welcoming smell of warm animal bodies and their feed. But in the summer the stables are empty. The door of the main house is open. I quietly enter the kitchen. It is empty. It's after the noontime meal, and nobody is there. Everything looks immaculately clean. In the middle, stand a large table on which the light falls, chairs all around it. My father's easy chair is a bit away from it, it is there where he rests after his meal.

There is an atmosphere of cleanliness and order. My mother must be resting now. Often, around noon, she gets her headache. Something seems to be closing in around her. She has remained politely friendly, but then, comes the retreat. Her moment of solitude, and a pulling back from all the duties in keeping her home. My father has disappeared. He must be somewhere in the fields. He prefers to be alone and remains like that throughout the day. He is a man of little words, and in an inner world not available to anyone. My sisters are not there. They have gone to school or are at their friends' homes.

I go to my childhood bedroom. I open it and enter. The striking thing about this bedroom is that it has dark velvety red curtains, completely different from the understated beige and browns my mother normally prefers. It has shiny floor, and two metal beds. A modern plywood cupboard stands next to the door. The atmosphere of the room is in real contrast with the rest of the house, which is filled with traditional furniture. It gives a glimpse of the new world of which my mother is dreaming.

I look around slowly and take in as many details as I can-- the slightly sloping ceiling, the branch of leafy green outside the window. I feel protected here, but also strangely disconnected from the rest of the house, not really belonging anywhere.

Premartha meets Wimke

As my eyes finally rest on the metal bed to the right, I notice my little boy. He is around seven years old. His name is Wimke. He is lying on the bed, staring at the ceiling. It is summer, and he is listening to the silence that enfolds the house in the midday heat. From far away come the sounds from the fields, where work is being done. He feels like a boy with a quick and alert mind, accustomed to his solitude. I can see that he is creating a dream world of his own, not fully satisfying, but oddly familiar. A world of words and colors, that cover up his loneliness and separation. He looks slender and quick, but there is a resignation in his movements. And something else is there, a silent waiting and a strength held subtly out of view. I feel for him and I want to come close to him.

Premartha through the eyes of Wimke

To know him better, I take a deep inbreath, and on the outbreath I slowly allow my essence, my consciousness, to float up and out of my adult body, here in my childhood bedroom. I slowly enter my child's body. I become the child now. I start to feel myself living in a boy's body again. I am lying on my bed, looking at the ceiling. I have discovered that I can create moving patterns in the air. These patterns change continuously. I feel intrigued with producing these invisible currents. The house is very quiet. Further away I can feel my mother resting. I have observed her tiredness and headache after lunch. A tiredness that leans on me, that softly presses me down. I hear the sounds outside, of work in the fields. The movement of it attracts me. But it is my father's world, in which he likes to be alone, so I cannot go and join him. I am waiting.

I detect a movement in the room. There is a tall man standing at the door. It is the adult-me. He has a youthful and handsome face, surrounded by curls of golden brown hair. When I look into his eyes, I see a depth of steady blue-gray that invites me in. I don't know what to do. In his face I see lines of wisdom and compassion. I feel I am opening up to him, in need to connect and share with him. Then I hear his voice. It is a melodious voice, and this touches me the most. He calls me by my name! He looks at me. What is in his eyes? There is a gentle caring there, but also a strength that touches me. "Don't resign," I can read in them. "I know your longing. I know how much you love life. I want to connect with you. Come close again. Share your feelings with me."

I am very touched by his message, his words, and I want to reach out to come close to him.

At this point, I take another deep inbreath, and on the outbreath I let my consciousness float back into my adult body. In front of me, is the child me reaching out to me. I see in his eyes an innocent longing, a smile and a shyness too. I love him. I want to take him in my arms and tke away his loneliness. I want to tell him about the beauty of life that I found in my adult life. I would like to receive from him

40

his freshness, his looking at the world with new and innocent eyes. I would love to support him in discovering his creativity.

In the hug we share, all this is contained and more.

Then I let him know it's time for me to leave, for my life. But it's the beginning of a journey, and we will come closer and closer, and become best friends. I can see he likes that a lot.

That makes me very happy.

THE RECIPE

GOING BACK HOME

In this journey you will go back in time.

During it, you will be able to observe both parts of you: the inner adult and the inner child.

Find a comfortable position to sit in for the next period of time. Close your eyes.

As the adult you, start slowly walking down the road that leads you to your childhood home. As you approach it, you can observe it from a short distance.

What is your first impression? Feel yourself before entering the house.

Step inside. Start walking through the house. Find the place of father and mother inside your childhood home.

How are they relating to each other?

How are they relating to the family?

Continue moving through the house, on your way to the bedroom of the child-you. Step in softly.

Observe the child-you in its own space. Focus your attention on it.

How do you ad the adult respond to this meeting?

Slowly allow yourself to move out of your adult body into your child's body, becoming the child-you.

Through your child's perception, you can notice the adult you. How do you feel with the adult? Is there something which you would like to say, or share with the adult about yourself?

With a deep breath, move out of your child body, and reenter you adult body.

How do you feel with what the child you has been expressing to you? Is there something that you would like to respond with?

Take your time to complete your meeting with the child-you.

Now say goodbye. Slowly leave the bedroom behind. Start moving forward in time, until you reach this moment, now, in this place, here.

CHAPTER 2

HEARING THE CHILD (0 TO 7 YEARS OLD)

> If you just sit silently and listen to your mind, you will find so many voices. You will be surprised, you can recognize those voices very well. Some voice is from your grandfather, some voice is from your grandmother, some voice is from your father, some voice is from your mother, some voice is from the priest, from the teacher, from the neighbors, from your friends, from your enemies. All these voices are jumbled up in a crowd within you, and if you want to find your own voice, it is almost impossible; the crowd is too thick. In fact, you have forgotten your own voice long before.
>
> ...But if you want to become an individual in your own right, if you want to get rid of this continuous conflict and this mess within you, then you have to say goodbye to them...Even when they belong to your respected father, your mother, your grandfather.
>
> (Osho, *The Golden Future*)

THE POWER OF SOUND

It is difficult to avoid the power of sound. Sound penetrates. Our more dominant sense of sight can control an overload of visual information through a very simple mechanism: closing our eyes, or looking away. Whereas, when there is too much auditory information, our ears are not equipped with anything equivalent to the eyelid. We are vulnerable to anything we receive through hearing. What we hear passes through part of the brain that in essence is responsible for our feelings. The result is that what we hear does not leave us untouched. Automatically, we respond to it emotionally.

Sounds accompany us from the very beginning. When we enter our mother's womb, we enter a world of sounds. During pregnancy the mother's abdomen and uterus are very noisy: the rumbling of the stomach and the rippling of the amniotic fluid surround us. Through it all, we are centered on the rhythm of her heartbeat. Frederic Leboyer describes the quality of these sounds:

> How do the sounds reach it? The child receives them in the same way as fish do, through the waters in which

it bathes, modulated and transformed by them. For us, barely recognizable.(1)

All these sounds make us feel secure. Because of their regularity, we feel that all is well. In the first months, we do not yet differentiate which sounds accompany our life rhythm. Only in the sixth month of our fetal life can we actually start recognizing the sound of our mother's voice; our body rhythm attunes itself to it. We also respond to the sound of conversation, to music, and even to individual words. Later, we also are affected in the uterus by the sound of our father's voice. Thomas Verny, explains:

> In cases where a man talked to his child in utero using short soothing words, the newborn was able to pick out his father's voice in a room even in the first hour or two of life. More than pick it out, he responds to it emotionally. If he is crying, for instance, he'll stop. That familiar, soothing sound tells him he is safe. (2)

OUR NAME BECOMES A SYMBOL OF WHAT WE ARE BECOMING

For most of us, at birth, the safe surrounding of organic sounds changes into an overwhelming cacophony of noise and voices. The first sounds we hear outside the womb are loud, shrill, and insensitive. We have no way of preventing them from being heard. The only way we can protect ourselves is by contracting our body. We long for the reassuring voices of our parents. Their cooing and whispering give us a feeling of recognition and homecoming, and help us to orient ourselves in this new world. To feel well emotionally, intellectually, and physically, we need this kind of loving auditory environment. As we receive this we can relax beyond the world of sounds, into a deep space of silence.

At first, all sounds are formless. After a while, we start to differentiate them and we become sensitive to and creative with what comes to us. When our mother varies the rhythm of her sounds, lets her voice repeat sounds to us, and invents new ones, we begin to focus on her face longer, and show pleasure to her in return. We respond to loving voices by wriggling our whole body, opening our mouth wide, and giving big smiles. We feel confirmed in our existence and in the value that we have in life.

Soon we learn to play with sound. Our own sound reaches out, interacts with objects and persons in the world around us. In this time, we start to remember names for things, although we cannot verbalize them yet. This silent understanding opens up whole new areas of learning. Out of this, grows our capacity to express our recognition of the outer world through such words as "mamma, papa, hello." If our parents are there for us in that time, they will support this by pointing out names for objects, showing us things, encouraging our freedom to explore all this. Through sounds, and movements, we individuate ourselves from our mother, we practice finding our place and discovering the world. When the "rapprochement" stage of development comes, we use our voice for insisting and expressing want. We discover that we can move away from our mother, but our mother can also move away from us. We also want to control her, and get angry when we can't. We have to learn the difficult task of realizing that our freedom depends on others' freedom too.

When we start experiencing this separation we can start to say our own name: "Wimke" or "Manú" wants this or that. We are able to associate our subjectivity with the objective, the name given to us by our parents. Our name becomes a symbol of what we are becoming. It is a bridge between us and the outside world.

While separating, we become aware of our own name. With our own name, we inherit a multitude of feelings. In the choice of our name, our parents already express the hopes and dreams they carry for us.

If we return to the time in which we received our name, and we open up to the message that this name gives to us, we might be surprised. In that simple word already the whole world of our conditioning is revealed. Before we received that name, our essential self had no definition. Noww that the name has arrived, with it arrives the first imprint of who we are supposed to become.

It can be a name that reflects the dreams of our parents. With it, come all the longings and desires that they have for us. Maybe it's a name of someone they read about in their favorite novel, or heard of in their favorite movie. Someone they identified with or admired. Someone they wanted us to become. It reflects in its meaning the specific aspirations of our family: the name of a hero, a poet, a saint.

Our name can have deep roots in the family system. We may be given the name of another member of our family. It can be our grandmother, grandfather, uncle, or aunt. Sometimes, with this name we are symbolically given away to that person; often, we are expected to inherit the personality traits associated with that person. If grandma was felt to be sweet and submissive, and we inherit her name, we are supposed to become like her. Sometimes, there is a child born before us in the family who dies, and we are given its name. With it, we are handed over the hopes and dreams that are left unfulfilled, but also the grief for its early death. Without knowing it, we are meant to fill the place and perform the function that these members had in our family system.

Or our name has no meaning to it. It is only a label hung onto our existence, with no sensitivity to whom we really are, the miracle of life, the mysterious guest of the beyond.

> *Gitte G. was an introverted woman who had few friends. She looked ageless, and chose to wear very plain clothes. Some longing which she could not define brought her to us. While doing the name meditation, she suddenly realized that her name did not belong to her. It was in fact her maternal grandmother's name. As a child, she loved her granny very much, and yet, while calling out her own name in the session, a feeling started to overcome her. This was not her name. Nobody had ever called her by her real name. We invited her to give back to her grandmother the name that she had been carrying for her. After doing this, she felt an empty space. She was nameless. We invited her to chose a new name for herself. After a few seconds of silence, she shouted, "Jasmine!" And Jasmine she became.*
>
> *When she came for the next session, her plain clothes had gone: she was wearing a colorful dress, and her whole attitude had changed. She could laugh and speak loudly. The little girl inside had gained the right to reclaim her uniqueness.*

We might have a strong connection to our name. In its sound and meaning it reflects something that feels intrinsically ours. Or we may not connect to our name at all, or even dislike it. Whatever is the case, the name we receive after birth is the first public definition made about us.

As we grow up with this name, we are very sensitive to the way we are called by others. Specially by those people that are close to us, our parents, family, teachers If there is reproach there, or anger, or disappointment, or disapproval, our name becomes a container of everything which is unwanted. Or if there is love, acceptance, support, it becomes a symbol for everything desirable. Our name starts to represent everything we are and do. It becomes the doorway to all the conditioned messages we receive. It tells us who we are supposed to be and who not.

We learn quickly which of our actions and behaviors are echoed by supportive and affectionate sentences, and which ones are echoed by negative ones. .They becomes a reference for us. Some of them are messages that are openly given to us, others come silently through behaviour or criticism.

We listen to these sentences, to their tone and content, and we learn to know what is expected from us, what we should do and not do, should be or should not be. Slowly we start to internalize them and we literally hear them inside of us, judging about what we do and who we are. The superego, our internalized authority that regulates and controls our life, takes on these voices: it runs a constant commentary inside, of all our activities, thoughts, and emotions. This commentary is rooted in the messages we received in our early childhood by our parents, siblings, and other close family members. It can poison our whole life energy, sabotaging and repressing everything that comes natural to us. It makes us an enemy of ourselves.

> *During the "name meditation" session, Deva S. realized that she was always addressed by "that": "That is now big enough. That will be grateful one day." She heard her mother's sharp voice calling her impatiently," Do this, do that! We do everything for you!"*
>
> *When we asked her, "Did your mother want you?" she said, "No, she wanted to have more time for her son, born three months before she got pregnant with me."*
>
> *Hearing her father's voice, she realized that the child in her wanted to do everything right for him. To have a position in the family, she focused on him. When she noticed her father's disappointment and loneliness, she wondered how she should be and feel, so that he wouldn't leave her. She promised herself that she would understand him in a way that her mother never could. The little girl hoped that this would make him love her the most.*

Our name and the messages that come with it slowly create our personality, the mask we wear to hide our true face. Our being, which originally was nameless and limitless, gets defined into a static, predictable, and narrow form..

> *Just close your eyes for a moment. Start connecting with your own name. Repeat your name. Be aware of what comes up each time you say your name. Consciously listen to the "running commentary" that accompanies the sound of your own name: this commentary holds total power over you as long as it operates from an unconscious place inside you. Turn up the volume, recognize where the different tones of voice are coming from, what they want from you, what messages lie underneath. Write down some of the things you have experienced.*

We need to heal the negative imprint that our name has received, and to heal the critical or demanding messages that are given to us. We have to create new positive messages.

Loving words can touch and open up the deep spaces of pain which are hidden in us. They can heal these wounds and create profound inner changes. When, as the loving, compassionate and understanding adult we take the responsibility to express to the child in us those messages it always needed to hear, we give the child a feeling of being seen, loved and appreciated in its existence. In this way, the negative imprints lose their power over us, and once again our innocent childlike being can surface, and express itself in its own natural way.

> *In our groups on Childhood Deconditioning, usually all the participants have, at the end of the exercise described in the recipe of this chapter, touched a real understanding of where the inner voices that produce conflicts inside them originate. They can acknowledge the way they have internalized their parents' voices. Then when they, from the adult part of themselves, share healing and nourishing sentences with the child part of themselves, often lots of tears flow. The recognition of the need for love we all have, creates a new connection among all of the participants. They realize that they do not need to be ashamed of or isolated with this need anymore. Some participants express this by embracing themselves, others come together and hold each other close. It is very touching to see people of all ages and backgrounds sitting on the floor together, sharing the sweetness that has come after expressing their wounds.*
>
> *Then, there is a moment when all the sounds in the room settle down, and only silence remains. But it is not a silence that is heavy with unexpressed emotions. Rather, it contains a compassion that makes it full and vibrant.*

SOUND IN ITS PURITY

As the negative imprint of our name disappears, the original sound of our name remains.

Detached from its components of personality, our name simply functions as a vehicle for our being. To experience this, we need to separate the sound of our name from the negative meaning that has been attached to it. Connecting with this original sound is a step toward meeting our unpolluted individuality. We can call out our name, and with it call forth our true self.

48

Sound in its purity is one of our easiest links to the world of spirituality. When we are no longer trapped in the meaning of words, our mind can relax. In between the words, we find gaps of silence. These gaps become doors into the deep peace of existence.Once we can call our name in its purity, the silence that follows leads to our inner being. We have returned to the silent limitless space we lived in before we got defined by any name or description.. Osho says:

> Those who have said that sound is absolute being have said the ultimate which can be said about sound. There is no greater experience than that of absolute being, and they had not known anything deeper than sound through which to express themselves. (3)

Rumi says (4):

> Leave the words.
>
> Look at the mirror of Essence.
>
> Because all fear and suspicion
>
> Come from words.

THE EVOCATION

MY PERSONAL EXPERIENCE WITH THE NAME MEDITATION

SVARUP

Manuela Piera Gladys. Quite a mouthful for a tiny, yelping, disoriented baby.

Piera or Pierrette in her language, was my mother's choice. A short and sober name in Italian. It fitted with the understated clothes and good solid shoes which my mother favored.

But my father's sister won the right to giving my first name. Manuela. My parents had some trouble registering it, in the Catholic Italy of the fifties. The initial E was missing: only Emanuele was a saint, and Manuela sounded dangerously exotic. It brought up images of a woman with a rose in her mouth, dancing wildly on the table on a dark, lusty Spanish night.

I wonder how I would have turned out if my first name would have been Piera. I wonder why my mother gave in. However, Manuela fitted my dark curls and fiery eyes. Gladys was the tribute, to my father's mother. It was an odd name, straight from the romantic novels adored by a great grandmother with an otherwise very middle-class background.

My parents didn't choose my name. In their modern spirit of jazz and revolution, they had no place for rituals. to cast all their traditions away. And, with them, their roots had vanished as well.

Mother through the ears of three-year-old Manú: lost in this foreign land together

Padova. Manú is in a field. She is blowing dandelions to the wind. She is getting lost in the deep, deep blue of some tiny flowers which are her secret connection to the Virgin Mary, after whom they are named.

I allow the magic to happen: I leave my adult body, and float into her child body.

My senses are open to the smell of the moist earth. A few puddles here and there are drying out in the timid spring sun. This field is across the street from her home. It is being eaten away bit by bit by new buildings.

I look up, as I often do, to the moving, shifting clouds. I get lost in their shapes. They are hints of something even wider, more magic. I hear the whisper of the beyond, uplifting and unattainable, and a bit scary too.

"MANUELA!" There is a mixture of reassurance and fear in my mother's voice. This land is alien to her. She tries to face with common sense and courage what her instinct cannot recognize.

"Why don't you collect some wild flowers?" I like it when she gives me a purpose. She becomes calm and safe, and her own fear recedes, it's just a tiny pitch in her voice.

As I collect the flowers, the smells and sounds of this scrawny but alive nature start waking up my senses…I want to run, to dance and shout.

"MANUELA!" My mother's voice is firm: "You are sweaty, it's time to go!" I stubbornly stop in my tracks and refuse. If I can't run, I won't move. And by not moving, all that is tender and alive around me, loses color. OK, it's time to go home.

At home, I sit and feel a bit stuck. In this well ordered world, the only outlet is fantasy. Me and my mamma drawing, remembering life outside together.

Sometimes, my physical restraint starts raging inside. I want to provoke, I try to make my mamma lose control.

"MANUELA, don't roll your eyes!" The threat in my mother's voice stops me then and there. There is danger, the real danger of a slap coming. I become defiant, I challenge her.

"MANUELA, come here!" I cringe as the slap descends on me.

"MANUELA, you will send me to my grave!" That's it. I feel guilty, I am afraid to lose her. Mother doesn't talk to me anymore.

I'll do anything, anything to make you love me again, Mamma. We are together, lost in this foreign land, together forever.

Father through the ears of three-year-old Manú: My favorite playmate

"MANÚ!" Father is home. It's just before bedtime. I luxuriate in the soft feeling of my flannel pajamas and talcum powder on my body. When I hear his voice, I am so excited…. Daddy will play with me.

"MANUELA, go to the kitchen, and check if I'm there!" Trustingly, I do this for my big Daddy. I move through the dark corridor, conquering my fear by whistling.

I suddenly hear mother's and father's laughter in the brightly lit living room. He has made fun of me. Of course he can't be in the kitchen! I storm back, feeling humiliated. I sulk.

"MANUELA, don't laugh." He manages to make me laugh.. I am his little girl, who admires him. I can't help it. He understands, and stops. He has a child inside who knows too much about humiliation. I feels so much that little boy, maybe sometimes too much.

"MANOU, when you grow up I'll teach you to drive a spaceship", and all is OK again, here is my favorite playmate, who knows everything about the universe!

Then, suddenly, the grownup man withdraws:

"MANOU, go to your mother, it's bedtime."

There is tiredness, maybe defeat, in his voice, I don't know…I would have liked to play so much longer.

He smiles an absent smile, drawn at the corners. His hand moves toward a book; our contact is over. I feel left with a longing, a hope, and a bittersweet taste.

Svarup calling Manú: I am here

I float out of Manú's body, and reenter my adult self. I can see the little girl just as she moves to the bedroom, a bit hardened and resigned.

"Manú.," I want to call her, invite the little girl in her yellow pajamas to run toward me.

"Manú.," She is confused. She loves her parents, she adores them, and yet in her heart she feels alone, she can't show them her innocence and her longing...maybe it would just be too painful for them...

"Manú.," I call her gently, from my belly, from the simplest and most honest place inside me.

"Manú, I'm here." My voice has reached my heart, it's a bit tremulous, it's a whisper. "Shall I lie next to you?" She looks at me, the dark, dark eyes blazing, the tiny mouth pulled together, and she nods: "Yes."

MY PERSONAL EXPERIENCE WITH THE NAME MEDITATION

PREMARTHA

A mother who wants a king's name for her child

My childhood name is Wimke. Wimke who was baptized Wilhelmus. "Wilhelmus, a noble name," the priest says to my mother. "Call him Wilhelmus, Wilhelmus de Koning. The name of a king."

My mother responds to this, she wants a royal name for her child.

"WIMKE," she whispers at night, looking at the child's face, fine features, soft curly hair. Little hands like silk. "No property should swallow you, no religion should alienate you, no woman should break her heart in trying to reach you." But then she feels guilty. And her voice changes.

"WIM!" The punishing tone of a trapped mother. Enclosed in the family and the neighborhood.

"WIM!" A voice punishing him for being different. Shaming the little boy, as they shame her. Her child who doesn't fit in the neighborhood. A child who doesn't want to catch the birds. A child who, at harvest time, wants to save the mice, and protect all that is soft, small, and gentle.

And her voice continues: "WIM! Don't be like them". But also: "WIM! Don't be different".

Enough to make this little boy whirl. Enough to make him dizzy and confused. He feels paralyzed and forced into resignation. But he cannot give up.

A father who cannot communicate

The father's voice. Silence.

A distant silence. There is an abyss between my father and me . Neither of us is able to cross it and to reach out. We cannot bridge

52

emptiness between us.

My father, who most of the time doesn't notice me. He leaves me in the care of my mother.

I don't understand my father. I look at him with curious blue eyes. I am attracted to him, but I don't know what to do. There is a longing for my father, but I cannot express it. I feel I am not good enough. Every effort to approach him fails before I even try. My father does not communicate. He would like to share his world, his talents, his love, but he doesn't know how to reach out.

And the distance remains. Sometimes, suddenly, our hearts meet, just for a simple unexpected moment. After that, we both feel embarrassed and turn, to go our own way.

How much I would like to hear my father call out my name: "Papa, call my name. I need to feel your respect and pride in me. Call me friendly. Invite me in your life. Share yourself with me. Play with me. Make me laugh, make me cry. Papa, call me. Any name will do".

From Premartha to Wimke
Wimke.

I want to let you know that I am here for you, that I am happy to take you in my arms. I want to say these sentences to you. With all my love and tenderness.

Wimke,
I am happy that you are born;
I am proud that you are a boy;
I love your sensitivity;
And I support your curiosity;
I respect your strong will;
I love it when you laugh and feel silly;
You can cry with me;
I am there for you.

THE RECIPE

THE NAME MEDITATION

As the adult, create a place for yourself. Then, place a soft pillow, representing the child-you, in front of you. Connect with yourself as the loving adult. Close your eyes, take a deep breath,. Observe the child-you.

Become that child. Start hearing your mother's voice, the voice of your childhood. Hear her calling your name. Hear other sentences coming with it. How do they affect you?

Feel what is happening to you, when your mother speaks to you. What is your response?

Allow yourself to speak out, until you feel complete.

Now start hearing your father's voice, the voice of your childhood. You can hear him call your name. What other messages come with it? How do they affect you?

Feel what is happening to you when your father speaks to you. What is your response? Allow yourself to speak up, until you feel complete.

Now, as the child-you, start hearing the voice of the adult-you.

By what name does the adult call you? What other messages is the adult sharing with you? How do you feel?

Become the adult-you. Connect with the child-you. Take a moment to feel your connection to the child. What would you like to say to it? Allow feelings to come. Continue going deeper with it.

Now reach out to the soft pillow in front of you. Take the pillow in your arms. Feel that you are holding the child on your arms. Continue sharing with it whatever comes up.

CHAPTER 3

FREEING THE CHILD (7 TO 3 YEARS OLD)

> I have been constantly telling you that the personality has to be dropped so that your individuality can be discovered. I have been insisting that the personality is not you; it is a mask people have put over you. It is not your authentic reality, it is not your original face. And you are asking me, "Is it really worth putting any energy into improving my personality?"
>
> Put your energy into destroying your personality. Put your energy into discovering your individuality. And make the distinction very clear: individuality is that which you have brought from your very birth. Individuality is your essential being, and personality is what the society has made of you, what they wanted to make of you.
>
> (Osho, *The Golden Future*)

ROLES AND THE EXPERIENCE OF ALONENESS

"Personality is what the society has made of you. Personality is the mask people put over you"

When you meditate on these words, what gets touched inside? Do you know the moments in your life when you act from your personality, from your conditioned self? What changes when you drop that, when you express yourself through your individuality, your true self?

How is it to be in your individuality, "In that which you have brought from your very birth"? Do you remember times in your life when you touched the space of being essentially yourself? You in your color, you in your own quality, uncompromisingly yourself? Yet, at the same time, at home, relaxed with yourself?

Take a moment time to recall how you feel in the company of even the best of friends. Notice your body, your feelings, and the thoughts that cross your mind. You might become aware that even in these moments you carry a certain amount of tension inside. A tension which draws you out of yourself, away from your inner center, which forces you to act as somebody you not really are. A tension that separates you from the others.

Tensions like this are the result of our conditioning to present ourselves within a role. Our roles tell us how we should behave.

They dictate what we can feel and what we cannot feel. In this way, we cannot be who we are. We can only try to fulfill what we think is expected from us.

We believe that in relating to others we have to perform. We carry the fear that if we do not play a role in the company of others, we might not be loved, acknowledged or respected. We will not belong

We will be alone.

For the mind and its conditioning, the experience of aloneness is often frightening. Aloneness has become synonymous with loneliness, separation and rejection. We have learned that to belong we need to present ourselves in the way others expect from us. At a deep unconscious level, we are convinced that playing a certain role is the only way that entitles us to be part of a larger system. And yet, as we present ourselves with our separate roles, we miss that very sense of belonging that we yearn for.

We have been taught that we are separate, that only by acting from our roles can we bridge this separation. To create these roles, we fall back on old conditionings and beliefs. We act according to what we learned in our early childhood: how we should or should not be. Relating in this way is very dissatisfying. Neither can we be ourselves, nor can the people we relate to, our lovers, friends, family, be themselves. R. D. Laing says:

> Let no one suppose that this madness exists only somewhere in the night or day sky where our birds of death hover in the stratosphere. It exists in the interstices of our most intimate and personal moments.
>
> We have all been processed on Procrustean beds. At least some of us have managed to hate what they have made of us. Inevitably we see the other as the reflection of the occasion of our own self-division.
>
> The others have become installed in our hearts, and we call them ourselves. (1)

In this way, we meet each other on the surface, but intimacy is not possible. The frustration that comes with it is often projected outwards. We feel misunderstood and not respected by others. But the real wound is that we are not respecting ourselves, that we betray our own nature by covering it up with something artificial and false. Out of shame for this, we hide our real being at the bottom of the well inside, or we push ourselves onward, trying to cover up our loss of self-worth by acting and doing. We have lost the true feeling of merging with life. We can no longer trust that life is friendly and that it loves us, that existence likes expressing itself through us in a relaxed and unique way. Instead, we feel we have to control ourselves, that living our life and relating is an effort. Whatever roles we take on, it seems that none of them allows any relaxation or trust. We have to stay on guard continuously to keep ourselves from presenting any holes in our image. And even if for some of us, the role we identify with is a negative one, we persist in making an utter effort to maintain the picture we have of ourselves. We are afraid we will be condemned, rejected, or ridiculed if we don't present ourselves in the form that we are known.

> *In our groups on Childhood Deconditioning, there is an exercise in which the participants play out their parents. They dress up and act like them, in a setup where they are invited to socialize with each other. It always feels like we are breaking a taboo. Quite a few of the participants remark on the feelings of betrayal coming up toward their parents that come up. They initially feel insecure about the exposure of their parents' traits, until they discover how they have internalized these traits, and how they have taken over, in their own behavior, the things they reject in their parents. With this realization, for some of them comes anger, for others laughter, or relief. For many, to admit that what they play in their own life is often only a copy of their parents, results in a deeper understanding of their conditioning.*
> *At the end, they embrace their inner child and connect with what this child, through absorbing its parents' traits and roles, had hoped to receive. Afterward, they often are able to feel the deficiency that lies underneath it all. By sharing with each other, much of the shame they carry about this starts to disappear.*

By being caught up in a fixed expression of ourselves, we destroy our natural spontaneity and creativity. In trying to fill up the holes in our image, we prevent ourselves from having moments of emptiness and silence. And it is out of this emptiness that new stars, new impulses are born.

When we try to control our impulses, we cannot live our own lives. We act in set patterns. We stick to the expression of ourselves that we think we are recognized for. This creates much tension in our being. To try to produce impulses when actually there are none at that moment, can be a real trap. The only things we produce under these conditions are repetitions which have no freshness and innocence.

A child in its innocence has impulses and expressions which don't carry this split yet. Being naturally part of this undivided consciousness, its impulses are born as an unfolding, just like waves unfold in the ocean. Its expressions come out of a relaxation and an emptiness.

When as adults we regain these qualities, it becomes a joy to watch how impulses are manifested through our individual form--that which we have already brought with us from birth. We start to enjoy our own expressions to the same degree as others' expressions, and we are equally surprised by ourselves as we are by others. The issue of competition doesn't need to arise anymore. There is no question of having to hold on to our own separate expression. We start to understand that the impulse that has ignited it is as much born out of the same mystery as the impulses of others. Our meetings become relaxed and playful. They are like the dance of separate streams converging into one river.

A SMALL CHILD YEARNS FOR RECOGNITION

Yet it seems that every child has to renounce this mystery to become part of its family: In its natural need for being connected, the child takes on the roles which are given to it, and learns to substitute the original sense of oneness with the feeling of belonging, having a safe and known place within the family. The spontaneity and wonder of the greater belonging, and the freedom that arises out of it, are replaced by the fixed and predictable rules and roles of a small group of people.

A small child yearns for recognition; it is as if the soul needs some outer mirroring, some reflection, to become aware of itself. It starts at the very beginning of life, when we need coming from the eyes and voice of our mother, the acknowledgment that we are welcome and that we are seen for who we are.

But small children can't discriminate whether what is mirrored relates to their deepest nature or to the projections and unfulfilled dreams of their parents. A. H. Almaas explains:

> One of the most significant characteristics of the soul is that it can identify with the content of experience. It can take any impression, for example self-image, and make itself believe that the impression is itself...Identifying with an impression or content of experience makes the self feel that it has an identity, and through this identity it then recognizes itself. (2)

This process of identification, reaches its refinement between the ages of three and six years old. It is as if we become an existential "Who am I?" asking for guidance in our search for an identity.

In this question, there is an unquenchable curiosity, a sense of wonder about the growing complexity of what we can do and what we can communicate. It is the "why? why?" in this time that often drives parents crazy as they try to come up with some kind of answer or dismiss the questioning. It is sometimes difficult for an adult to understand that the pleasure a three-year-old experiences in asking questions has more to do with expressing its own excitement and curiosity, than with receiving the right answer.

During the first stage of this process of "finding our social identity," our ideas of ourselves are still quite magical, sometimes grandiose, poetic, symbolic, and mostly "unrealistic" to the eyes of our elders. We are still open to our dream world. Here we can be anyone, from an infinite creator to the emperor of the world.

But, as we share our dreams, mother or father might not be able to handle them, because these dreams confront them too closely with their own failures and anxieties around belonging and surviving in the world.

In fact, although these dreams might sound funny or close to impossible in the particular social context in which the child lives, in their essence they reflect and contain a quality of search, which in itself has great value and beauty. The openness to different possibilities, the ability to look beyond the obvious in a situation, are qualities that might get lost when these dreams are shamed or dismissed.

The realism that needs to enter the visionary world of a three-year-old has to do with the actual limitations of its body, which is still small, and with having to learn how to follow up an idea in time and space. Yet, the "realism" that the parents might bring in at this stage is often of a very different nature.

Most of the time with good intentions, mom and dad warn us, through their words and through their actions, that our purpose in the world has very little to do with our dreams. Maybe what they intend is to protect us from the disappointments and wounds they were subjected to, maybe they just happen to have the "perfect" idea about what we should become so as to fulfill their own unfulfilled dreams.

On a deep unconscious level, we start responding to what our parents see in us: we still very much need them, not only for survival and nourishment, but also as role models, and as the first representatives of the opposite sex. Through them, we need to create our own sense of "I" as a little boy or girl in the world.

No one gets to be who he is

In current psychological literature, much has been written about cross-generational bonding. As Bradshaw illustrates, when parents have remained "adult children," and haven't developed the capacity to relate to each other on a mature level, sharing vulnerability, facing conflict, and owning their choices in life, they start bonding in an unhealthy way with their children:

> Adult children, having long ago buried their authentic selves and lost their sense of IAMness, cannot give themselves to their partners because they don't have a self to give.... In like manner and to varying degrees, all dysfunctional families violate their children's sense of IAMness.... In dysfunctional families, no one gets to be who he is. All are put in service to the needs of the system. (3)

When mother is not happy with father, she might take whatever she can't get from her spouse from her little son, and make him her substitute husband, secret lover, hero. Father might resent this and make his son a rival. Equally, father might put onto his little girl all the expectations not fulfilled by her mother. His daughter might have to become his little princess, his substitute wife, his secret lover, or nurse. Mother might not like this, and call her a whore. Or, when the parents' unresolved conflicts are funneled and released through one child, this child will live out the mental or physical symptoms of the family imbalance, and become the "identified patient." Or again, parents might unconsciously use one child to cushion their struggle, and this child, caught up between the two, becomes the harmonizer, or mother's or father's lawyer. And, when a child is not wanted, it might take on the role of the rejected one, the "garbage bin of the family," or become invisible.

We assume these roles out of our need for love and recognition, and accept them in order to get a place in the family system. They become our first social identity. Later on in life, as adults, those early roles function as blueprints of how we will relate to ourselves and others.

In our present relationships, we are still busy filling these roles, or trying at all costs to escape from them. They become virtually identical to the way we perceive ourselves, like a second skin. Even when that skin is too tight and uncomfortable, shedding it feels like disappearing and losing all hope of belonging. Whether we try to conform or rebel, the focus remains on who we were taught to be. In this tension, we lose the contact with our natural being.

Danielle Z. was a very successful manager. She had difficulties in her relationship with her husband. Connecting with her inner child was the first big step for her. On her journey, she found a timid and fragile girl who had retreated into her dream world.

When we worked on her roles, she could experience in the place of the child, the tension that was running through her as she stood in the middle of her parents' permanent conflict.

She felt very divided. On one side, she experienced the expectations of her father, who wanted her to become the son that he had dreamed of. On the other side, she experienced her loyalty to her mother, who felt neglected and cheated by her husband. Danielle had taken upon herself the role of mother's defender and lawyer.

The roles that Danielle had to play for her parents were creating a big split in her: they were both very male and aggressive. As she truly loved her husband, she could not continue playing tough with him. She was longing for her femininity.

When she became aware of the situation, a deep sense of grief surfaced in her. She felt the loss of her integrity as a child, but at the same time she felt unable to change her way of relating to her husband. Slowly, this sense of helplessness took on a different quality. It became a sense of not knowing, and an openness to surrendering without collapsing.

A MISGUIDED ACT OF LOVE

In some families, the roles that are given are more extreme, especially when these families are "dysfunctional." This term refers to families which are falling to pieces, with alcoholic parents, histories of abuse, or extreme living situations. In these families, a child often carries the heavy burden of the whole family dysfunction. But also in families which are considered normal, and in which parents are "doing their best" and trying to give as much love as they are capable of, the children are assuming the roles that are asked of them.

The lack of IAMness is part of our human condition. In the world of spirituality, it is exactly the experience of this deficiency that drives us in the search for ourselves. In this way, it is most often not a pathological situation to be treated, but a state which is common to everyone: the loss of a sense of integrity or wholeness, of presence and being. And we all long to regain it.

Most parents are simply bound to give to their children their unresolved issues around their own IAMness. Without intending to, they transmit all the ways that they developed for filling up their holes, covering their own deficiency, and compensating for their own feeling of being lost.

If we have been denied the full experience of ourselves as unique and lovable beings, how can we recognize anybody else's uniqueness? Instead of working on the wounds we received, we try to protect our children from them. It might be well meant, but the outcome is that they will absorb our pains, and take on roles and attitudes that don't belong to them.

Children unconsciously adjust themselves to their parents' feelings, often blaming themselves for their parents' unhappiness and trying to take it on themselves. Whatever it takes, they will do it. They need to feel acknowledged and seen in order to have a sense of identity. If it is impossible to be themselves in the family, then they will take the role which is offered.

The loss of our true nature is very painful, but blaming ourselves for it is not helpful. We did it for love. As children, we could not do other than to try to relieve mother's pain, father's failure, by taking it on our shoulders. We created roles out of this, to balance the family system. We were so dependent on its oneness, that the sacrifice of our own needs seemed a small price to pay for the harmony of it.

As Bert Hellinger has shown in his work on family systems, this is far-reaching: where there is an imbalance, a secret, a sickness, or a death in the family, our need for love and oneness impels us to take a place in the system which is not ours, and live someone else's life. Our sense of identity is then rooted in a misguided act of love, in an attempt to recreate a merging where there are big holes that we cannot actually fill, because they are not ours in the first place. (4)

> Sam G. was the first child in his family. He had lived his life always striving to be the first in school, in his job, in sports, in everything in which he could prove his worth. However, he was nagged by a sense of exhaustion and by the inability to stop his efforts. What emerged when we looked at his family setup, was that his mother had had stillborn twins before him.
>
> As we explored his mother's expectations of him, it became clear that he had taken upon himself the task of consoling her for the loss of the twins. Out of his need for her love, and also out of his desire to gain a special place in her heart, he had unconsciously filled the place of first born which was not his by right. He was the third in the

line. This discovery gave Sam the space to admit to his longing for relaxing and being part of a bigger "team."

The pain and confusion of discovering that "I am not living my own life," the feeling of loss and isolation that comes with this discovery, needs to be addressed with compassion and love. The child inside needs the space to feel again what happened; the adult in us needs to understand how it happened. Out of this, something new can arise.

Basho says (5):

Poor boy--leaves

moon-viewing,

for rice-grinding

THE EVOCATION

My personal experience with the issue of roles

Svarup

Manú's parents meet: two noble spirits
My mother and father met in Tunis in 1941, when they were only 17.

He was a charming young Italian Jew born in the south of Tunisia, the dark son of a line of soldiers and shopkeepers.

She was a strong and beautiful French girl, of mixed Eastern European and North African Jewish ancestry: She was well spoken, artistic, and refined. She had spent her childhood in beautiful marble villas with shady gardens.

My mother and father shared a nobility of spirit, and a rage against injustice. They started reading forbidden communist books right under the open sky on a beach. They joined the Communist Party, and felt bonded in a secret conspiracy. They made love for the first time in a dangerous area of the city, half-destroyed by the air raids.

In 1948, when the war was long over and everyone's spirit was soaring high, they packed an old trunk full of memories of the colonial life they were leaving behind, and set off for Naples, Italy. They wanted to be part of the Communist revolution that for sure was going to take place very very soon... He started studying chemistry. She became a functionary of the Party.

But the Revolution never came. And they found themselves stranded in a land which was foreign to both of them. Holding on to their dignity and never looking back, they decided to hold on and survive. Years of silent waiting stretched ahead of them.

A little girl to brighten them up: Manú

They moved to Genoa, up north, to try and find a way to make a living.

In 1952, on a balmy August night, in the House of the Peace Committee where they had a room in exchange for caretaking, they conceived a child. This changed the situation drastically. Once their biology was in motion, everything settled. He found employment in a big multinational company. They learned not to mention their Communist past. They started living a normal life, on the third floor of a brand new building in a working-class neighborhood. The area was gray, polluted, and industrial.

Mother's dream

She stays at home, he works. She dreams of her child to come:

"I'll teach her to be strong and intelligent. I'll make sure she will obtain the highest education. We will understand each other She will be my companion in this foreign land.

Father's dream

On his way back to the apartment, he dreams of his baby:

"This is going to be my little girl, she will be my princess. She will admire my strength and courage. And if I have to, I will compromise and bend for her sake so that she will never have to do that herself. She will be a rebel, my rebel!"

Who are we, then?

Padova 1957. Daddy's job has brought us here. It is early morning in Manú's home. I see her in her little bed. She is opening her eyes and looking across to her parents' big empty bed.

I allow myself to float out of my adult body and enter her body.

It's early morning. I finally have the right to show I am awake. I inhale the strong smell of my parents' bodies lingering in the room, and I disentangle myself from the wet, crumpled sheets. I am wearing "Ho Chi Min," my white flannel pajamas (the yellow ones are called "Mao Tse Tung"). I feel raw. The hyperlucid anxiety of the night slowly fades into the day..

But I am learning to be reasonable and not to show my anxiety. They love me better when I behave like a grownup. If there is tension between them, I am supposed ignore it. At the most, what I can do is to make them laugh, or impress them with some wise remark beyond my age.

It's just that every night,when we go to sleep, it all comes up again, and all that nervousness travels up and down my body.

But now, sitting around the breakfast table, I want to believe that everything is fine. And in a way, it is. I am their bright child, their funny, precocious child. I am lulled into oblivious comfort by the friendly, intelligent chatter between them. The way they hold their conversation creates a golden wall of separation from the surroundings. I feel very special, sharing an atmosphere which no Italian Catholic kid knows of. Sometimes, though, I would actually prefer to be like everybody else. I secretly wish I could be carried along by the solidity of having roots, Sunday clothes, the magic of Jesus, roses in the garden.

But I don't say this. My mother, all nicely polite in front of the neighbors, criticizes them in private for their utter lack of culture.

So, here we are, in our small kitchen, around our battered old table, behaving like aristocrats, helping each other to forget who we are and where we are.

Who are we, then? This is a secret, an unmentionable question for me to ask, or for me to answer. Deep down, I know it. What I do not know, and cannot even imagine, is the devastation of a Holocaust which is only 7 years behind us. We don't talk about this at home.

In my parents' conscious world there's no space for fear. The focus has to be kept on the light. Not the divine light, just the daylight.

Daddy's little princess

I somehow know I have to cheer up Daddy, and let him tease me, take me in his arms and swirl me around. I feel transported by his charm, his frown disappearing, as he sings romantic American songs to me. They contain great promises of a different tomorrow, that linger with me and nourish my fantasies long after he's left for work. I promise myself that I will grow up to be a very, very special woman, a sexy, beautiful, cultured woman. For my Daddy.

Much later, when he comes home from work, he will be distracted and absent. He will reach out for his newspaper, hardly noticing my presence. He will talk to my mother in suffused and embittered tones about the meaninglessness of his work.

65

I will feel outraged, rejected by his neglect. I will try harder. I have to be extraordinary to get his attention, undemanding and extraordinary.

On Sundays, a whole world of incredible stories and adventures opens up. Our tiny apartment and our neighborhood walks become the theater for great science fiction stories. He explains the theory of relativity to me. I fantasize about the moment, which is coming closer and closer, when he and I will vanish from this earth at the speed of light, to return only when it's a better time.

I am Daddy's little princess, admirer, accomplice.

Mommy's genius

I am now alone with my mother. Everything slows down. I enjoy the comfort of another piece of bread with margarine, dipped in the large bowl of barley coffee and milk. She talks to me; she talks in her proper Italian, learned only recently with the aid of newspapers and crossword puzzles. Hers is a solid, rational world, based on black and white information She treats me like an adult, wants me to learn to speak properly and fluently. We share an atmosphere of intellectual superiority.

I know that this is the way to please her, to keep her warm, milky-white large body a bit closer to mine. When she teaches me how to read and write, I can smell her face cream, the sweet odor of her armpits, I can brush my hand against her soft arm.

I am Mommy's little genius, Mommy's showpiece. She revels in satisfaction when the peasants, the shopkeepers, and other people around us are stunned by my precociousness, my serious way of talking. And I shine, feeling that for this moment I have made up for all the troubles I have caused her.

And I'll grow up as a wise, independent woman, one who won't need to live her life through others.

I learn to keep my love for Daddy, flowers, and birds as something vague, a girlish dream which will fade in time. I am Mommy's secret rival.

I will betray them in the name of God, patent leather shoes, and bean soup

Tomorrow I go to kindergarten, where I will meet the normal, ordinary world consecrated by Jesus and the Virgin Mary. There, I will betray my mother and my father in the name of God, patent leather shoes, and bean soup.

I will learn to fend for myself. None of the failures, mistakes and humiliations I encounter with the other kids and the nuns will ever be mentioned to my parents. I am their strong girl, their little adult.

I come back to my adult body, feeling both, the shame and the innocence of the little girl. I also feel a deep compassion for Manú's parents, who also did not know how to respect and protect their own innocence.

PREMARTHA

The natural child: sapphire blue and sparkly gold

I am looking at the little boy me in his essential state.

He is full of light and play. His curly blond hair is tousled and his face shines. In his eyes, there is curiosity, with a sparkle of mischief. He is running through the rooms of the main house. Faster and faster. He is laughing as he turns around each corner, with a high clear sound. His face looks flushed and excited.

He is teasing his sisters, jumping up and down, provoking them into response, but always outwitting them in his fastness. Everything around him looks like blue and gold. Sapphire blue and sparkly gold. Then, he lets go.

Just in the middle of the living room he drops on the ground. Now he is motionless, still. He slows down his breathing until there is no visible breath anymore. Everything has stopped. His face is infused with bliss.

He is at home.

Mother's child: quiet and invisible

He would like to share his excitement with his mother. To run to her, and hug her, kiss her, make her laugh. But he cannot. She is too sad. She is sitting in the kitchen on her chair, her hands motionless, her eyes staring into the void. He doesn't want to disturb her. It feels as if she would break in pieces if he would come too close.

Once in a while, he manages to reach out to her, and when he curls up in her lap, he smells her comforting smell and feels safe. But he cannot move too much, he as to control himself, and wait for her response.

Sometimes, her sadness enters him. It makes him heavy and immobile. Also his movements slow down into a stillness. But this stillness is not comfortable. It makes him dizzy.

When he forgets about this, and spontaneously runs around, jumps and shouts, there are times when she looks at him and laughs. These are the unforgettable moments of his life. And, otherwise, she can suddenly snap out of her resignation and shout at him. That scares him to death. He feels guilty for upsetting her, and anxious for creating turmoil.

So, he decides to be more quiet, not to move too much, to let the movement become almost invisible.

To become a quiet, invisible child, ready to renounce, for her happiness, his desires.

Father's child: distant and lonely

His father simply ignores him. He does as if the little boy does not exist. Why, nobody knows. He is like that with everyone in the family. He takes his meals in silence, and leaves the house without a word. Mother and sisters try not to disturb him, and so does the little boy.

Sometimes, he secretly looks at his father, while eating, and he feels a wave of tenderness towards him. An unexplainable feeling of regret and longing. Too big for a little boy to understand.

He is also afraid of him. Often he looks so closed, or angry, that the little boy feels it is his mistake. That there is something that he did wrong. He would like to go to his father, put his little hand in father's large hand, and feel protected by him. He would love to run along with him, go to the horses, walk through the fields. Ask him the many questions he has inside, like: "Why the birds fly low when the sky is overclouded?" or how has father made the little chair for him. But it is not possible.

Rarely his father smiles, but when he does, his whole face relaxes. In these moments, the little boy loves him so much, he would want to do anything to keep this feeling a bit longer. But it doesn't last. It seems the only way he can be close to him, is to be silent too. He learns t also not talk. When his father is around, he withdraws in his own world. It's silent there, but not really. It's lonely and a bit empty. There is not much sharing.

He feels embarrassed when this need for intimacy comes up. It becomes something that he has to hide and be ashamed of. He becomes a distant child, a child that doesn't need anything from his father.

Premartha to Wimke:

Come to me, my little boy. Yes, it hurts to feel the emptiness and rejection. Yes, it is exhausting to control your energy, to give up and to keep yourself quiet. But take time to feel it. I am here with you. You never had anybody who listened to you how you felt about this. You kept it all for yourself. You did your best to take on the roles that would make it bearable. Now I am here, I am an adult now, in a world that respects sharing, where you can run and shout, where you can be yourself, unconcerned.

Little boy, I see your real colors now, I feel your essence. I am proud of you.

THE RECIPE

Exploring the Layers of Conditioning around the Natural Child

As the adult, connect with the natural child, the child who is still wholesome, full of the essence it was born with. Remember a situation in the past where the child-you felt it had enough space to enjoy its own energy and be itself, a golden memory.

Acknowledge the quality of you as a child in that situation; feel it in your body. Give a name, like beauty, courage, being, to whatever the essence vibrating in you in this moment feels like.

Now feel what happens when mother is around. Feel what happens to your body when she is there. Express what is coming up, through movement and posture.

• What expectations do you feel coming from her toward you?
• Which are the positive ones; which are the negative ones?
• What is (are) the role(s), positive and negative, that you have to fulfill for her?

Now feel what happens when father is around. Feel what happens to your body when he is there. Express what is coming up, through movement and posture.

• What expectations do you feel coming from him toward you?
• Which are the positive ones; which are the negative ones?
• What is(are) the role(s), positive and negative, that you have to fulfill for him?

Connect again with the natural child. Become aware how you can support this child in your life.

CHAPTER 4

FEELING THE CHILD (7 TO 3 YEARS OLD)

The child's whole body is erotic. He can enjoy his fingers, he can enjoy his body; the whole body is erotic. He goes on exploring his whole body; it is a great phenomenon for him. But the moment comes in his exploration when the child gets to the genitalia. Then it becomes a problem because the father and mother are all repressed. The moment the child, boy or girl, touches the genitalia, the parents become uneasy. This is to be observed deeply. Their behavior suddenly changes, and the child notes it. Something wrong has happened. They start crying, "Don't touch!" Then the child starts feeling that something is wrong with the genitalia, he has to suppress. And the genitals are the most sensitive part of your body...the most sensitive, the most alive part of your body, the most delicate. Once the genitalia are not allowed to be touched and enjoyed, you have killed the very source of sensitivity. Then the child will become insensitive. The more he will grow, the more he will be insensitive.

(Osho, *Vigyan Bhairav Tantra,* Vol. I)

Between the ages of three and six, we begin to experience a growing independence. We are busy trying to find out how the world works. In this endeavor, we are very self-centered. We test our surroundings to find out how things happen, particularly what influence we have upon on them. We test life to find out what is possible. For such a pursuit, we have to ask lots of questions. We think about what we notice and feel around us. We are at the beginning of learning who we are and how we want to live our life. And part of finding out who we are is discovering our sexual identity.

SEX PLAY ALONE AND WITH SAME AGE FRIENDS

In this time, both boys and girls start to notice the difference between them. Their natural curiosity makes them want to explore this with each other.

Both boys and girls at this age are extremely curious. Their curiosity is also expressed physically. There is an urgency and joy in exploring oneself and others: children want to know their own bodies. They like to touch themselves everywhere, especially in the genital area, where they are most sensitive. They also like to know the differences between themselves and others. Often this is done in rituals, such as "mother and father play," or "doctor play." If the parents are repressed in their own sexuality, they might punish the child for these very natural urges.

But if the parents can allow the child to have its exploration, they make space for something wonderful to happen. The child starts to recognize its own genital expression.

It finds out that boys and girls not only are different, but also fit with each other.

Remember the passionate loves affair we entered in at that age. These were the first tastes of falling in love. Even though we were children, our love had all the qualities that belong to it: attraction, fascination, curiosity and passion. We were practicing for the first time the language of love.

THE CHILD IN THE OEDIPAL TRIANGLE

As we as children are learning the language of love, this attraction to love also spreads out to our parents. Our relationship that has been until now a relationship of protection-being protected evolves into something completely new, attraction-being attracted.

Suddenly, the child starts to see and feel its parents in a completely new way. They become people separate from himself, people he can interact with. He not only can relate differently to them, also his little body responds differently to them. All the awakening libido looks for physical mirroring. The child wants to hug, kiss, play and jump and rub itself on the parents.

This physical outburst of sensuality and passion specially turns towards the parent of the opposite sex. There naturally he feels the strongest potential of being mirrored in his difference, the greatest desire to be received and loved.

As we discover that we are either a boy or a girl, we start feeling mother and father in a new way: we feel attracted and want to explore this connection. Although innocent, this attraction is very powerful. It pulls us naturally toward the opposite of our own vibration. For a boy, the mother becomes the object of fascination, worship, and adoration; for a girl, it is the father. To be guided through this new and exciting territory, each of us also feels the need to connect with the parent of the same sex as a role model. Our parents' response to both this attraction and this need for support affects us deeply. The period in which these issues arise is known as the Oedipal period.

It is not an easy time for many parents. Though consciously they might want to support their child in its exploration, unconsciously their issues around sexuality and intimacy are activated. Their own issues with their bodies, with making love and relating, their own childhood issues originating from this time are all potentially provoked.

Yet, if the parent manages to keep a natural approach towards itself and the child, the results are a blessing for the child. He will learn that his body, including his genitals, is beautiful, sacred and respected. He will remain in touch with the miracle of his existence, his physical sensuous form, the human body in all its glory.

He will remain a wholesome being.

As you continue reading, what issues might be provoked in the child in that time, please keep in mind that the perfect upbringing does not exist. When we point out what are the mistakes that can happen in the Oedipal period, and what effect they have on us as adults, it is simply to bring awareness to how we got wounded, so that we can allow healing to reach there. Compassion, passion, respect and support are the ingredients to heal the genital child in us.

So, allow yourself to fully understand what happened in that time, and stay in touch with the healing power you have access to today.

THE ISSUES OF THE BOY CHILD

The boy's erotic feelings are focused on the mother. She is all and everything, a goddess for him. In his passionate love for her, he wants to have her all for himself. With this, his connection with his father changes: he becomes a competitor for his father's place.

How many men in their childhood have been sabotaged and humiliated for this by their father? The only thing left for them was to start hiding their attraction towards mother. Does here start the basic conflict with father?

No wonder men don't trust the identification with their father. If you don't feel supported by him, and you have to submit and retreat, you don't want to be his best buddy. But this loss of support has its consequences. How much of a man's fear and inadequacy is born out of this?

And when the boy manages to jump over the hurdle of father's jealousy, there is the obstacle of mother waiting. She may not be able to handle the passionate love directed toward her at all. Because of that, she prefers to pull her little boy back into her lap, smother him and engulf him with overcare. Her own need for safety and non confrontation is fulfilled. She is not aware of the tragedy she creates. While he is trying to be the helpless infant for his mother, the boy slowly loses touch with what he likes and what he wants.

Specially if she bears a strong resentment toward men, she might reject and humiliate him for the attention he craves for. What else an he do than to hide his attraction, growing ashamed or secretive about it, becoming unable to enjoy his sensuality.

> *Ugo N. was a man in his thirties. He came to us with a big "father issue." He could not value his own decisions in life and feel like a man. His father was a strong patriarch from farmer stock. Although on repeated occasions in therapy sessions he had expressed his anger toward his father, nothing seemed to change. We asked him about his mother. His response indicated great love and idealization of her. As we went deeper, we noticed how, with the lack of intimacy between his mother and father, Ugo's mother had given her son the role of her protector. But, besides that, a deeper energetic truth surfaced: Ugo's mother had held onto him as her last baby, thus preventing him from connecting, although perhaps in a conflicting way, with his father. Ugo lacked the experience of polarity between male and female: in his bonding with women, he was a baby, resentful and puzzled about his lack of initiative. Our work was first to bring him to say goodbye to his mother, and then to encourage him to reclaim, through breathing and bodywork, his own life source. He reconnected with the sexual energy he had withheld in order to please his mother and feel connected to her. It came like a rush, a trembling in his body, accompanied by a loud and joyful "Yes!"*

Once the adult man opens up to the wounds of the little boy in him, he can start fathering that little boy, supporting him in the right way. Holding the space, putting no pressure, reducing performance, opening the heart are all qualities that support the genital boy-child inside. Looking out for healthy feminine energy, becoming available to woman's sensuous energy, exploring sexuality in a safe and respectful way, will spontaneously grow out of that.

THE ISSUES OF THE GIRL CHILD

The girl's eroticism is focused on her father. She recognizes him as the other, and a desirable other. But she can only allow herself to experiment with this attraction if she feels support from her mother. The mother who has resigned herself into a submissive role towards her husband, passes this on to her daughter. She in turn will curb her own sensuousness into passivity, and repress her wild side in order to be like her. Jealous mothers prevent their daughters from expressing their attraction to their fathers. Becoming their rival, their daughters feel isolated, with no female roots.

> During the "jellyfish exercise,"[1] Deva S. came in touch with the creativity, playfulness, freedom, and strength that originated in her natural sexuality. She could see how it had been repressed and pronounced dead. She also felt the immense anger there with it. She realized that, through her mother's conditioning, she had absorbed the attitude of the church toward her female sexuality. Now, as an adult, she felt that she could trust her inner child more than all those people of the past. And, that this child had the right to be sad and confused about the attraction and rejection that her body, her female body, had provoked, as well as about the aggression that had been directed toward her through hidden glances and double messages. When she realized that her mother was completely caught in this net, she became aware of how she herself was burdened with guilt without even knowing it. After the session, she felt very natural in her body. She noticed she could move freely, without fearing she would appear provocative.

Lacking the right example or support from her mother, the girl has no other choice than to turn to her father for this. But now he not only becomes the focus of her libidinal drive, he also starts to represent the authority and power women don't have. Once he exercises this power and expresses it in a repressive way, her longing to reach out is blocked. As Alexander Lowen says:

> In the Oedipus situation, much depends on the actual role played by the father in the childhood and youth of the girl. A strict authoritarian father can produce great fear of the male in the young girl. In such a case not only is the genital desire inhibited but the anger which arises as a result of the frustration is blocked and repressed in turn…. Repressed anger and pride block the approach to the suppressed longing. [1]

---

1   This exercise will be explained in the recipe at the end of this chapter.

To come close to her father, the girl learns to suppress her natural self. She tries to fulfill what she thinks her father likes in her as a female. How many women had to become asexual and submissive, just to please their fathers? Or how many women could only receive love by becoming their father's secret lover?

When the father, out of fear or shame for his own unresolved issues around sex, rejects the erotic affection of the girl, she returns defeated to her mother. The symbiosis continues, but this time it isn't nurturing, it is engulfing and suffocating.

We are tremendously sensitive to the feedback we receive. Criticism or rejection makes us shrink and hold back. Shame enters our body, and we feel guilty about the attraction we experienced. Many neuroses and physical blockages we experience later as adults originate from this time.

Yet, when the adult woman opens up to the wounds of the little girl in her, she can start supporting her in a new way. By affiliation, she teaches her to become like her, sensuous, strong, loving. Se can help her to enjoy her body, to discover her femininity, and to trust her natural attraction to male energy in a soft and playful way

SEXUAL ABUSE

There are parents, who try to get from their children what they themselves lack. Their children abandon themselves to give them what they are asking for. When this turns into sexual abuse, the natural unfolding of their energy gets strongly affected.

All of us have received sexual conditioning. But for some of us the this is overshadowed by experiences of sexual abuse in our childhood, by our parents, siblings, or caretakers. Abuse includes playing with genitals, oral or anal sex, penetration and masturbation of the child. But it also includes voyeurism, exhibitionism, using a child for sexual stimulation, and inflicting constant verbal abuse (sex talk) on it. When this happens to us in our childhood, the trust and safety we need to experience with the adults we depend on, is broken. Shocked by being abused, our natural sensuous impulses become associated with invasion and violence. After that, often the child takes the blame upon itself, and condemns its own natural sensuousness as the reason for the abuse. In this way, innocence is lost.

As adults, we can experience the symptoms of abuse in our daily life in the form of panic attacks or unconscious acts of self-destruction. Antisocial behavior, sex addiction, perversions, or abusive behavior can become the substitute for what has been broken and destroyed in us as children. The abused child inside of us needs to hear that it was not its fault.

It deserves the full space to express its anger, despair and disgust towards those people that wounded it. Creating healthy boundaries, learning again to say no and to say yes, are tasks that we as adults need to learn to protect the abused child inside of us.

Only by regaining its innocence and its self respect, can the child find the trust again to feel and explore its own nature and beauty.

LEARNING FROM BOTH PARENTS

What the child needs in this period, is to learn from both parents. The Oedipal period is unavoidably full of the contradictions that come with the discovery of the opposite sex and the difference between adult and child. Nevertheless, in its essence, it is a very playful and stimulating time for both boys and girls.

Parents who love and respect each other, and who respond naturally to each other's desire, create the right ground for their child to experiment. Their child is safe to test its awakening passion. Including the child in their love, yet making it clear that their sexual commitment is to each other, will set the child free. It can safely identify itself with them and in that way move beyond them. Jessica Benjamin says:

> Moreover, by accepting that the parents have gone off without him, the child may go off without the parents. If father and mother fulfill one another's desire, the child is relieved of that overwhelming responsibility. By allowing their full sexuality, the child can identify with them as sexual objects. (2)

THE EXPERIENCE OF SENSUOUSNESS AND THE BODY

Each time we are breathing, there is a pulsation in our body. There is a rhythm of charging and discharging. On the inbreath, fresh life energy, together with air, flows through our bodies. On the outbreath, toxins leave our bodies. The deeper we breathe, the more we energize ourselves. Freshness, aliveness and alertness start to arise. Our bodily sensations, as well as our emotional feelings intensify. Repressed physical and emotional expressions come to the surface and want to be released.

As Wilhelm Reich has explained in depth in his literature, we learn to control our breathing as a result of our early-life conditioning around sensuousness and eroticism. We train ourselves to breathe shallow and controlled:

> In breathing out deeply, strong feelings of pleasure or anxiety appear in the abdomen. But it is precisely the avoidance of these feelings that is accomplished by the respiratory block.... It is only in the course of this work that the machinations are revealed which the patients used as children to master their instinctual impulses and the "butterflies in their stomach." As heroically as they once wrestled with the "devil" in themselves, i.e., sexual pleasure, they now senselessly defend themselves against the cherished capacity for pleasure.... Holding one's breath for a long time was considered an heroic achievement of self-control, as was making the head and the shoulders rigid. "Grit your teeth" became a moralistic command.... Initially, such typical admonitions are rejected by children, then accepted and carried out against their will. They always weaken the backbone of the child's character, crush his spirit, destroy the life in him, and turn him into a well-behaved puppet. (3)

The life energy, which is stimulated through the natural flow of our breathing, has a need to expand from our core to the periphery of our body. It can have different expressions in different moments: it can express itself as love, anger, sex, etc.

The whole body naturally wants to support this pulsation. But the repression imposed by our parents and our environment, forces us to reject this flow of unlimited energy that starts moving through us. Our body and mind take control. A split is created: between what we want and like, and what is forbidden.

With this inner division, we don't breathe in enough and on our outbreath we repress whatever we would want to release. We learn to fight and obstruct our nature. The natural flow between charging our energy and discharging it is interrupted.

As our body starts losing this intrinsic quality of "liquidity," it becomes "armored" and rigid. As time progresses, we actually identify more and more with this armor, creating a whole life style around this imbalance.

Helen P. was a very sweet looking woman, younger in appearance than her actual age. Her main issue was feeling rejected by men, as well as a difficulty in saying what she wanted or did not want sexually from them. It was easy for her to understand how, as a little girl, she had taken the side of her weak father against her dominant mother who would burst out in sudden rage attacks against her husband and daughter. As we moved into experiencing these issues through her body, we noticed the absence of flow in the legs and pelvis: she could move and breathe, but it was as if nothing could vibrate and be really felt. Once her breathing reached the area of her diaphragm (the place that contracts and maintains the split between heart and sex), a tremendous rage erupted with such intensity and force that her voice and her rather small body seemed to occupy the whole space around her. By having surrendered her own right to rage to her mother and having molded herself into a harmless father's angel, Helen had also given up her right to be a sexual and alive woman. The rage finally subsided into vulnerability, and the vulnerability slowly turned into a trembling and a big laughter

SENSUOUSNESS AND THE CHILD

The rigidity and control that so many of us experience in our personality and our body is the result of our childhood conditioning around sexuality and pleasure. The large amount of energy we felt around that time got divided. Instead of streaming through the whole body, we learned to cut this energy in the middle, at our waist. In this way, our heart and sex lost their harmony. This results in what is known in Reichian bodywork as the "rigid" body type. As adults carrying this wound, we have well-developed bodies filled with energy, yet we cannot freely express ourselves. We replace our spontaneity with control and competition.

During the Oedipal period we did not only receive directly our mother's and father's response to our attraction, but we also absorbed their attitudes around sexuality in general.

In our openness and sensuousness, we received their messages about controlling and judging sexuality. The way our parents exerted their control was not only verbally, but also through the way they related to their own bodies. These messages entered deeply into our child's heart and sex.

We learnt how to control our energy with our mind. This gave us a certain satisfaction. By harnessing our energy for our parents, adapting to their demands, we could be like them. We started feeling a sense of identity and belonging through holding: "I can control my sensuousness like or for my parents." Reich says.

Parents suppress the sexuality of small children and adolescents, not knowing that they are doing so at the behest of authoritarian, mechanized society. Their natural expression blocked by forced asceticism and in part by the lack of fruitful activity, children develop a sticky attachment to their parents, marked by helplessness and guilt feelings. This, in turn, thwarts their liberation from the childhood situation, with all its concomitant sexual anxieties and inhibitions. Children brought up in this way become character neurotic adults who, in turn, pass on their neuroses to their children. (4)

The process of holding obstructed the organic flow of energy in our child's body. As adults, we carry the armor that grew around it. Shame and guilt replace our desires and longings. Our sex and our heart are split.

What we search for is the connection, the flow between our sexual energy and our love. We want to open our heart again and let go.

THE ESSENCE OF PASSIONATE LOVE

When our heart and sex are connected again, the essence of this state is passion. We live passionately, creatively, and with a depth of involvement. This is exactly the state a boy or girl between three and six years old is in. In this age they are passionate in their expression, their dreams, their games, their way of relating to others and life. Their budding and innocent sexual energy, not yet focused on any sexual act, provides an enormous reservoir for creativity and curiosity. The openness in their hearts provides the fuel for unlimited dreams. Their life style is one of spontaneous daring, of a reaching out beyond everything known.

This essence of passion, nurtured in our childhood, makes our adult life richer in tone, makes it a celebration. Not focused on a goal or target, its burning flame keeps going. It unites again our sex with our heart, making us true lovers of life.

Rachel W., a young woman in her twenties, was drawn to our work by the question, "Why can't I succeed in having an intimate relationship?" She was aware of her lack of daring with men, her hasty resignation, and her secret romantic dreams. When she was asked whether she had been in love with her father, her whole attitude became defensive: she was ready to

*admit to the futility of her attraction, the impossibility of stand-
ing up to her mother in the competition, etc.*

*When we acknowledged her attraction toward her father as
something normal, and, more than that, as the seed of her passionate love, a precious inner space opened. She flushed, and her
eyes brightened: the little girl, veiled by reasonability, felt seen
and supported in her wanting. The object of her wanting slowly
became irrelevant, compared to the promise of living the flame of
her desire with totality in her life.*

Saraha says (5):

> The buds of joy and pleasure
> And the leaves of glory now.
> If nothing flows out anywhere
> The bliss unspeakable will fruit.

THE EVOCATION

MY PERSONAL EXPERIENCE WITH THE ISSUE OF SEXUAL IDENTITY

SVARUP

Use metaphors

Sex was an unemntioned subject in my family: too many secret
affairs and escapades from both grandfathers, aunts, uncles, and
much evasiveness around the subject from my father. For my
mother, all had to remain hidden to protect the children from "it".

"Metaphor" was a common word in my cultivated family. "Use
metaphors," my mother would say when a man of father's side of the
family, one of those dark, hot-blooded yet tame men, would refer to
the subject of sex in my presence. "Not in front of the children."

The pure and simple fact of sex hung unspoken in the shadows.
In between the lines, the wisdom of my grandmother: "Close your
eyes, let it happen, wash yourself after and then ask him for whatever you want." . My mother would not have dreamed of saying
this: in her loyalty and friendship toward my father she was tender and committed. Yet this message dwelled deep within her cells,

80

like a spite or a distrust toward lower passions. She overlooked her man's sexual needs, reminded him constantly of higher values, was physically unresponsive. He would then turn away his lust from her, ashamed and resigned, to dream of black, luscious women, or blond Amazons. They would still love each other, with loyalty and commitment, a bit like brother and sister.

An experience with the jellyfish exercise
I am about to start a shaky journey: my body, once vibrating with the full aliveness and sensuousness of a little girl, has learned to hold back, hide, and cover whatever doesn't fit within the spoken or unspoken rules of behavior in my family.

I close my eyes. I allow the little girl inside to take the whole space in my body. Her wounds and blocks are written all over my muscles, my thighs, my sex, my heart, my eyes. I breathe deep: I can feel the fluttering, the shakiness inside my belly. I stopped breathing this deeply a long, long time ago.

The first sexual memory: a hot summer afternoon, the shutters drawn to fend off the sun, the unmoving air in the room. I am five. I close my eyes and something comes over me. A wave of sensuousness, something piercing, that makes my knees weak. I explore this strange feeling. I have no single moment of doubt that this will have to remain my secret. I wake up from this reverie and walk out of the room grumpy and perspiring, wearing a clammy undershirt and panties, feeling a bit too fat, restrained in my movements.

I breathe deeper: I allow myself to feel this chubby body, stuffed with too much white bread and control. My legs hold the secret between my thighs. My mother's silent message, a message delivered by her body: the fear of ridicule, the shame of being too large, too clumsy, a shame which needs another layer of fat not to be felt. The betrayal of my father, his rejection: "Don't be fat like your mother. Don't touch yourself there." His embarrassment, turning away from me as I reach out for the warmth of his body. Hold it.

Sexual feelings are a dark, unspoken river that flows through my veins, intermingled with rage. For more than half of my life I couldn't reconcile my sex and my heart. As a teenager, I was looking for romance and finding only sex, the dark, often shaming one. And when the heart was there, it was boring, I would end up becoming cruel and rejecting.

I breathe into the heart of this little girl: it's closed, like stone. It opens only when it flies up to the sky, to visions of the pure Virgin Mary, of a goodness that can be glimpsed upon only at a distance.

Breathe deeper; my little heart is trembling underneath, the insecurity of no guidance, no love for the budding mysteries of my body. No one to talk to. The way my mother humiliates me when she discovers me and my little friends playing doctor in the shed: she dismisses it all with a laughter, and no explanation, no protection against the outraged Catholic mothers.

The door of my heart opens.The sadness is very deep: it's the loss of my innocence, the heart burdened and resigned to only dream and be disappointed. The tears are hard in coming. I carry so much fear about making a fool of myself.

I open my eyes, and feel the eyes of the little girl. There is a veil over them, like a dark filter blocking out sunshine and air. On top of that veil, burns the charcoal of anger and defiance. That's how I look at my mother and at my father. Nobody is going to detect my need for closeness, nobody is going to see my vulnerability. Later on, I will learn to fire streaks of lightening from my eyes, to cast threatening glances, to put out a seductive look. But I will always have to do something with my eyes, to be fast and first, so that no one can ever see that helpless and thirsty being in there.

The tears come now: the longing to dance in a vast field, to roll on golden carpets of ripe wheat, to let the sun and wind caress my body. Such a vastness, so much beauty, inside and all around. I am singing, waving my arms in graceful patterns through the air. Innocence regained.

My eyes relax: I can see you now, and I can be seen. It feels a bit dangerous, vibrant. Diving into a shady pool of rest. I am not hiding anymore. I can feel this sensuous little girl inside my body: she is flushed in her cheeks, vibrating. Her eyes shine; her hair is wild. She needs to feel me, as an adult, supporting her, bringing space for sensuousness and nature back into my life. I honor and value her gift of wildness, and I take her close to my belly and heart.

My personal experience with the issue of sexual identity

Premartha

Mother
My mother's presence is very soft. Sometimes almost
absent. In those moments, it is difficult to feel her. She
has gone somewhere where there is no access for me. She
disappears in her own world, and becomes invisible.

Physically, she is there. She moves, she works, she talks, she touches, but it is without substance.

In a way, it is pleasurable. It allows me to disappear too. I can dream and dissolve. After a while, though, I feel a bit nauseous and panicked. I am losing my center and cannot find her center either. We are both floating away, each one its own way.

I don't understand why she leaves me like this. I don't want to disturb her, so when I am playing I watch her secretly. She is preparing the food, but she is not there. Her eyes are empty, as if looking into a different world. Her movements are slowed down, almost like underwater. I cannot stand it very long.

Then the panic comes. I am going to lose her now, if I don't do something, she might not return. The panic takes over, forces me to act.

So I go there, sit in her lap. I ask her questions. I wait for answers. When she answers, I can relax. I found a lifeline with which to pull her back. We talk together.

I watch her carefully. Sometimes I touch her face, and tell her how much I love her. She is embarrassed, but I know she likes it. She takes me deeper in her lap. It's warm there, and cosy, and it smells of her, a mixture of warm skin, kitchen herbs, and fresh laundry.

She tousles my hair, and tells me I am too big to sit in her lap. I know she is right, but I don't want to go. I am afraid that, when I go, she will disappear.

In each movement she makes, in the way she touches me, I can feel her sensuality. But it's always sad. It's a sensuality that makes me lose my will. It throws me like in a river, and I float, though I would like to swim and enjoy. I can feel that I should not be too much for her.

When I become passionate with her, she withdraws. She doesn't punish. She simply pulls back and out of reach. I am standing there with all my love, helpless, powerless.

After a while, I withdraw too. I bury my sensuality deep inside me, calm myself down. I wait for the moment when I can connect again with her.

When it comes, I love the merging with her. But at the base of my pelvis, in the core of my senses, I am sad.

Father

In my sadness, I look for father. He is not much inside our home. Most of his days he spends on our property. He organizes and arranges everything. He loves to be outdoors.

In contrast to my mother's skin, who is milky white and very soft, his skin is ruddy, browned by the sun, and weather beaten. His complexion is dark olive skin and black hair. My mother is honey blond. They are opposites in everything.

I love my father when he moves around. He has energy, his movements are focused, he is always busy. He is dressed in outdoors clothes, thick cottons and Manchester., boots and hat. I watch him and wait for him to invite me.

He never does. Maybe the waiting and watching that I have learnt with my mother, alienates me from him. I don't know how to jump. Sometimes I feel so tense, my muscles ache from holding back that jump. But I am to insecure with him to take the initiative.

So, he forgets me. He is anyway a man with very little needs. His meals, he takes with us, but it is as if there is an invisible wall between him and us. Even his food is different. He likes red meat, rye bread, black coffee, while my mother prefers white bread, cream, cheese and tea. I lose myself in between them. I follow my mother's taste, though secretly I am attracted to what he likes.

My body wants to be held by him, by his big man's hands, close to his big man's chest I love his smell, which is the smell of earth, smoke, body, something almost tribal and primitive. I would want to share in his passion, in his capacity to act and to take care. I am always ready for it to happen. Like a wound up spring waiting to be released.

But he doesn't need me.

Talking, he doesn't like. But it's the only way I have learnt to bridge the absence of my mother. When I talk to him, I am always afraid he will get irritated. I already protect myself. In that way, I am not an easy child for him either. Maybe he mistakes my insecurity for unwillingness or silent criticism. I don't know.

It happens that we meet, rarely, but it does. Usually it's outdoors, in his world. Away from the family. Then, when hen he turns to me, he is very loving. Warmhearted and also careful. I don't know how to respond. I am terribly shy and afraid that this will make him turn away from me. I do my best to listen to him, but deep down I am panicked and afraid to miss the moment.

Afterwards, I feel guilty for not having responded well enough and I think of a thousand ways in which I could have done better.

The jellyfish

It takes me a moment to relax in the body position. It feels quite delicate and exposing, my knees up and apart, lying on my back. But slowly slowly, with the in and out breath, my pelvis gently starts to rotate. It's a movement at the same time charging my energy, and discharging. Filling up with breath energy, and letting go.

Sometimes I disappear and forget, and it seems I am staying in one long outbreath. It's clear that my childhood conditioning has made it more easy for me to discharge than to charge. Charging myself makes me always shaky. A bit panicked. As if I am not able to contain that much energy, and better let it go...

After a while, the movement changes, and now comes the part where my legs are moving very slowly together, and apart. It's not an unpleasant feeling, though again, I notice my emphasis turns automatically in letting my knees fall apart. But now I know this pattern, so I consciously focus a bit more on the coming together.

Soon my legs start to tremble. It's an involuntary trembling and I have no control over it. It produces a mixture of pleasure and fear.

Fear to lose control.

After all the pelvic area, with its eliminating functions of urinating and defecating, is an area that is intensely conditioned in our childhood. Plus the additional charge of sexuality that comes from the genital area. It's a hot spot.

The trembling evokes the feeling of the child inside me. His insecurity and shame with father, his panic and control with mother, come to the surface. I feel them as subtle blockages, interferences in my energy. With very definite images and belief sentences.

Together with the trembling, all these old physical and psychological toxins are being released. It's an art not to get overwhelmed by them, or to stop the exercise or to space out. Here comes in a good dose of will. The will, the decision, to not resign, however scary continuing feels like.

By moments, my whole genital area becomes ice cold, a terrible feeling, but recognizable. After a while, when I continue, warmth flows back in again. With it, the sensuality starts to wake up. And a strong coming home feeling follows. It's so clear in this moment that I am also my pelvis. I am also my senses, my sex, my pleasure. The warmth of this discovery spreads to my belly and rises up to my solar plexus. There, the trembling meets a narrowing. It's not completely blocked, but it hardly flows anymore. I can feel the powerful control that society has installed there, in my childhood, and the fear and exhaustion of my child in trying to fight it. I realize that pushing it will not help, and that I will have to slow down and feel it.

After what feels like an eternity, my midriff relaxes and the trembling flows through. It is difficult to describe the release and the sense of victory that comes with it. It is as if my father stood up for me, did not abandon me, on the contrary supported me.

Now the trembling reaches the heart, a release of joy, of love, of compassion. Tears and laughter. Welcoming my mother back into my heart. My little boy spreads his arms wide. Like wings, and the energy is flowing till his fingertips.

By now, the breathing as become spontaneous and easy, so when the trembling continues spreading through the throat, in the face, to the top of the head, the whole body feels sensuous and orgasmic, flowing, natural, and innocent

To be hugged in this state is what my child never experienced. To feel love and respect and support flowing from the other, unconditionally, is what my child never knew. Now he does, and it feels like his birth right has been given back to him.

THE RECIPE

THE JELLYFISH EXERCISE

This exercise is called "jellyfish" because it focuses on rediscovering a subtle trembling in your body, like that of a jellyfish in the ocean. This trembling is a sign of your sensuousness loosening up and streaming throughout your body.

In this exercise bring your awareness to your sex center. Notice a subtle trembling there. Observe how the energy spreads from the thighs and the pelvic floor through the solar plexus upward.

Observe this overflow reaching the heart. It becomes a sharing, a giving and receiving.

Feel how it brings back the light and wonder to your life, like when you were a child.

CHAPTER 5

PROTECTING THE CHILD (5 TO 2 YEARS OLD)

Somewhere near the age of three the child becomes civilized. We force him. We initiate him into civilization... And civilization up to now has been a kind of insanity, a madhouse. We force the child to become more and more intellectual and less and less intelligent. We force the child to be more and more prosaic and less and less poetic. We force the child to become more and more concerned about the non-essential...Money, prestige, power, ambition... And more and more uninterested in the real joys of life. We turn the child from a playful being into a worker. The work ethic enters. Now duty becomes more important than love; formality becomes more important than informal flow; manners become more important than truth; policy becomes more important than authenticity.

(Osho, *Sufis: the People of the Path,* Vol. II)

SPACIOUSNESS

Imagine yourself shortly after birth. You have been nine months in the womb of your mother. You were never alone. There was no division between you and her. No boundaries. Each second of your life, you were part of her.

You were coming from universal space, the cosmic womb. Still in her womb, you experienced this spaciousness in its manifested purity. Nothing defined you in being separatefrom the womb surrounding you. Until birth came.

Through birth, you received the beginning of a great teaching. The movement from unlimited spaciousness into being defined, formed, contained. A teaching that gave you the experience of spaciousness permeating space. Space holding spaciousness.

From there, the journey of discovering boundaries started. In your little earthly body, you were for the first time confronted with all kinds of limitations and separations. You discovered that you were part of an existing system already. You were challenged to find your own boundaries. You forgot about your original spaciousness. The journey to find back home had started.

Mother and father as the first representations of our boundaries

The practicing phase

After birth, our main connection is still with our mother. We are still merged with her in a feeling of a oneness. Our senses remain like an extension of her senses. We perceive and feel the world through her. All our attention is centered on her.

But there comes a moment when we lift up our head and start looking beyond her. With this simple movement, the search for our own self starts. We have started our jounry towards our own individuality.

As Margaret Mahler describes thoroughly in her book The Psychological Birth of the Human Infant (1), between the ages of six and fourteen months, the separation-individuation process fully starts. For the small child, it is a subtle learning between its dependency and independency. On one side, the child at that time experiences a growing fascination about the world which lies beyond its mother's embrace. It contains all kinds of new sights and sensations. On the other side, while delighting in its discoveries, the child still needs her protection against falling or getting hurt.

As the child grows and its muscles develop, it starts experiencing an increasing amount of physical energy. Moving more and more, its energy comes to a crescendo of testing, trying, and reaching out. It thrusts itself forward toward anything that catches its attention. Still, it feels close to the mother. Almost as if there remains an invisible cord keeping it connected with her body. Through this bonding, the child feels much bigger than it really is. This creates a feeling of omnipotence. It is not yet aware of the size of its own body and its limitations.

At this age, the play between our enthusiasm and our safety is a very delicate one. Our impulses need to be supported and given space so we can explore the world around us. Through this exploration, we develop a feeling for what we like and what we don't like. But we are not yet fully independent. We rely on our mother's capacity to hold space, to create a safe environment around us. Her presence enables us to move away and experiment, but also to return and relax. In our inner world, we perceive the boundaries she sets around us as containing positive or negative charge, either protecting or repressing us in our exploration.

An engulfing or overprotecting mother, makes us feel suffocated. Our natural need to explore the world is stopped. On the other hand, a mother who is not really present to hold the space for us, does not create the safety we need to feel to be able to explore.

What is happening with mother at this stage of development in our later life greatly influences our capacity to create space for ourselves and still feel connected and protected by the world around us.

> *Bodhi K., a man in his mid-thirties, had extreme difficulty in expressing what he wanted. He was living a rather isolated life, and had no intimate friends except for a girlfriend with whom he could not live for more than few days at a time. He was addicted to drugs and drowning in overwork. During our session on the issue of boundaries, he became aware of how his mother, a stranger in the country where he was born, had held him within her space in order to avoid her own loneliness and estrangement. He, as a child, had succumbed to this engulfment. His unexpressed "no" remained inside. Whenever it surfaced, drug and work addiction recreated the atmosphere of safety and numbness that he felt within his mother's space.*
>
> *When Bodhi became aware of this, he began to experience this engulfment as being surrounded by fog, pierced only occasionally by the lightning of his mother's frustration. He recognized the pain and anger of his imprisoned inner child and realized that his "no" needed to be expressed, that drug or work addiction wouldn't help address these feelings. He decided to face the issues which prolonged intimacy with his girlfriend would bring up, and told her what he wanted and didn't want from her. He made it a point to set up a time and a structure for their meetings, which became more relaxed and authentic. After facing an initial fear of rejection and loss, Bodhi started relating in a wholesome way for the first time.*

The rapprochement phase

As the rapprochement phase sets in around the age of one and a half, the child starts walking, moving with greater speed and determination toward objects it wants. It can provoke a lot of frustration to discover that mother doesn't agree with what it wants and where it wants to go. Its sense of omnipotence is challenged. Suddenly, there is a limit and there are boundaries.

However frustrating, healthy limits are needed for the child. They create a sense of a feeling of safety, and at the same time support the child's budding individuality.

But the boundaries that mother sets for her child during this time can reflect her own fear of separation or her lack of initiative.

If she is very rigid, and represses and stops the child a lot, the child cannot experience its need for freedom. It doesn't know when to hold on and stay, and when to let go. In this dilemma, passivity and obedience become the only alternatives.

In our adult life, the phenomenon of "separation anxiety" reflects the difficulties we experienced at this stage. When we feel confused and panicked when we need to go our own way. We might decide to not act, and rather let others decide for us. In these moments, the child in us is afraid to lose mother's protection and approval. What we need to learn is that we have a natural inner balance that regulates our capacity to be with others and our desire to go our own way. Left undisturbed to develop, this balance functions spontaneously and perfectly.

FATHER AS THE OUTGOING PRINCIPLE

During the rapprochement stage, the child starts to become aware of father. It is fascinated by the way he comes in and out of its world. The difference between father and mother is very attractive to the child. Full of life enthusiasm, the child turns its attention toward father. It starts identifying with its freedom to move.

For a little boy, this is his initiation into the male world. The love for father prevents him from being pulled back into the symbiosis with mother. A love affair starts: the little boy admires, adores father in an ecstatic and noncompetitive way. He wants in every way to be like him.

A little girl also falls in love with father. Through father's response to her adoration she feels included in his world. By trusting him she starts to trust her own independence.

In identifying with father, the child starts synchronizing with him. The attraction toward him gives it the strength to follow its curiosity for the outside world. If mother is the ground for the movement, father is the fuel for it: the child now has someone who is safely there, and someone who points the way and knows the territory. In this way, it is learning its first lessons about the world and how to move in it.

But father's beliefs about the outside world, can enter deeply into the child's system. Before it can experience the world directly, it already "knows" through father that it is a hostile place, or that there is nowhere to go, or that moving outwards is an uphill task.

Later on in our lives, we translate these early beliefs onto the world around us. They become the core of the rules that dictate our actions. It is difficult for us to stop acting according to them. We absorbed them at the very beginning of our adventure to become separate individuals. They still represent the support that we needed from father.

Guido Z. had extreme difficulty in being flexible in his ideas about the world and how it should function. His ideology was open-minded and modern, yet it reflected a rigidity and a split. Guido himself could not live up to his ideals of purity, compassion, freedom, etc. He blamed himself for that and never felt good enough.

Guido's father, orphaned as a child, was a military man who had compensated for the lack of guidance in his early years by adopting the strict and clear rules of the army. When Guido explored his father's boundaries, he felt how their rigidity covered up a deep feeling of inadequacy. He himself as a child had felt suffocated and restricted by these boundaries. He remembered how later throughout his adolescence he had chosen to take up any ideology which opposed the official status quo. He recalled his own fanaticism and intolerance, and acknowledged how he, in fact, had adopted his father's way of setting boundaries, only with different labels.

Standing a bit longer within his father's space and feeling how it had barely overlapped with his own space as a child, the deeper feelings of the child started to surface: first, the anger and rage for the physical violence that had been their only bodily contact, then, a very profound grief for the lack of support from his father.

He admitted to his great need for support from men, that it was time for him to connect with them in a more personal way. Joining them through work, sports, or politics couldn't provide him with the intimacy, physical exchange, and play which he had never received from his father.

THE POLARITY BETWEEN MOTHER AND FATHER

As the child's identification expands toward father, mother still carries a very important role. She needs to "introduce" father to the child, to support its curiosity for him. If she cannot do this, because she doesn't trust him, or is frustrated in their relationship, the child will feel a split.

However, if mother herself has a sense of independence, then both boys and girls can remain connected with her in their outward going discovery. They experience that she understands and respects their fascination with father, and that she is happy to share this new phase of their growth with her husband. As Jessica Benjamin explains:

In this spirit, we can value both traditional figures of infancy--the holding mother and the exciting father--as constituent elements of desire. As we have seen, holding and the space created by it (the female principle) allow the self to experience the desire as truly inner; so, it is not merely the recognizing response of the exuberant, exciting father that ignites the child's own sense of activity and desire. The mother's holding, or containment, is equally important. (2)

CONFLICT RESOLUTION

The way people approach conflict in their adult life is directly related to how their parents approached conflict during their childhood.

Because of being focused on standing on its own feet and learning to go its own way, the child is keenly aware of how its parents solve their issues around living their own lives and yet remaining together.

If our parents had difficulty in expressing their disagreements, and covered them up by silent tension or politeness, we haven't learnt how to solve conflict, and we try to avoid conflict at all costs. Or growing up with two parents who always fight, and never come to a resolution, teaches us not to believe in the possibility of harmony and peace.

FAMILY BOUNDARIES

The combination of mother's and father's beliefs around their own boundaries, their joint view of the world and their place in it, and the abidance to these rules by the child and other family members (siblings, grandparents, etc.) create what we call the family boundaries.

The family system with its boundaries is more than the sum of its members. It takes on a life of its own. It is like a small nation whose needs for stability and balance take precedence over the individual needs of its members.

In her session on the issue of boundaries, Deva S. experimented with taking the place of each one of her family members within the family boundary system.

In her father's place, she became aware of how isolated he was from the rest of the family. He had never spoken about it, and had instead taken up working day and night.

Standing in her mother's place, Deva S. felt how her mother had given up on him, and wanted to make sure that her daughter would not become so dependent on a man. Going deeper into this place, Deva S. realized how her mother kept everything under control by being the contact person between all the family members.

In her older brother's place, she experienced his refusal to live, that crippled him, even physically. She felt how he was even more isolated than their father, and that he could never live up to his expectations.

In her own place, Deva S. understood that she had become what her father had expected from her brother: aggressive and assertive. When, at the end, she placed her family members in the order she would have liked them to be, she put herself outside. We asked her to focus on what this position contained for her.

Each family system carries a set of values, rules, and a hierarchy which defines its boundaries toward the outside world and inside the household.

When a child is born, it already occupies its place within this system. As the time to experiment with its boundaries comes, the child will not only have to meet its individual parents' limits, but also the structure that its family carries in relation to the outside world.

In relation to their boundaries the family can be divided into three main categories (2):

THE THREE FAMILY TYPES

• The "cultic" family, rigid toward the outside and within the family, in which everyone has its place and function. Rules of behavior: perfectionism and sacrifice.

• The "chaotic" family, in which boundaries are enmeshed and confused both within and outside the family (children take care of the parents, messages are incongruent). Rules of behavior: failure and inconsistency.

• The "corrupt" family, in which everything is allowed within the family and nothing of it is visible on the outside. Rules of behavior: secrecy and abuse.

In each one of these fixed structures, the child is bound to take the place that has been assigned to it. If it wants love, protection, acknowledgment, belonging within the system, it has to give up its privacy and natural boundaries. A great split is created between its natural desires and drives and what is expected from it. [1]

THE CHILD BECOMES ENGAGED IN WARFARE WITH ITS OWN ENERGY

These family patterns create a fixed character in us, and solidify around our bodies. They reflect the split that happens in each one of us.

If these patterns affect us the most in the practicing phase, they

result in a body and personality structure that in Reichian therapy is known as the "psychopath" body type. As adults, when we carry this conditioning, we usually carry a lot of energy in our upper body, it can even be overcharged. But our lower body lacks energy. Our chest is strong, but our legs are weak.

As children, our conditioning was carried out in a manipulative and indirect way. We were seduced to give up our own will. Mostly, this happened through the parent of the opposite sex. Before we were really ready, we were put in a special position. We tried to be bigger than we really were. We didn't have the time to trust the timing of our own impulses. We disconnected, lost touch with ourselves, and physically drew our energy upwards. We became little adults. Our energy became in the service of self-control and control over others. The natural flow of breathing and feeling in our belly was interrupted, and a deep outbreath of relaxation was no longer possible. On this sonstant inbreath, we did not have the time anymore to explore our own natural ways.

If the family patterns affect us the most in the rapprochement phase, they result in what is known as the "masochist" body type. As adults, when we carry this wound, we have compressed and compact bodies. We are full of energy, but appear to be overloaded. We are resistant in expressing feelings, and often feel stagnant or stuck. Our unexpressed flood of natural power weighs heavily on us. We are engaged in warfare with our own energy. These blockages are part of our self-image. We mistake this holding as the only form of strength which is allowed us. Our "no," unexpressed toward parents who were unable to respond to it, has turned into a "no" toward our own aliveness and spontaneity.

As children, this conditioning was carried out in a verbally

---

1   We will expand on this subject in Chapter 6.

repressive or physically rigid or violent way. It taught us to hold back our will and impulses, especially in our legs and solar plexus, which are in the process of being fully developed around the time of boundary setting. We learnt to train ourselves to hold the not welcomed power in those parts of our body, shut down our voice, and take our "no" to the limitations imposed by father and mother and hold it in shame and guilt upon our neck and shoulders.

THE INTERNALIZED PARENT AND THE LOVING ADULT

As we grow up, this split between how we should be and should not be is internalized. However much our child inside still has a yearning for space and experiences beyond what is familiar and known, as adults, unconsciously we control that child in the same way our family system kept us within its boundaries.

If we come from a "cultic family," we have the tendency to discount and judge our inner child's desires as useless and unproductive.

If we come from a "chaotic" family, we have a tendency to neglect its needs for privacy and rest, and to ignore what it wants.

If we come from a "corrupt" family, we have a tendency to punish and abuse our child inside for its innocence, or let it run wild and go too far until it gets hurt.

To stop listening to these toxic voices of the past, and to start listening to our inner child in a new way is the simplest and most direct response to this. As adults, we step out of the invisible prison that we keep creating for ourselves.

In the process of regaining our healthy boundaries, flexible and responsive to situations as they come along, we first need to understand that our map of the world does not originate from our own experience. The fears and limitations we carry are passed down and transmitted by our wounded parents. We need to allow the young toddler inside us to express that powerful original "no" that has been suffocated by their rules. This "no" is just the spark that once more will set fire to our "yes" to initiative and lust for discovery.

WILL POWER AND SURRENDER GO HAND IN HAND

When our time comes to start exploring the space around us, and the boundaries that define it as safe and inviting, our essential quality of willpower is budding. In the child, this is a natural phenomenon. Its whole body is ready for the experience of moving.

Its movement has no goal, just an enormous amount of enthusiasm and determination toward whatever awakens its interest.

When we look at a child, we notice how it easily moves through extremes: total activity is followed by total rest, in a natural flow. Willpower and surrender go hand in hand. In the moments of rest, the little boy or girl returns to its center, fully relaxing into an inner boundless space. When action arises again, it is the expression of an overflow, of being so full inside that sharing that energy is a natural consequence.

The child's attunement with itself is the seed of spiritual experience. It consists of ease, trust, and a readiness to move outward. The Taoist tradition, through Lao Tzu and Chuang Tzu, points out that it is exactly from this space of relaxed non-doing that meaningful actions arise. These actions have a truthfulness and solidity about them which is grounded in the quality of being. This is also called the "watercourse" way. It is the most refined expression of the combined force of surrender and will. When we move like water through the rocks and obstacles of life, we surrender to their solidity and shape, and at the same time, we keep flowing around them in an easy and relaxed way.

SPIRITUAL BOUNDARIES: OPENING UP FOR NEW TERRITORIES OF EXPERIENCE

The pain of the original loss of space, and the memory of how we had to curb it within boundaries that were not our own creation is very strong. We trained ourselves to be contented with the space that was allowed to us, and created our body-image within that space. To open up to the boundlessness of our inner world again is threatening. It makes us feel exposed once more to the fear of invasion and loss. A. H. Almaas says.

> This illustrates the primary reason for the extreme difficulty encountered when an individual attempts to achieve a clear experience of open space through meditation techniques, as in Eastern spiritual schools; for the experience of space, because it involves the dissolving of defenses, will bring into consciousness any distortion of the body-image. The defense mechanisms of the ego will then automatically mobilize. This mobilization of defenses in effect amounts to the repression of space. (4)

In the way we were brought up, not much acknowledgment is

given to that inward-going movement back to the quality of being and boundlessness. Underneath this, perhaps, is a fear of being unprotected, of being invaded, or of dissolving into the unknown.

But, if we want to reach that place inside all of us which is beyond boundaries, where all is one, we cannot stay within known limits.

When we want to step beyond these invisible boundaries that restrict our spiritual experience, we may be confronted with a feeling of defenselessness. For a while, we may feel lost and disorientated.

But, no longer following a fixed direction to go, and being awed by the vastness of our inner world make us more alive and human. We become deeply connected to the child inside. We regain our childlike trust, we start to open up for new worlds of experience.

Then, the boundaries we need around us are part of the space, they hold the space lovingly and respectfully, they are made of the soft protection of our self-love and our own appreciation for the journey we are on.

Soseki says (5):

> Don't ask why the pine trees
> In the front garden
> Are gnarled and crooked.
> The straightness
> They were born with
> Is right there inside them.

THE EVOCATION

My personal experience with the issue of boundaries

Svarup

Fiery and light, sensuous and strong

I see the 5 year old Manù at the beach: a kerchief knotted up around her short black curls, squinting in the glare of the sun, digging a hole in the sand. She is wearing a yellow bathing suit and she looks wild, intent, and happy.

I dive with my consciousness into her body. Through her senses I perceive my surroundings. The intensity of the salty air mixed with fine sand blowing on my body, the smell of the sea, the heat, the sound of the waves, the laughter of other children, some distant music. The space around me is wide, golden as the sand, orange and red. Around it, the light blue of the sky. I can expand in all directions, feel fiery and light, sensuous and strong.

My mother's boundaries: dark blue

I feel the presence of my mother. Her concern for me encircles me with dark blue.

I can hear her voice: "You can't go in the water before you've digested your meal, someone got cramps and drowned because of that. I don't care what other children do, come into the shade!"

The dark blue blots the lighter blue of the sky, and the golden orange-red of my aliveness becomes a bit brown. To defend my impulse, I try to create a black ring of stubbornness around me. I will keep my fire for myself then. But with that, movement is gone.

My father's boundaries: a warm, gray fog, gentle and distant

Somewhere at the periphery of my space I feel the presence of my father. It has the quality of a warm, gray fog, gentle and distant. It is out of my reach. Protected by this cloud of absence, the glowing earthy red of his sensuous nature is burning lazily in its own flame. I would like to touch that flame, but the gray haze prevents the contact, although it is transparent enough to reveal the flame at the core. Instead, it is his grayness that seems to touch me, to enter me in an ever so subtle and invisible way. It softens the black ring around me, it makes it more bearable for a moment, and then it's gone again. I am learning the art of disconnecting and retiring into a dream world. There, I share my space with Daddy.

My sister: she stole the merging

Valeria, my little sister, is there. Her energy is trembling, golden, new and fresh. She occupies no space and all space. Her boundaries are not defined yet, they are one with mother. Her golden glow shimmers at the edges of my mother's blue and softens it. I feel tremendously jealous: she stole the merging with mother. I can't show my jealousy. And I can't show the longing to connect which lies underneath it. Our family is made of separate units, and it has to stay like this.

My parents together: we are dancing a pretty dance together

I turn my attention toward both my parents at the same time.

They are talking with each other. Her original blue and his earthy red quiver and reach out for each other in a hush of sensuousness, and then suddenly retreat completely to their respective cores. There is a gap, a moment of silence, a tightening of control. On their inbreath, they reach out again, but this time only with their minds: a new pattern weaves itself between them. It is lacy, and it has light and diaphanous colors. It's pink and peachy, unfolding higher and higher. It is pretty, insubstantial, gracious, and safe. Nothing is really touched, but everything seems to move. Until the next tender impulse will draw the closer for another single moment.

I absorbe this dance. From the way they relate, I am learning that conflict and passion must be reined. They are dangerous, raw and physical. They would upset the fine balance that we are all trying to keep.

I also want to become gracious and understanding. I try it out. I am instantly received, taken in, encouraged. I have a new sense of space, a shared space. Our bodies do not touch, and neither do our secret longings. But we are dancing a pretty dance together.

Soft exposure, and a good fight with a laugh

I gently lift myself up from the little girl's body.

In my adult body I can easily recognize those patterns still woven all around it. I also can feel inside the longing that is leading me out and away from them, on the search for sensuous authenticity. I look at the intricate lines of colors and threads lying all around the little girl. I feel the need to free the space around her.

The little girl needs to feel safe. What she needs is a green boundary of relaxation around her. A space which allows the truth to grow inside her, that gives her a sense of rest within herself. The green will moisten the core, allowing her inner glow to radiate in a gentle way. She needs soft exposure.

I dive back into the little girl's body, feeling the green all around me: a sense of no hurry, of being, of moving gently through. The dark blue of my mother becomes what it originally was: a sense of awareness, presence. The gray fog of my father dissolves, and the earthy red wavers to find its place somewhere in the sun, where it can vibrate and be sensuous.

I feel the presence of my adult self, the reassurance that it gives me. I can have time and space. And she will teach me how to have a good fight, and to laugh and celebrate at the end of it.

I come back to my adult body. I am here with my little girl, in a tender breeze, taking my time, feeling my body, learning the dance of nature and the language of truth.

Premartha

My mother's boundaries: slightly pastel or faded

My mother's colors are all slightly pastel. Or faded. Something in her has disappeared. Maybe the real wish to live, or the trust that she can fulfill her potential. She is often tired.

She can also be very irritated, then suddenly it all seems to be enough, and she verbally attacks and scolds. Her voice is sharp then, and her words hurt. Sometimes she is cruel and cold. And her pale colors are not symbols of absence, but of control and withheld anger.

She can also be gentle, and in that state, for moments she appears almost formless. Her boundaries not contained then, but large and loose. A mother to sink and disappear into. Even then her colors appear faded, like the colors of old and much loved clothes. She takes a central space in the life of my family. When she is at ease, we all have the tendency to gather around her; we become absorbed by her. We all relax, we laugh a lot, and talk all at once.

When she gets irritated, or when her authority gets challenged by our rebellion or disagreement with her rules, she scatters us around like a ferocious wind. We try to hide, and duck our shoulders and heads to make ourselves invisible. But nobody is safe.

Apologies are the only way to calm her down then. But not only through words. We have to prove it. Until she relaxes again, and we all relax with her. Then her gentleness returns, and embraces us all.

My father's boundaries: a dark presence

My father's colors are always dark. Deep red and black. And lots of brown. As if he wants to lose his own definition in the surroundings. The depth also has a natural warmth to it. Something one can trust deeply. It does not contain the lightness of my mother's energy. Even his voice has a deep sound.

But when he has his sudden anger attacks, the dark and deep core in him splits open, and fire bursts out, burning and all-consuming. The attacks are short and quickly consumed. Then he closes off. All his colors turn into an indefinable brown.

At the slightest demand by my mother, he retreats. He leaves the room, and the house. He disappears in his work on the property. Or when there is nothing to do, he steals into an inner retreat, where he is incommunicable and out of reach.

If conflicts happen in the evening or later in the night, or when things remain unresolved for a long time, he comes and sleeps in the empty bed in my room. He doesn't connect with me; he just turns away. The space is full of his mood. Sometimes, I get taken into my mother's bed. I feel warm and comfortable there, but guilty for taking his place.

Even though he is on the periphery of the family, he maintains a solid position. His presence creates a feeling of safety. But it is as impersonal as the presence of a tree.

The family

I am drawn in by mother's form and shape. My energy field is still light blue and gold. But when I come too close to her or stay too long, my colors fade away, and I become pale like her.

Even her formlessness invades me then. I want to stay close to her forever, and fear each moment we are separate. I cling to her, her dress, her leg. I become too pale, and no longer able to find my own way. There is a deep, unconscious fear that she might not love me as I hope she does. Because of that, I should never hurt or disappoint her. It could destroy her; she would go and disappear forever.

But then, she suddenly breaks her faded boundary lines, and attacks sharply. Often she focuses her anger on my sisters, and I am afraid for them. But I cannot interfere. Her way of dealing with them is out of my control. I can only wait until it has passed.

My sisters stick together. My mother's anger pushes them into this. Although they are often sweet with me, I don't really belong to them. I love them a lot, but cannot show it too overtly. I might lose my special place, and the safety of being out of her field of attack.

And when I try to break out from her world which pulls me in, what stops me is that I don't want to leave her alone. I understand her too well. Her loneliness, her lost dreams. Her apathy, her sorrow. I feel enveloped by it, and I carry it around with me. I cannot hurt her. I believe I am her last hope, that it all depends on me, that I keep her alive and going. The worst defeat for me is her sadness. When she closes off, she still functions in the house, but her gestures become slow and heavy, and there is an absence in her eyes. In these moments, I want to do everything I can for her. Anything to make her happy. To make her smile and laugh again, and answer my questions with so much gentleness.

My father's energy remains that of a stranger. I reach out for him, but he is not there. The few times he responds, I am too panicked to receive it. I am learning to be afraid of him.

I understand my mother's feelings well. I don't know what he is feeling. But I love him. I admire his handwork and the way he can make things. I long for his presence and wait for a sign of love. But the connection remains very fragile.

What happens when my parents turn to each other?

What happens when they turn to each other? It feels like a powerful meeting. There is magnetism there, and an electric undercurrent. Good sex. Earthy and creative. His colors are becoming more vibrant and visible. Still deep. Her colors are brightening up and sparkle in their subtle pastel shades. He is vibrant red, some black, and also some deep, deep blue. A blue of longing. She is pink and yellow and white, light and happy. His depth infuses her and gives force to her potential, her sparkle and light brings laughter to him, and joy in sensuousness, love of life.

Seeing this, I am stunned by the fireworks between them. A witness to something very alive. I feel in their happiness that they love me. It is a natural overflow. I am infused by their contrasting energies.

I feel alive and vital. Unburdened of guilt. I am not responsible for them. They can take care of themselves.

I know they rejoice in me and in my freedom. That they too are touched by the innocence of life. I see their eyes as they look at me before turning to each other again. They say, "Enjoy life, it is our gift to you, for free."

I receive their gift with gratitude, free to go my own way.

Ptino's 2 new boundaries: a stillness of utter tenderness

It is a sunny day as Ptino walks along the beach. In the night there was gentle turquoise rain. The remaining droplets shine like rainbow-colored jewels. The green is alive and vibrant; branches full of soft, downy leaves reach out in the early morning sun. There is a fragrance, young as the dawn. Of transparent violet and blue. Lingering soft colors in the air.

Ptino's whole body feels liquid. It doesn't need defining, safe in the loving presence of a nature which stretches out and yawns in ever so delicate sounds. And when he yawns, everything around him pours in, tickling him with fresh life. The last sleep floats away like puffed-up clouds, to rest in the hollows of branches and on the soft beds of leaves.

Ptino is happy. For no reason. His feet are splashing in the sea, which gently laps over them. He listens to the songs of the birds, some nestling in the green, others flying around with their wings spread in new abandon. The parakeet, the cockatoo, the bird of paradise.

---

2   Ptino is the name that I gave to my child for this particular story.

Pale-cream pheasants, royal blue peacocks, and red-breasted robins. All twitter and quiver, singing songs of the new dawn.

Ptino is a colorful bird himself. He wears his velvety orange shorts, and a turquoise Hawaiian shirt to match. He is happy to be alive and awake. His little legs walk rhythmically along the beach. He listens to inaudible songs which float around him and make him dance. His whole body responds to the rhythm of it now. It starts from his feet, which make their own movements. His legs follow, up and down. The warmth spreads to his belly, upward to his chest. From there, it is only a moment before his arms open wide. They swing around and sway. Then, his throat opens up and his voice comes out singing. He sings nonsense songs that make him laugh. His eyes are sparkling the brightest blue, his curls swaying in their honey-colored light.

Ptino has entered the world of the senses. A sacred world. Where everything is clear, and delicately drawn; where sound becomes color, color one can feel. Where no sense remains separate from any other, but all are one. Ptino dances his own dance to his inner melody. The birds, the trees and the flowers, the waves, the sky, the sand: all are one now. Distinct and unique, yet blended into one whole.

Ptino's heart is bursting. He spins around, whirling himself to abandon. He is at the center, and the universe whirls around him.

Stars and planets, and a deep-blue night sky stretch beyond the morning. He can trust his trust.

He whirls and whirls. With less and less effort until it becomes a floating. A silent, royal floating. Majestically, with arms outstretched, he is whirling in deep blue. His form becomes irrelevant, his separation not needed now. Tears spring from his gentle eyes, to float and whirl around him, like planets in orbit. Everything is very still. A stillness of utter tenderness.

A silent floating around the axis of Ptino's being. A coming home. The day drifts by. The sun rises to its peak, then starts its descent. Ptino turns and turns. His ears attuned to an inner melody. Until Ptino lets go, and lies on the velvety-soft sand. His arms and legs outstretched. The cosmos whirls within him and he lies at its center. On the curve of his mother earth.

Ptino cries; a stream of long forgotten tears bubbles up from deep inside his belly. Tears fresh like morning dew, and salty like the sea. Through these tears a lake inside is released. Of deep, dark blue waters contained. That finally can pour out onto the sand, and into the sea. It leaves him full of emptiness.

The sun is setting now. An orchestra of vivid farewells plays all around him. The birds sing their early evening songs, and the wind gently covers the leaves, as a mother covers her child. Ptino slowly sits up. His little body all emptied, he is here. Silently sitting on the shore. The deep, opaque colors of the setting sun turn everything into gold. A turquoise sheen remains, the last light of the sleepy sun. He sits and waits. Nowhere to go, nothing to long for. Until it is dark, and the stars and moon have filled the sky. Ptino knows all, and yet life continues its eternal wheel. There is no beginning and no end. Ptino waits. Until from far away he notices gentle footsteps coming closer. In the darkness, he can see the shape of a little girl.

Ptino values his friends. And loves this one. He is contented in their friendship. Happy feeling the warmth of her skin when she sits close, and the sweetness when their hands touch. The darkness caresses the little girl's curls which are as dark as the night itself. And like the stars, her eyes shine. Her body is soft and round, and lovely to touch. It has the smell of earth, and flowers opening at dawn.

Ptino sits by the sea. His lovely in his lap. They are silent, alone together. A universe on their own. Ptino is at rest. He does not need to know what more life will bring. The darkness doesn't ask for any revelation. He rests inside and thanks this friendly universe. Ptino smiles.

THE RECIPE

EXPLORING YOUR FAMILY BOUNDARIES

In this recipe you will observe the layout of the child's family boundaries, and how the adult can recreate healthy boundaries for the child.

Close your eyes.

Remember the composition of your family as a child. Take a moment to connect with both father and mother.

Observe their interpersonal dynamics.

Now tune into the boundaries of both of them.

Which color do you associate with father's presence in the family? Trust the message that comes with the color. (For instance, red could show anger, dominance; blue could show coldness, distance; white could show absence or death, and so on.) Allow your own associations that come with the color you observe.

What place did your father have in your family? Observe the boundaries you feel his presence had in the family. They can be large or small. Their shape can be for instance smooth and round, or square and solid.

Now become aware of mother's presence in the family. Observe the boundaries, their color and shape. Notice mother's place in the family in relationship to father. What do you observe?

Now, observe the place of the child-you in the family. Notice its boundary, its color and shape.

Watch the place of the child in relationship to its parents. Ask yourself what the child-you would have needed from your parents. What healthy boundaries would have supported and protected the child. As the loving adult, imagine providing the parents with these new boundaries.

Notice how the child's space is affected by them.

Be aware, of how in response to the parents' healthy boundaries, those of the child might change

• Do they come closer to the child or do they create more space?

• Do they become less defined, or more?

• Does their color change?

Now take your time to visualize and feel yourself as the child, in your new space, also in relationship to the new boundaries of your parents.

CHAPTER 6

SUPPORTING THE CHILD (5 TO 2 YEARS OLD)

A disciple of Buddha was taking leave of him. He was going on a faraway pilgrimage to spread Buddha's word. He touched Buddha's feet, he waited there for his blessing. Buddha blessed him and said to the assembly, "Look, brothers! This is a rare disciple! And what is his rarity? He has killed his mother and father!"

He had never said such a thing. And nobody had ever thought that this man could kill his mother and father. He was one of the most silent, peaceful, loving persons they had ever seen. He was compassion incarnate.

Somebody asked, "We don't understand. What do you mean by saying that he has killed his father and mother?"

And Buddha said, "Exactly that: he has killed the voice of his father and mother inside him, the parental voice." That is very deep rooted in you.

(Osho, *The Wisdom of the Sands*, Vol. II)

Satyam shivam Sunderam

The need to express ourselves truthfully is essential to us all human beings. Freedom of speech is unquestionable in a civilized world. Not only for adults, but also for children. Specially they should have the right to say whatever they feel is true and important for them. They still live close to the source of truth. As adults, we have moved away from it a lot, we might not even remember it anymore. We have learnt to lie to ourselves and others.

Sometimes we do it consciously, but mostly it happens unconsciously. We don't even know anymore we are lying.

Children still speak the truth. When they like something, their whole being rejoices in expressing it, when they don't like something, they reject it without shame and openly speak against it. This is not always comfortable for the grownups surrounding them. They get embarrassed, feel confronted and challenged, or they get afraid. Because of this, they will try to stop the child from expressing its truth.

The Indian Sutra Satyam, Shivam, Sunderam, puts truth on the same essential level as goodness and beauty. Truth brings goodness and beauty in our life, It clears out the fog of denial and resignation, and it challenges the weight of repression and fear we carry.

In its purity, truth brings nobility to our existence. It makes us a sacred child again.

THE CHILD DEPENDS ON THE RESPONSE OF THE PARENTS

As small children, between one and a half and three years old, we express ourselves freely. It is the way through which we contact life and our surroundings. We touch, look, taste, make sounds. We test the world around us. We interact with it .

Sometimes the response we receive is a delight. It supports us in our exploration, it is exciting and it makes us curious. It activates an exchange with our surroundings, and we feel part of life.

There are other times, though, when the responses we get as children are in conflict with what we really need. Instead of love, comes anger. Instead of support, comes judgment or punishment. We learn that if we like to come close to mommy, she might get irritated, or when we want to play with daddy, he might not have time for us.

When this happens repeatedly, we start losing trust in what we want to receive and share. We might respond to the world around us with fear, shame, or guilt, unable to continue our exploration.

In this time, there needs to be a deep recognition from our parents of what we want or need. Even though they will not always give in to what we express or demand, they need to remain in tune with us. The limits they need to set should not come out of anger, irritation, or rejection, but out of love and support. We need limits in this time, so that we can start to define ourselves, find our own "I." But if the limits given to us are inflexible, or full of our parents' repressed emotions, we can never be ourselves.

THE "GOOD" AND THE "BAD" PARENTS

As children, we start absorbing our parents' limits because we have no other choice. We need father and mother for nurturance, support, and recognition. Very early, we have to create a split inside, between the "good, ideal parents," who have what we need for survival, and the "bad" ones, who want to stop us from becoming ourselves. We learn to accommodate ourselves to the "good parents" by becoming what they expect, and we learn to hide our feelings from the "bad" ones, knowing that if we challenge and provoke them we will be deprived of their love. Our own desires and needs cannot be expressed openly if they contradict those of our parents.

Our body-mind-feelings respond instinctively to this dilemma. We prepare for fight or flight. To fight, to protect ourselves, we need to draw from resources that are meant to support our growth instead. We use our own energy to build a wall, an armor around us. We harden ourselves, our bodies become like fortresses behind which we carry out the battle. Behind the wall, our impulses turn into rage, which can only turn against us. As Jessica Benjamin says:

> In much of early life, destruction is properly directed toward the other, and is internalized when the other cannot "catch" it, and survive. Ordinarily, some failure is inevitable; for that matter, so is the internalization of aggression. When the parent fails to survive attack--to withstand the destruction without retaliating *or* retreating--the child turns its aggression inwards and develops what we know as rage. (1)

When fighting feels too dangerous, or useless, we have to choose flight. We renounce our aliveness, and collapse into resignation and passivity. We retract from our own impulses and our own sensuousness. Our body-mind-feelings, no longer get the life juice they need in order to grow. They weaken and shrink. We are left with a hate inside for what has been inflicted upon us. Because we cannot show this, our life is poisoned by it. Wilhelm Reich remarks:

> When a person encounters insurmountable obstacles in his efforts to experience love...he begins to hate. But the hate cannot be expressed. It has to be bound to avoid the anxiety that it causes. In short, thwarted love causes anxiety. Likewise, inhibited aggression causes anxiety; and anxiety inhibits demands of hate and love. (2)

As long as the child inside feels a lack of love and support from us as adults, it keeps its "parents" alive to get that love and support from them. As we grow up, these internalized parents start dominating our life. They take on the shape of the Superego. They become critical and demanding.

Meanwhile, our actual parents might have changed, and might have deeply understood and acknowledged the mistakes they made while raising us. And yet, because of the unresolved search for love and recognition, we persist in holding on to these parents of the past. Deep down, we continue to believe that in order to receive love and support, we need to keep fulfilling the same conditions that we had to fulfill as children. This affects our intimate relationships. We start to project onto the people whom we need or want something from, the same responses that we experienced from our parents. They start to reflect for us what we have internalized. Then, we respond to this with our conditioned mechanism of fight or flight, and in this process we lose the joy of sharing with each other.

A SAFE SPACE TO EXPOSE

A wounded child still lives inside each one of us adults. It is either ready at any moment to attack and strike back, or it has given up, resigned, and is alienated and lost. It has learned from the past that it cannot change its surroundings. It does not know that there are other ways of living. It has no experience of having a supportive environment.

How many times do we ourselves try to prevent this wounded child from speaking out and showing itself? As children we already learned early on that to deserve a place in life we had to win the love and acceptance of our parents. For this, we had to hide or deny our feelings.

As adults, we need to create a space in our life where it is safe to expose, share, and show the old wounds of the past. We need to express the anger, hurt, sadness, and hate that the child in us has learnt to hold. These wounds can only heal when the poison is drained from them. Arthur Janov says:

> Make anger real, and it will disappear. Until that happens, many angry outbursts against people in the present will be acts, and therefore not real. (3)

But we need to do it with the awareness of an adult. If we do not consider choosing the right moment or the right place for this, then we will attract rejection.

> *Giovanni D. was a successful, self-made man in his forties. His life had been an uphill struggle; he was very proud of his achievements. The reason he came to us was because of his growing feeling of isolation. He felt misunderstood and alienated from his colleagues and his wife. In his first sessions, he touched the shame that had hardened him into his decision to never feel smaller than others. He experienced sadness and compassion for his little boy inside.*
> *When it came to the point of releasing his deeper feelings*

109

of rage and anger toward his humiliating father, we came to a standstill. Giovanni argued that throughout his whole adult life he had been expressing rage and anger, and that he was proud of being so honest and straightforward about them. The result of this, though, he continued, had been only more humiliation and isolation, and he couldn't see any value in creating an artificial situation in which these feelings would be fueled.

We asked him in what circumstances he allowed his rage to erupt. He answered that he would do it any time it was provoked. It was very much part of his now daily explosions with his wife and employees. We were on the verge of an argument with him ourselves: his ability to create outer tension to justify his explosions was now operating on us.

We suggested he ask his little boy what was going on. The answer surprised him. The rage was there, untouched by his adult explosions, brooding under a deep fear of more rejection and humiliation. Because of his growing attunement with his child, we could suggest Giovanni try something new. We told him to prepare a room where he could be loud, make sounds, and move. We suggested he connect with his child and invite him to express its pent-up rage in this safe setting.

When Giovanni came back for the next session, he reported to us that his body had felt much lighter after his "private release," and also that for the first time he could see how anger can be an enjoyable phenomenon.

We need to create the right environment and the right support for us as adults to express what we could not express as children.

BE PATIENT WITH THE CHILD

In the beginning, the child in us might be afraid, or resist to us as adults and refuse. It had to learn its lesson of holding back and hiding its feelings so early that it might feel threatened by becoming vulnerable again. Instead of being able to direct its energy to those who hurt it in the past, it might attack us, the adult. Or it might mistrust us, and blame us for not being on its side.

> *t is one of the hazards of being a therapist to sometimes be the target of these attacks. Louise H., a trained body worker, had learned very early in her life that the way to be part of her family was to help. Already as a little girl, she had developed the knack to be sensitive to mother's needs without having to be asked or*

110

told anything: mother was sick and weak, and the household was revolving around her illness.

After a few sessions, Louise started admitting to a growing anger inside. She could understand intellectually how she had been used as a child, and how in her life now she still gave priority to other people's needs.

But when we started focusing on releasing her suppressed anger toward mother, she turned against us. She accused us of manipulating her, pushing her into something which she did not feel. Her reaction was verbally violent and accusatory.

Being attacked brings up shock and defensiveness: we had to incorporate this response with awareness. By breathing deeply, and remaining compassionate to the issue of manipulating that she carried from her past, we could bring Louise's focus back to her mother. We told her that by throwing her rage on us she was diverting her focus, and once again protecting her mother. Louise then realized that by doing this, she had lost touch with her own inner child. She could return to feel herself and acknowledge where the anger really originated.

As adults, we need to be compassionate to the child. By staying strong and supportive to the child, slowly it will regain its trust again.

To help the child to release its repressed feelings, we as adults need to release these feelings in a safe environment.

We have to create the right setting. We need to find a soundproof room and surround ourselves with mattresses and pillows. It is important not to hurt ourselves, as we might have done as children when we were unable to release our feelings.

THEN, WE CAN START

Then, we can start. We can express ourselves verbally, by making sounds, talking gibberish, or shouting. Or, we can express ourselves through our bodies by kicking, stamping our feet, moving around or running, beating a cushion, or biting into it.

Once the release has happened, we are able to experience our bodies as alive and fluid again. The anger and rage we felt can transform into love and compassion.

It is important to understand that we are not doing this to change our parents, or to convince them what they did was wrong. We are simply doing it for ourselves. By taking the appropriate space to express all that we could not express as children, we complete the past and get ready to let go of it.

Honoring the gift of life

At the end of expressing what we could not as children, we might want to turn to our parents and say: "Thank you for the gift of life that you have given to me. Now I can receive it. I will take good care of it, and take it into my life in my own way".

This gratefulness is expressed by honoring life and ourselves as part of it. Hellinger says:

> I accept my life as it comes through (my parents) without any objections. I take it as a whole from them. Then, the second thing is that I honor the life they gave me. That means I preserve the life they gave me--even against my parents if need be. Honoring my life implies honoring them also. So if my father becomes violent or my mother becomes violent, I honor them by protecting their gift to me, by preserving my life. (4)

The burdens our parents carried were not truly theirs. They carry them also for others in their lineage.

When we are ready, we can acknowledge that we carried their burdens out of our need for their love. Now we need to hand back these burdens to our parents, so that in their own time they have the freedom to return them back to their past.

> *In her session on completion with father,[1] Deva S. made a drawing of him. The title she gave it was: "Papa, why are you so sad?--I can't speak about it!" When she focused on the last sentence, she suddenly remembered what she knew about her father's story during the Second World War. He had never spoken to her about that time. He had been in Russia for three years, at the front, and had been the only survivor in his company. His only brother had also died in the war.*
>
> *We asked her if her father carried guilt feelings about being the only survivor. She responded with disbelief: her father, the patriarch? Guilt feelings about being alive? She realized how her brother had been crushed under the weight of her father's withdrawal and anger. She could feel her father's pain underneath his anger, and that she had been trying to carry it for him. She*

---

1   See "The Recipe."

panicked when she realized that she needed to give this burden back to him. She felt she could not leave him alone with it.

But when she remembered her commitment to her child, she finally bowed down to her father, saying, "I return your burden, your fate, back to you. I accept my own life."

THE ORIGINAL FACE

In due time, we learn to express ourselves in a calm and peaceful way. But to get there, we need to give space to the pent up feelings inside of us first. To express these, we might need to be loud and cathartic. This has its own grace, like when the sky is loaded with heavy clouds, and thunder and lightning discharge the atmosphere. Then, when the storm passes, a silence remains. A lucidity, a clarity, a freshness and innocence. In the same way, after a healthy catharsis, a deep cleansing, our inner world becomes vibrant and

alive again. Our mind is more at ease and silent, our feelings warm and flowing. And our body feels more sensitive and vulnerable, yet stronger, juicier, and younger. The child in us has regained its original face.

In our groups on Childhood Deconditioning, there is always a golden moment at the end of the completion with father session, as well as at the end of the one with mother. When everybody has spoken out and expressed, often physically, held back feelings with the parents, a sense of freedom suddenly surges through the room. When we put on dance music, everyone gets up from their places and turns to each other, and in no time the room is transformed into a crazy and playful stage for all the liberated kids to go wild. Some laugh, some run around, some dance alone, some dance with others. And some are silent. Sometimes the whole group comes together and spontaneously creates a circle of delightful celebration. It is a moment of transformation, where all the feelings of anger, hate, and sadness turn into love, compassion, and aliveness.

Osho says:

The baser can be changed into the higher. Nothing is lacking in the baser. Only a rearrangement, a recomposition is needed. This is the whole of what alchemy means. When you are sad, celebrate, and you are giving a new composition to sadness. You are bringing something to sadness which will transform it. You are bringing celebration to it. Angry?... Have a beautiful dance.... (5)

WISHING OUR PARENTS A GOOD JOURNEY ONWARD

Once we feel free from their burdens, and the anger and pain from carrying them, we may feel a true compassion for our parents. We are able to see the wounded child also inside them. Then, from the depth of our hearts, we can wish them a good journey toward completing their own unresolved past.

COMPLETING WITH FATHER

If you are conscious, you can watch. Go back; now your father is no more but for the eyes of the memory he is still there; close your eyes; again be the child who has committed something, done something against the father, wants to be forgiven but cannot gather courage...Now you can gather courage! You can say whatsoever you wanted to say, you can touch his feet again, or you can be angry and hit him...But be finished! Let the whole process be completed.Remember one basic law: anything that is complete drops, because then there is no meaning in carrying it; anything that is incomplete clings: it waits for its completion.

(Osho, *And the Flowers Showered*)

Father, you left me, I never left you.

I needed you so bad, you didn't need me...Oh, no.

So, I just got to tell you goodbye, goodbye...

(John Lennon)

THE THREE FACES OF FATHER

When we start to move away from the symbiosis with mother, we need father's love and support. By example, father teaches us how to move our own way and deal with the world.

However, there comes a time when the support we receive from

114

him needs to include the permission to question and challenge him on his values and principles. It is the only way we can develop our own insights, we can become rooted in our own strength, and make our own choices in life.

But fathers rarely respond to this rebellion in a flexible way. The reason for that often lies in their childhood. As children, they themselves had to give up a lot of their own ideas about life and obey the adults around them.

To gain respect, they had to learn to criticize, and be ashamed of their own vision of the world. They had to develop fixed ways of behaving, to cover up the loss of their true value. These strategies with which they covered up their own truth, they will later pass on to us, their sons and daughters.

By taking them on, we become deeply affected in our sense of integrity and our capacity to live our own life.

To find our own truth back again, we need to explore the strategies our fathers adopted and passed on to us.

For this purpose, we divide the figure of father into three main typologies. They are related to his basic way of setting his boundaries in the family: the rigid father, the weak absent father, and the corrupt father.[2]

The patriarchal family
The position of the father in this type of family remains unchallenged. The system is fixed: on top comes the man, the father, then follows the woman, the mother, then follow the male children, the sons, and then lastly, the female ones, the daughters. Being a male includes having certain inborn privileges, such as the right to take initiative, the right to dominate, the permission to demand and command. To be a man, means to be the provider, the one who brings safety and security, the protector.

The rigid father
The patriarchal family is based on the absolute rule of father: the rigid father. He has the right to mold his wife, but even more his children, into the shapes and personalities he considers right. The patriarch doesn't leave much space for intuition, play, and freedom. His sons and daughters are taught early that to deserve the love and respect from him, they better learn to fit in, to surrender to the system.

Growing up in this patriarchal system, the desire to complete our unresolved issues with father is very strong. From very early

---

2   See Chapter 5 on boundaries: family types.

on, we experienced the fear of being wrong, of being inadequate or incompetent regarding what he expected from us.

The only way we could receive the love of our rigid father was to try and become what he expected us to be. We had to follow his desires and his opinions, prepared at any time to renounce our own feelings and understanding. To be ready to exchange them for what he, and the outer world he represented, considered to be normal and appropriate.

We had to create an inner division, hiding our softer sides in order to receive the support we needed for moving out into the world.

The sons and daughters of the rigid father

As sons of a rigid father, we learned that to associate with him meant to associate with a source of power. It demanded from us a contempt for the "weaker race," women, and, with it, a spite for all that was weaker in us, for our female side.

In our adult life, this has great repercussions on our capacity to feel. Love, gentleness, sharing, become qualities that have to be fought with and discarded. Sadness, crying, needing are signs of weakness.

But secretly we long for these feelings, and we try to find them outside, in the women we love. But, no longer allowed to experience it within ourselves, we often hurt and punish those in our lives who represent those softer sides.

As daughters, we learned that to be a woman meant to be inferior.

As daughters of the rigid father, we have only two choices: we either have to submit to father, becoming all that he needs and wants, or we have to become like him and renounce our feminine side. If we win his admiration and acknowledgment for being like him, we lose the connection to our biological roots. We identify ourselves with the male world giving up the nourishment of Mother Earth. To quote Marion Woodman:

> "Daddy's little princess" is her father's chosen child. Blessed by his love, she may be cursed by his love. Her special place in his dynasty sets her on a throne too remote for most princes to reach. Her throne is carved in ice far from the nourishing warmth of Mother Earth. (6)

Completing with the rigid father: regaining playfulness and longing

As adults, we need to complete many things with this father. We need to tell him all that we could never say and express as a child.

116

The pain, the anger, the fear he instilled in us, which poisons our adult life, needs to be released so it can dissolve. We need to say what we didn't want from him, and also what we wanted and longed for. We need to reclaim our strength. The impotence that so many of us feel in our actions and in our desires is created by the early decision we had to make regarding our relationship with father. To receive his love and attention we renounced much of ourselves. Either we learned to imitate him, but we were never allowed to measure up to his standard, or we resigned and submitted to him, and forgot about what we really needed or wanted.

If we look a bit closer into this rigid patriarch, the man who imprisons his children and wife with his rules, we come to the realization that he himself is the victim of the past.

This man, so rigid on the outside, is in fact a child shamed to his core. He had to learn to hide his natural insecurity and close off his heart. Besides the feminine qualities of sensitivity and intuition, the patriarch has to renounce a great spiritual quality: playfulness.

Playfulness is, in its essence, the capacity to enjoy experimenting without focusing on results. Every child is born with it. When cultivated in our adult life, playfulness gives joy and meaningfulness to every action. But playfulness leads to rebelliousness, because by its nature it doesn't follow any rules. This does not suit the patriarchal system, rooted as it is in obedience and suppression.

To gain his title, the patriarch had to let the playful child inside him be crushed. And, with double vengeance, he will crush and condemn the playfulness in his inheritors.

To reclaim as adults the power we surrendered to our father, we have to reconnect with the playful child inside of us, releasing it from prison. Underneath the rage, the impotence, and the fear, waits a shout of joy. Song, dance, laughter, and play are the natural expressions of our life energy. By releasing the child inside from the bondage of seriousness, its longing for father, and its delight in discovering and exploring the world with him can reemerge.

When our longing for father finds its expression, and the healthy wanting of his love and support surfaces again, the healing begins.

The weak father
In the last 50 years, we have witnessed the birth of a "new society," which Robert Bly so well describes in his book, The Sibling Society (7). This society is made up of brothers and sisters. It is fatherless. In it, the rigid father has been thrown off his pedestal, shattering into pieces. His function has been analyzed and denounced. He has been removed.

Regrettably he has been replaced with the absent or weak father.

This father no longer has a real function. It looks like he is there only for appearance, having no part in fathering us during child-hood.

Many of us have grown up around such a father. The meetings we had with him once in a while were empty, meaningless, and frustrating. We could make no claims on him and could not express any expectations. We learned to protect him from ourselves.

In the effort not to feel the pain of his absence, some of us created the figure of an imaginary and ideal father, the faraway hero. This replaced the weak or absent father on the outside. This imaginary father figure, though, lacks substance. The challenge of being intro-duced into the world by him is missing.

The sons and daughters of the weak father

As sons, without a clear mirroring with a real father, we do not know what it means to be a man. We feel as if we are standing on quicksand, trying to fulfill a male role without any support or guidance. We keep up this role with a lot of tension, or we become absent and irresponsible men like our fathers.

As daughters, we feel that we do not deserve the full attention and support of a man, or we cherish and nurture the myth of an imaginary father, the unreachable hero whose affection we strive to conquer. As we grow up, we find ourselves reaching out for unavailable men, blaming them or ourselves for not being enough. Through the indifference and immaturity of our father, we lose the definition of ourselves. Our beauty, our strength, our independence remain unreflected. There is no man to really mirror us.

Completing with the weak father: regaining strength and desire

The weak father can be hard to confront. His weakness invites pity and protectiveness. We might feel guilty about our anger toward him because he presents himself as helpless as a child. In his helplessness, though, there often lies a dark and hidden under-current of manipulation feeding exactly on our protectiveness. As Robert Bly describes, the weak father can be a tyrant:

> Each father inherits thousands of years of cunning and elaborate fatherhood. The apparently weak father can control the entire family from beneath with his silences. Should the father be an alcoholic, his alcoholism may be a massive operation, carried out with Napoleonic thor-oughness, so that he rules his house by the most economi-cal means. He withdraws energy from his community;

energy pours into his dynamos, rather than out of them, in a way familiar to us from the lives of great tyrants. (8)

The weak father is wounded in his maleness. He either decided very early on not to follow in the footsteps of his own humiliating rigid father, or had no father to guide him. Out of reaction, he decided to remain a child. But, by doing this, he gave up the confrontation with authority, which would have strengthened him. This undeveloped strength makes him absent with his own children. He cannot support them to gain their own strength. When they challenge him with his absence, he responds by asking them for understanding or pity.

To liberate ourselves as adults from our enmeshment with our weak father, we have to dare to expose our own strength. The frustration and the anger of the child in us for being abandoned need to come to the surface. By telling him to be here, that we need and want him, we will break through layers of resignation, defeat, and compensation. In expressing it, giving it voice and body, we regain the strength we lost.

Within us lies a source of strength and vitality, of desire, drive, action, and willpower. That source has remained dormant too long. When we infuse this stagnant pool with the river of life, it starts overflowing.

Emily D. had had a very sick and absent father. When the time came to confront her inner picture of him, she started experiencing great weakness and many physical symptoms. We almost took the place of her child, feeling drawn to protect her and excuse her, just as she had done with her father in her earlier years. We pointed out to her that this was her energetic bonding with father: to withhold her strength and give up confrontation. She realized that this was exactly what she was doing in her adult life with men. First tentatively, breaking through a very powerful numbness, then with a sudden explosion of power, she started moving. It was not easy to tell her the hour was over, such was the enjoyment she experienced in being so alive.

The corrupt father
The corrupt father doesn't belong to any particular type of society. He has always existed on the edge of all societies, and has at times acquired great power within them.

He can look like a rigid father on the outside, and be very articulate about his moral values and social principles. But his outer rigidity is a facade, to cover up and safeguard a complete lack of boundaries within the family system.

He is the obvious Godfather, the "Mafioso." But he is also the apparently normal family man, who, as soon as he enters his household and closes the door behind him, turns into a violator and abuser.

The sons and daughters of the corrupt father

The corrupt father's power lies in secrecy and cheating. By imposing the law of the jungle on his family, he teaches his sons and daughters that there are, in fact, no boundaries, and in this way, chains them to him. His credo is: "The rest of the world might believe in rules and limitations, but we do not follow these restrictions. We will go as far as we want, joined as we are by secrecy." The only rule that this man values is not to get caught or exposed. He prides himself in his ability to do whatever he wants at the expense of anyone around him.

As sons and daughters of such a man, our choice can be very limited. We might end up growing into abusers or become victims of them ourselves. If we choose the latter, we find situations in life in which again and again we give our power away and submit ourselves to invasion and disrespect. If we choose growing into abusers ourselves, we spend our lives running away from our fear by taking what we understand as a position of power, and become, in turn, abusive and violent with other people's boundaries. In both cases, we have no chance to experience finer and softer feelings that make intimacy possible.

Completing with the corrupt father: regaining innocence

The corrupt father has probably been heavily abused in his own childhood. He rejects innocence in himself and others as naiveté, and has learned that being naive invites only exploitation and humiliation.

As adults, to release ourselves from the grip of fear and seduction that chains us to such a father, we need to reclaim our freedom. Breaking the secrecy that has bonded us to him can create fear. We have been carrying for him the shame he never owned. We might feel responsible for him, or justify him by denying what we really saw, felt, and experienced with him.

A great rage and disgust might surface. And a deep pain and grief for the loss of our trust. When we allow that grief to surface, out of its depth our original childlike innocence can unfold itself again.

> *Ulrich H.'s father had a very high powered position in the German Army during World War Two. As a child after the war, Ulrich had lived in great secrecy about his father's past, and*

in tremendous fear that it would be discovered. Throughout the whole of Ulrich's childhood, his father had carried a dose of lethal poison in his pocket for the whole family, in case his crimes would be exposed. To hear Ulrich's voice, broken by sobs, stuttering, hardly being able to breathe, reveal his father's crimes, was one of the most touching experiences of our lives. A deep silence followed, and we felt immense respect for his courage. For the first time in his life, Ulrich felt innocent.

Receiving father's gift of life

Robert Bly concludes:

> The father's birth gift cannot be quantified. It has something to do with a love of knowledge, love of the mind. And a way to honor the world of things. (9)

When we feel complete with the father of our past, we become able to start acting and taking initiative from our own source, from our own authority. Our dignity and integrity are no longer restricted by the images of our past.

We might touch a precious space of gratitude within, for the gift of life that father gave us, and reown this gift in a most mysterious and impersonal way.

A Zen poet says (10):

> The raging wind's companion:
>
> In the sky,
>
> …the single moon.

THE EVOCATION

MY PERSONAL EXPERIENCE IN WRITING A LETTER OF COMPLETION TO MANÚ'S FATHER

SVARUP

Daddy, look at me. Am I not the way you want me? Didn't you promise to be there for me? What is this look of pain in your eyes? Why can't I feel you when you are sitting there? You used to hold me and put me to bed when I was a baby. You were the soft companion of my dreams. What happened now? Why don't you hold me anymore? Can we only meet in a dream?

As I sit here and look at you, I feel a great pain. Is it your pain or my pain? Your body hurts and my body hurts too. What hurts even more is than I cannot relieve you from your disappointment...

I am tired, tired of waiting for you to heal and move on. Deep down, I feel betrayed. You are already gone. I can't reach you. I want to scream and scream: you cheated me!

I am angry, and I want to move. If I don't move, this anger becomes rage, a rage against myself. It becomes a poison.

I want to let this poison out. My body shakes with the fear of losing you. But this time I won't stop. I have a body, and a voice, and a fury, and a dance inside me.

I have so much energy. When I let it happen, it becomes anger, and this anger makes me feel beautiful and innocent. I cry, and I laugh. There is a volcano in me, a thousand sparks of life, sex, madness. And joy: I am enjoying myself tremendously, I feel alive, vibrant, I am having fun!

And when I finally stop, spent and happy, I have to laugh. The fog is lifted. Underneath it, you are the source of this abundance in me!

You are a man full of passion and lust for life, a dancing mystic...

Thank you for the magic, the song and the vision you gave me. I will live it fully, and keep it alive by sharing it

Your daughter

My personal experience in writing a letter of completion to Wimke's father

Premartha

Father,

What I could never tell you before is that my whole childhood I have been waiting for you.

I dreamt that one day you would find the time to be with me. To share your interest in my world, to show your interest in me.

I admired you for your strength to be alone. I wished I would grow up to be like you, a silent, self reliant man. I was ashamed that I liked to play, that my world was colorful, and full of fantasies.

Father, I get paralyzed when you talk to me, frozen in fear that I will respond in the wrong way, and in irritation you will turn away and leave for your work.

I want to be your ally, but you want to fight your battle alone. Sometimes I feel I have become the enemy, and your anger turns to me as if you would want to destroy me. But you hold your temper, and leave me standing there in utter shame and guilt. In these moments I wish you would beat me, so at least I would receive a place in your battle.

I feel your melancholy, your wounded side, through which you don't know how to relate to us, the family, to mother and to me. I notice when you want to be part of us and you carefully try to enter into the atmosphere of the house. But you are like a wounded animal, sensitive to the slightest rejection or criticism, ready to take your hat and coat, and leave for the land.

Sometimes you disappear for days. I never know where you go. When you reappear, you don't speak to anyone. You can keep silent for months on end.

I see you looking at mother with longing and affection. But you cannot go to her and share it. You leave her alone.

You leave me alone.

We all protect you. We know your hidden sensitivity, your love for music, your mastery in classical languages. We all smile when you are happy.

But you never become part of us, and we of you. We remain strangers.

My body aches from holding back. Until the love for you turns into anger. Until I only want to scream at you, and push you away, keep you on a distance forever. Until my body feels like a wound up spring, ready to release the tension of separation.

Only through releasing this anger and despair, I can find that space in me where I look at you again in an innocent love. And I can tell you finally that whatever you gave me remains precious to me forever.

Father, I am proud of you, and I miss you. I would have loved to introduce you into my world.

You are part of me, and I am part of you.

Your son

THE RECIPE

COMPLETION WITH FATHER

Write a letter of completion to your father.

Start with the sentence: "Father, what I have never told you before...". Take time to tell him all the things you had to hold back as a child.

While writing, you might become aware of different emotions coming to the surface. There might be anger, sadness, need, and grief. Allow them to be there, without any judgment.

At the end, sign the letter with your adult name.

CHAPTER 7

SUPPORTING THE CHILD (5 TO 2 YEARS OLD)

> Look at mothers, just simply watch!…and you will feel
> they are trying to dominate their small children. Their
> aggression, their anger, is thrown on them…They have
> become objects of catharsis; and by this they are already
> burdened. They will move in life carrying mountains
> from the very beginning, and they will never know that
> life is possible without carrying such loaded heads; and
> they will never know the freedom that comes with an
> unloaded being. They will never know that when you are
> not loaded you have wings and you can fly into the sky
> and into the unknown.
>
> (Osho, *And the Flowers Showered*)

COMPLETING WITH MOTHER

We all long for a completion with mother.

We dream that our adult relationship with her becomes one of
respect and love. In the longing to connect, lies the wish to relate to
her as someone to whom we can truly bow down. We want to honor
the great gift we received from her, the gift of life.

When we come close to a gesture of gratefulness, issues with her
can arise.

Where do these issues come from? When we go to the roots of
them, they are most often negative issues of our childhood which
have remained unresolved. They are the wounds of the little girl, or
the little boy inside. They belong to the daughter or son who in the
past has felt unwanted and uncared for, or invaded and overpro-
tected by her.

THE NEGATIVE MERGING WITH MOTHER

Because our mother gave us life, we feel her very much a part of
us, and ourselves a part of her. We are conceived in her womb, and
for about nine infinite months we float in her inner waters, sensitive to all her emotions, thoughts, and actions, perceiving them as
part of ourselves and our bodies. We live together through the time
shortly before birth, and together we go through the birth process.
We are forever influenced by the way she connects with us during

our transition from life in the womb to life outside it. In these early stages of our lives, we absorb our mother deeply.

We all begin our lives in a state of communion with her.

In the deepest recesses of our minds, we all carry memories of the golden glimpses with her. They taste like honey, they have a golden glow, they evoke feelings of total comfort and relaxation. They evoke the space of the sweet merging we experienced as infants.

After the "honeymoon" of pregnancy and the first period immediately following delivery, mother's body returns to a less "enlightened" state. The spaciousness, the surrender that made her go beyond herself, become less. Her "altered state" is starting to change, the hormones are returning to a normal balance again. When reentering her personal world, Mother may go into a rebound,. While she is taking care of us, perhaps breastfeeding us, the unresolved issues, problems, anxieties, and fears which were kept at a distance by the high of the birth process, can come back in full force. As babies, merged with mother, we absorb both the golden merging, as well as the possible rebound she goes through.

In our symbiotic connection to her, we are not able to make a choice. We want and need to stay bonded to her. Her issues, her pain, her fears, her anxieties, become the substitutes for that original golden flow of energy. If we cannot have this golden flow anymore, to remain bonded, we are ready to accept all the negative feelings that are there. To accommodate those feelings, we adjust and tense our little bodies. In this way. We try to preserve the sensation of communion with her.

As infants at that time, we have no other choice. We are totally dependent on mother. We are one with her. We know we will not be able to survive without her.

As adults, even though consciously we know we are able to take care of ourselves, unconsciously we carry the belief that without her we cannot live.

This belief expresses itself in our fear of relaxing and surrendering. It creates the feeling in us that we are not supported, that life does not provide enough. In our unconscious, mother and life become one.

It is time to learn to differentiate between what came from her as a nourishment, and what was poisonous. It is time to take care of the little child inside.

THE SEPARATION ANXIETY

When in life we want to go independently our own way, we might experience what is called "separation anxiety." We become afraid of not receiving the golden merging anymore. That is the moment when the negative merging we had with our mother in the past is activated in our unconscious. Like in those infant years, we try to hold on to the situation we are in, replacing golden merging with a negative one. We attack and criticize the people we feel bound to. Deep inside, we believe that in this way we can continue holding on to mother, and receive the nourishment and security she promises. As A. H. Almaas describes:

> Negative merging is still merging. One can always acti-
> vate it in times of separation anxiety. It is painful, mani-
> festing in frustrating affects and emotional conflicts, but
> when it is used as a defense against separation, one feels
> mother is around, and therefore feels secure in some way,
> even though the mother might be very angry or hateful.
> (1)

Through expressing the pain of negative merging, by releasing the despair and anger we carry inside, we can experience again the golden merging, the honey like flow that connected us from the very beginning. Only now that golden flow comes unconditionally, it comes directly from the motherly manifestation of existence. It nourishes and supports us to be connected and yet live our own life.

MOTHER IS NOT PERFECT

Mother you had me, but I never had you.

I wanted you, you didn't want me...

So I, I just got to tell you goodbye, goodbye...

(John Lennon)

To discover ourselves, we need to separate from the unconscious merging with the mother of our past. We have to face the fact that she is not perfect. As long as we hold on to a perfect image of her, we will remain unhealthily bonded to her. We need to confront that image. If we don't, our love for her will be false. It will be based on how we want her to be, and not on who she is. The unconscious anger that this effort to preserve the ideal picture of her creates, goes underground. We hurt ourselves with it. Each movement of separation contains an outward going element of natural aggression. As Jessica Benjamin explains, if we repress this aggression we will not be able to make an authentic connection to her. We will resent her and ourselves for being false. We will not be able to separate.

> Separation—whether really leaving or simply asserting one's own will— is often interpreted as a hostile act, by both parties. Both must manage not only separation, but the associated aggression. As we have seen, the inability to survive separation and aggression keeps mother and child locked in a field of omnipotence. The idea that mother is or should be all-giving and perfect (just a kiss away from all-controlling), expresses the mentality of omnipotence, the inability to experience the mother as an independently existing subject. This idealization testifies to the failure of destruction; hate has not been able to come forth and make the experience of love less idealized and more authentic. (2)

Once as adults we have expressed this aggression towards her, we can let go of the compulsion to make her perfect, with the more realistic image we gain of her, we might realize how hard certain situations must have been for her, and feel compassion for her as a human being.

Yet, this compassion does not imply that we have to carry her suffering and unresolved issues for her. It means leaving her the right to carry her own burden, without us trying to take it away from her. In a respectful way, we allow her to carry her own fate and the responsibility for her life.

In this way, we also carry our responsibilities. We are liberated from the spell of negative merging, free to meet each other in a nourishing and loving way.

MOTHER IN THE PATRIARCHAL SYSTEM

To recognize the origins of mother's tensions, we need to move to another level of understanding. Besides their personal histories, all our mothers carry the history of the whole of womanhood, in which there is a deep split originating far back in time. In the age of the matriarch, woman was free in her expression, owning her own authority over her life and family. The goddesses who were worshipped at that time, embodied both the "light" and "dark" aspects of the feminine principle. The creative nurturing principle had its place alongside the destructive death principle: together, they represented the cycles of nature. Feminine rituals could range from loving devotion to divine madness.

At the onset of the patriarchal age, when man took charge and became the authority over the family, a deep split was created within the feminine principle. The "dark" transformative side of woman was rejected, and the "light" nurturing side was overemphasized. We will never be able to determine fully how this split happened. Perhaps men forced it on women, or women limited their own freedom by accepting only their motherly side. Or, perhaps women surrendered the "dark" part of themselves to men out of convenience, a desire for protection and security. But its outcome was a distorted image of womanhood. This accounts for the feeling of betrayal and anger that so many daughters nowadays carry toward their mothers, as representatives of a collective that has sold out and capitulated.

The patriarchal system's rejection of the dark aspect of women is reflected in its mythology. As recorded in ancient Hebrew texts, Lilith (the dark aspect), the first wife (and mother) of Adam, was cast out of paradise as a punishment for her strong-willed independence, and Eve was created out of one of Adam's ribs. Eve (the light aspect) became the wife (and daughter) of the patriarch. Lilith was relegated to the realm of demons, and became the feared force who threatens childbirth and the peace of the patriarchal family.(3)

For centuries, women and mothers have trained themselves to reject their inner Lilith. They have exclusively focused on their nurturing and caring principle, and denied their dark, transformative, inspiring, and ecstatic nature.

In this way, both sides have suffered. By being overemphasized, the nurturing side has been overused. What in its essence is a joyful sharing of love and care, turns into a duty, a role. If a woman cannot no longer find inspiration in the other side where she replenishes herself through her wild and ecstatic nature, her giving becomes an effort. The overprotective, controlling and engulfing mother who loses herself in others, is the revenge of Eve.

On the other side, Lilith, imprisoned in the shadows of women's unconscious, creates havoc, unhappiness, and frustration in the lives of the mothers, wives, and daughters of the patriarch. The repression of their wild nature often creates sicknesses in their bodies and souls, and they ract to this by throwing their destructive feelings on the husbands and children they feel bound to. Even in these modern days, where male authority is stepping back a lot, whenever a woman breaks through the bondage she has cocreated towards men, she still has to confront within herself, centuries of guilt and self-doubt about her "dark" side.

THREE DIFFERENT TYPES OF MOTHER

As children of these "divided" women, we need to understand how their inner split has affected us. As daughters of such mothers, this is the only way for us to separate from them and heal our own inner division. As sons of such mothers, this allows us to develop wholesome relationships with women, enjoying all the sides they can share.

Each mother, according to the circumstances of her upbringing as a child, and the connection she has developed with either of her two sides, uses different strategies to deal with this inner division.

In our negative merging with them during the very first stage of our lives, we are already dealing with the consequences of these strategies. Mother can be either holding us too much, or too little. On a deep level, we absorb her denial of part of herself: we already feel her disowned rebelliousness that has turned into overcaring, or the rejection of her nurturing side, turned into coldness and absence.

But when we reach the "separation" stage of our development, we meet these strategies in full action. Mother is a part of the society we begin to encounter. Her behavior and responses define her place in it. Our own place in this is created through the values we received from her. Whether we can explore ourselves freely, or have to base our self-image on the strategies she confronted us with, depends directly on her conditioning.

To understand the effect of these strategies more clearly, we will again refer to the "modern archetypes" that we used in the chapter on father.

The rigid mother
The rigid mother is on the side of the man. She supports him at any cost. She carries the mission of safeguarding the male patriarchal structure. If her husband is weak or absent, she takes his place and becomes the patriarch in the family herself.

Her expression is rigid. The world around her has to obey the rules and regulations she considers right. There is a precise hierarchy around her: everyone has his fixed, unchangeable place.

To win her love, as her children, we have to obey and prove our dedication to her ideals. Already as infants, the nurturance we need is replaced by strict feeding schedules. We start to deny our own natural needs, and try to cover them up with behavior that suits her.

With such a mother, as children separation is a hard task. She does everything in her power to hold us back and control us: she sets limits before we can experience what our natural limits are.

As adults, it is difficult to assert ourselves or break through the strict discipline we have taken on from the rigid mother in our childhood. We might be successful in the world, but we can't follow our heart's desires. With the initiatives we take, we feel that they don't measure up to the standards the rigid mother imposed on us., Therefore, we can't enjoy what we created.

> *While completing her unfinished issues with mother, Deva S.*
> *realized that all her deeper feelings of sadness, laughter, anger,*
> *were always subjected to her mother's judgments. Often, her*
> *mother laughed about them. We supported her in reconnect-*
> *ing with these moments. She experienced great disbelief, "My*
> *mother? Did she really do this?" When she fully realized the*
> *impact of what she understood, she started screaming and*
> *screaming toward the drawing of her mother, "Go away, get out*
> *of me!"*
>
> *At the end of the session, she could really hold her inner child*
> *in her arms.*
>
> *In her homework after the session, she touched her inner*
> *child's fear of letting go of mother, and her mistrust that the*
> *adult would really be there for her. Deva S. promised her inner*
> *little girl that she would not force her, but that she would wait*
> *until the child was ready.*

The rigid mother has renounced her femininity. Deep inside her, father's daughter is still yearning for his recognition. She has become equally alienated from the surrendering principle of nurturance, as well as from her wildness and intuition. As Marion Woodman describes her:

> Whatever the cause, her own instinctual life is unavail-
> able to her, and, disempowered as a woman, she runs the
> household as she runs herself—with shoulds, oughts and
> have tos that add up to power. Life is not fed from the

waters of love, but from willpower that demands perfection, frozen perfection. (4)

It is hard to release ourselves from our negative bonding with a rigid mother. Our anger and rage, our aggression need to be expressed. Only through releasing our negative emotions, we get in contact again with our more vulnerable and soft sides. As children we hid these sides out of the fear of being hurt and overpowered by her.

As adults, we learn that life is only worthwhile if we can live all the different expressions of it. When we regain that flexibility, we can turn to mother, and finally share the love with her, that we so painfully learnt to withhold.

The absent mother
The absent mother has either renounced her independent will or has given up her nurturing side. She can be physically there, but she is not really sharing herself.

Within the family, she performs her duties, but inside herself she withdraws from this world into an inner numbness and lack of initiative. It is not easy to confront such a mother with her absence. Her situation brings up a feeling of pity.

Her lack of emotional presence is often covered up with an over-giving. Having renounced their own desires, such mothers become great automatic performers. They have a big unconscious investment in maintaining their image. Rebelling against it, would require to be there. But underneath their toxic absence, smolders their unexpressed dark side. Their children often experience it expressed in an attitude of rejection they have no proof of.

In the sibling society,[1] the absent mother acts out her rejection. She suddenly abandons the family, in order to cultivate her independence. Since she believes that her nurturing side is associated with submission, she decides to renounce it. She doesn't enjoy the relaxation of surrender. She wants her children to be as independent as her, to understand her, and not to expect too much from her.

As sons and daughters of this absent mother, we miss the nurturing space we need in order to relax. By not receiving mother's inspiration, we don't feel worthy. Or, we try to do anything to gain her attention or approval. Inside of us, the rage of feeling unacknowledged deteriorates into self-doubt or compulsive ambition. We have become abstinent to ourselves too.

---

1   See Chapter 6 on completion with father

As adults, to complete with our absent mother, we need to renounce the hope that keeps us bound to her. Underneath our understanding for her, and the justification of her choices, lies the rage of having been abandoned. We need to regain our self respect. Once we have regained our self worth, we can open up to her again. We can let go of the pain of having missed her, and start to connect with who she is now. We can acknowledge her courage for following her own way and make it an inspiration in our own lives.

In our work, we are meeting with greater frequency, the children of such absent mothers. George M. was a young man in his twenties. He was plagued by indecision and a sense of meaninglessness. His mother was a modern woman, who was interested in growth and had an independent life. George had grown up in a permissive household where everything was allowed. It

took him some time to reconnect with his own child inside. He was extremely protective of his vulnerability, and very reserved. When it came to mother, we noticed how understanding he was toward her. But, eventually, the memories came back. He realized how unprotected he had felt by his mother. He recalled her periods of tremendous insecurity and feelings of being lost, which deprived him of the possibility of confronting her with his own needs. He also realized that his mother had failed to hold a safe space for him in which he could experiment with his boundaries. All was allowed, but nothing had real value. George touched his anger and became more real. As he embarks upon his own adult life, he will need to meet the challenges and limitations that can mold his strength.

The corrupt mother

The corrupt mother lives her dark side in secret. On the outside, she can appear either as morally rigid, or as meek and submissive. But underneath se lives a secret life.

She herself often carries the wounds of abusive relationships and violence from the past. From this, she learns to present herself as a victim or she becomes an abuser herself. Socially, she might keep a proper image, but inside she carries enormous hate.

Everything confronts her with what has been done to her. In the revenge she wants to take, she knows no limits. She is ready to use her surroundings, including her children, to hurt back. She has learnt to be very clever. Secrecy, abuse, seduction are her politics. She knows how to divide the family, create separation and conflict to her advantage. She can wait.

The mysterious, intuitive qualities of her dark female aspect have turned poisonous and sour inside. These qualities have been so abused, that they have become destructive. This destruction is no longer in the service of transformation and rebirth, but an end in itself.

Sons and daughters of this woman are bound to her by the powerful tie of secrecy and hate. They either are forced to choose her side and create destructive alliances, or they become her eternal enemies, getting all her hate and rage. Either way, the energy they absorb from mother is used destructively toward others or themselves.

Or, out of shame, they try to reject it and they end up renouncing their own power and life-energy with it, feeling empty and hopeless.

As adults, we desperately need to find a supportive surrounding, in which we can release the terror of the nightmare we lived as children. We need to feel safe to express the fear, rage and hate, that we had to hold back. Specially in this situation, we need to find healthy resources. Once we have relieved ourselves of the secrecy of the past, we may for the first time feel really part of humanity. In this natural belonging, we can turn to mother, noticing her deep loneliness and alienation. Finally, we can break the negative bonding that has made us accomplices to her, and look at each other in freedom and respect.

> *Bob D. had a mother who presented herself as a victim. In his childhood and adolescence, he had sided with her against her violent husband, his father. As an adult, he experienced a period of intense depression. In the session, when working on his father, he realized he had made a decision early on not to follow in his footsteps and be violent and abusive like him. But as he connected with his mother in that time, he also realized that by being the "good" son, he had had to renounce all his male qualities. When facing the picture of his mother, he could not express any anger or aggression. He started feeling very heavy and disconnected. We asked him why his mother had never left her husband. After going through all the obvious reasons, Bob started experiencing something different. He realized that he had been used by her: she would criticize his father to him, and stop him as soon as he expressed outrage about it in front of him. She did the same with each one of her children. He remembered how she divided the whole family by telling different secrets about the father to each one of them, instructing them not to mention anything to anybody. She would side with father when he beat them. Bob*

started feeling her web of hatred around him. He became aware of her immense power. The release of anger that followed was intermingled with grief and pain for having been betrayed and separated from his brothers and sisters.

LOOKING BEYOND MOTHER

As adults, when we experience how much we yearned for that golden merged space with her, we can realize now that our mothers have given us the first taste of it. Although it may not have been sufficient, or not have lasted long enough, we received a precious taste of golden merging. Later on, we remember this imprint, and it makes us search for meaningful merging in our lives. We learn that negative merging can never be a substitute for the positive one. Criticism, neglect, or being accomplices, will never be enough to replace the real value of merging.

We also learn to understand that in life merging comes and goes, and that we do not need to reject it or cling to it, out of fear that it will disappear. If mother gives us the first true taste of golden merging, than beyond her is the feminine manifestation of existence, that provides this merging at any time we open to it, unconditionally. As Bert Hellinger says,

> Do you want to change your mother? You'll never change her—she is the only possible mother for you. If you realize this and agree to it, then it starts an inner movement. You let her be as she is on the one side, and you bow down in front of her on the other. You honor her as your mother. After all, you take life from her, and only she could pass it on to you—together with your father. If you do this, you look beyond your mother and you see life coming to you from afar—you don't know where—and it is a deep religious movement. If you have done this, you are free, and your mother will shine. (5)

Basho says (6):

> To the willow —
>
> all hatred, and desire
>
> of your heart

THE EVOCATION

MY PERSONAL EXPERIENCE IN WRITING A LETTER OF COMPLETION TO MANÚ'S MOTHER

SVARUP

Mamma, as I start writing to you I feel an upsurge of need.

I always felt and longed for your soft milky sweet nature, but could never reach it for more than an instant. Your walls of protection would quickly close around it, and cover it with duties and routines.

I couldn't understand why you had to make yourself so hard and critical.I would have understood better your tears...

You might have though it inappropriate for you to show them to me,but your self control made everything dry and parched. Not a good landscape for our rich hearts.

That's why I was all the time making you angry. To feel you.

But it wasn't your anger I wanted!

I wanted the soft and artistic quality of that long ago little blond girl that still lived somewhere inside you, the one who knows about taking her time and about the rhythms of nature...

Mamma, please come to me, open the gates of your inner sacred garden to me...

When those gates are closed, life becomes meaningless.

Mamma, let's take a holiday, let's walk on a meadow full of flowers...I don't need that much safety, I want to see you happy!!

I won't allow you to forget your beauty, Mamma. Why don't you enjoy it? Is it not OK to be visible? Is it not Ok to let go?

Mamma, let your own tenderness heal your heart. And let me be who I am, a little girl who loves being messy, dancing, and playing with boys. I give you back the self-criticism and rigidity that I absorbed from you, and I receive your poetry, your great sense of beauty, your wisdom...Thank you for who you really are....

Your daughter

My personal experience in writing a letter of completion to my mother

Premartha

Mother,

What I never told you before is that your absence hurt me most.

I felt as if I came with my natural gifts to you, and you weren't really there for them.

You didn't even remember your own gifts anymore.

You gave up and resigned.

As a child, I was afraid of the melancholic space of depression that enveloped you.

Afraid, because it was pulling me in.

It felt dangerously attractive to let go and disappear in your lap.

You were tired.

I learnt to measure my impulses.

I became sensitive to your responses.

Maybe it was not the right moment, maybe it was not the right time.

It shocks me to realize how much I became an ally to your passive battle.

I did it for your attention and love.

I feel betrayed.

I believed that you were the wounded Queen, and I your Knight in shining armour.

I though I had to protect you from the bad King-Father.

But you didn't want to be free.

You were like a bird who lived a life long in a cage, and now that the door opened, you had forgotten how to fly.

I locked myself in the cage with you.

I waited.

I shrank.

I gave up my needs.

I became sad like you.

But nothing helped.

Until a rage started growing in me, and I wanted to destroy the cage and you with it.

Mother.

I loved you too much. I adored your tenderness and sweet nature. I dreamt of seeing you free. Spreading your wings on your own flight.

Now I have to free myself.

By spreading my own wings, I can feel the gratefulness I carry towards you.
You allowed me to dream.
You gave me a vision.
You nourished my longing.
Thank you mother.
The cage has started to dissolve.
Your son

THE RECIPE

COMPLETION WITH MOTHER

Write a letter of completion to your mother.

Start with the sentence: "Mother, what I have never told you before...". Take time to tell her all the things you had to hold back as a child.

While writing, you might become aware of different emotions coming to the surface. There might be anger, sadness, need, and grief. Allow them to be there, without any judgment.

At the end, sign the letter with your adult name.

CHAPTER 8

EMBRACING THE CHILD (2 TO 0 YEARS OLD)

Man needs to be needed. It is one of the most fundamental needs of human beings. Unless one is cared for one starts dying. Unless one feels that he is significant to somebody, at least to somebody, his whole life becomes insignificant.

Hence love is the greatest therapy there is. The world needs therapy because the world is missing love. In a really loving world no therapy will be needed at all; love will be enough, more than enough. Hugging is only a gesture of love, of warmth, of caring. The very feel of the warmth flowing from the other person melts many illnesses in you, melts the ice-like, cold ego. It makes you again a child.

(Osho, *The Wild Geese and the Water*)

THE ORIGINAL TRUST

Enter the room where a newborn baby is resting...

As we enter, we become aware of a change in the atmosphere. From the daily noises and activity in the rest of the house, we are stepping into a completely different world.

There is a subtle and silent vibration, and a quality of delicate and full presence in a baby's room. Because of this, it feels natural to us to approach an infant with care. Tenderness and awe surface at the mystery of this new life. It is a mystical experience.

On the one hand, we perceive the physical fragility of the new small being, while on the other we are awed by the vastness of its presence, its spirit.

The newborn baby itself, does not move much yet. There is a a stillness coming from its being. Physically, it can suck and make sounds, and perform small leg and arm movements, but it does not yet try to hold its head up, or try to change its body position.

As the baby rests, it does not have to make any effort. It is in a state of being. On a basic biological level, this is called the healthy autistic state. This state is needed for the baby to recover from the intense experience of birth, and to fully receive the nourishment it needs to gain strength and grow. On a spiritual level, the baby is still in Samadhi.

In its physical surrender, lies the seed of a fundamental spiritual quality: trust. An infant lives in a state of deep trust. Because it has no perception of itself yet as a separate entity, its trust is not toward someone else . It is an unfocused state of receptivity and openness for what life brings.

In that quality of being, nurtured by a loving atmosphere, the child is able to totally relax. It knows that it is surrounded by warmth and care. As adults, this experience becomes the ground on which our trust is built.

When in our lives we are meeting or holding a newborn child, we spontaneously reconnect with that forgotten memory of surrender and trust. A baby emanates this. When the baby relaxes in our arms, for a moment we remember this, and we become part of a forgotten world of merging again. We get nourished by the silence and restfulness that its presence gives us. Its eyes, still unfocused, reflect a soul that is not divided. Its small body, with its sensitive belly and delicately beating heart, is open to receiving all the impressions that life offers. We are partaking in the baby's state of openness and trust. Through it we return to our own age of innocence.

THE PHYSICAL BONDING OF THE INFANT

The separation of mother and child

A newborn child, like any newborn mammal, has many physical needs. It is the most fragile and complex animal on earth. It needs good nourishment, warmth, and a lot of care. And, like any other mammal, it needs a certain time of recuperation and growth before it can make significant steps outward. Apart from care and nurturance, the greatest physical need of the infant is bonding. This simple biological reality evokes an instinctive response even in the youngest and most inexperienced of mothers.

After birth, the child needs physical bonding with the mother. To be touched, stroked, hugged, is essential for the child. The baby needs this especially in the time immediately after birth, in its first few hours. The baby's impression of life, whether it is protective and nurturing or not, is decided by the bonding it does or doesn't experience then.

> Isaac K., an entrepreneur in his fifties, had anything in life he could wish for on a material level. Yet, he easily felt rejected, and could precipitate himself into a panic, making him totally withdraw. His mother had died one year after his birth, so he was raised by his aunt with true love and care. As a matter of

fact, we had decided to focus on his aunt while dealing with the issues of anger and boundaries, because she had been extremely overprotective of him at that time. When we moved into his early infancy, he came in touch with his short but significant period with his mother. He started reliving a long-forgotten sensation of bliss and union. The traumatic separation from his mother had deprived him of the remembrance that she had really loved and cared for him in the first year of his life. Isaac was able to realize how this experience of merging had laid the foundation for his spiritual search, and could bow down in deep gratitude to his mother for the golden merging he had shared with her. Although he remained reserved and shy about his deeper feelings, Isaac started recognizing and surrendering to the love that his woman and friends wanted to share with him.

It is in this early time that the bonding between mother and child has the strongest effect. When for different reasons this cannot be acknowledged or is not allowed, by the mother, or the people who surround the mother, the child pulls back and starts to shrink inside. And this doesn't happen only to the child: the mother also withdraws and shrinks.

In our modern way of giving birth, this need for bonding is often ignored. Mother and child are separated from each other immediately after birth. The bonding, the natural merging, is not respected. The pain that this separation creates, is overwhelming. Often the mother does not know how to handle it. She feels helpless. The only thing left for her is to close off.

It is the baby's crying that activates the mother's milk production. It is the touch of the baby's skin on the mother's breast that stimulates the release of the hormones slowing down the post-birth bleeding. It is the baby's presence that naturally awakens all the instincts lying dormant in the mother. When the baby is taken away from her and only brought back later, an estrangement between the two is created.

When the mother sees her baby for the first time, her instinct reaches out to it. She wants to hold and cuddle it. The baby's vulnerability and innocence, its looks and the sounds it makes, create in the mother the instant response of love and protection for her newborn. Even if she has never learned how to do this, nature supports her, and she will find herself spontaneously offering the right responses.

But in our modern world, dominated by the belief that nature has to be bent to mankind, the basic nurturing of our children no longer arises from a direct connection with our instincts. Most babies born in the last forty years have been separated from their mothers at birth. Soon after, they are put on a strict feeding schedule and their physical needs as they arise are no longer responded to. Clock time substitutes real attunement and sensitive presence on all levels. Women are taught to lose their trust and understanding of their own bodily and emotional responses.

Science in this way has increased the number of children who survive birth complications or post-natal illnesses. But it has also created a deep disconnection on a physical and emotional level between mother and child. This has become the source of many of the psychological illnesses in our modern times.

Negative emptiness
With the arrival on the scene of the famous doctor Spock, a whole new ethic was introduced to a humanity, looking for practical solutions in child rearing. Mothers who were dealing with the new stress of having jobs and other commitments to society, were happy and excited to try out on their babies these new ways of strict and controlled child upbringing. Specially in the area of feeding and nourishment, to have fixed schedules meant having more free time for themselves, and less dependence on their babies unpredictable needs.

But a baby doesn't have any means of understanding that the reassuring, nurturing, and warm experience of drinking mother's milk is going to occur at regular intervals. In its hunger, sharply experienced with the totality of its small body, when not responded to, the baby feels a total panic and helplessness. No promise of a delayed response to this hunger can soothe it. It is too early for the baby to understand about time and schedule. What it really needs is mother's attunement and availability, her care and her love.

As adults, we compensate feeling undernourished and uncared for in various ways. We try to negate the basic sensation of negative emptiness. We try to fill up the hole. We fill up our lives with eating and smoking too much. We use drugs, sex, and work to fill up the unbearable emptiness we feel inside. Or we control all our intake, starve ourselves, and live on a minimum. Most of our eating disorders originate from our baby time.

But none of these strategies works for long. As they fail, we have to run away faster and faster from the feeling of undernourishment in our bodies and souls. To avoid feeling the disappointment and emptiness that lie within, we have to compensate more and more. To heal the sensation of negative emptiness, we need to face the lack of bonding and care that we felt as babies.

Sometimes, the compensations have solidified around us so strongly that they become addictions. Then, it can be very difficult to resolve them through our type of work. Jenny F. was a very beautiful young woman in her twenties. She was addicted to heroin. The time after her birth had been extremely difficult and tense. Her mother, who had been at that time struggling to swim above the surface of her own panic, was now giving Jenny all the support and care she could provide. Jenny came to us with deep shame about her addiction. Underneath her self-destructive behavior, she was very sensitive and fragile, just like a newborn baby. She became aware of her habit of endlessly taking revenge on the world for the hard circumstances of her early life, and felt the shame of her predicament. She stopped heroin, and we had great hope for her recovery. But then she stopped coming to us, and started to take heroin again. We heard a year later that she had had a child, and was under treatment for heroin addiction. We hope that the memory of the meeting with her own little girl inside will reflect in the relationship to her newborn son, and contribute to her healing.

As adults, once we consciously recognize the space of negative emptiness inside, and we can stay with it without filling it up with compensation, we start to experience how existence itself fills up this emptiness effortlessly and unconditionally. In our surrender, we receive exactly what we need.

THE EMOTIONAL BONDING OF THE INFANT

If love is denied

In the nineteenth century, a large percentage of newborn infants was killed by something called marasmus. Through religious and social conditioning, mankind was so much disconnected from its natural instincts, that exposure to touch, or even air, was considered dangerous to the child. Instead, immediately after birth, the newborn was tightly swaddled in cloth. The child would resign itself from love and its flame of life would slowly fade away.

If love is shared

For healthy growth on all levels, physically, emotionally, mentally, and spiritually, the baby needs mother's loving contact and tender care. Only a healthy, natural bonding can provide all of this. It gives the baby the experience that it is loved and cared for. In the intuitive bonding between mother and child, the child thrives. At birth, and after it, it is the time when more than ever love and touch are of absolute necessity for the child. The child's outer and inner structure is still sensitive and malleable. It needs all the extra care in the world to grow into a healthy, grown up being.

Mother's emotions become our own

In the first months of our lives, mother is the bridge to existence.

She is the main and constant presence in our new world. Merged with her in symbiosis, we do not differentiate between what we ourselves feel and what was she experiences. We experience the moods and attitudes she has toward herself, and life surrounding her, as part of us.

If these moods are positive and optimistic, we feel a happy attitude towards life. We coo and gurgle contentedly in our little beds. If her moods are negative, we suffer too. We become closed and unresponsive to our surrounding. Her moods become the first mirror of our existence. As Reich puts it:

> The infant has no means of expression at his disposal than various forms of movement…and crying. The mother grasps the expression of the infant's gestures…. If her organism is free and emotionally expressive, she will understand the infant. But if she is armored, characteriologically hard, timid, or otherwise inhibited, she will fail to understand the infant's language, and therefore the emotional development of the child will be exposed to a variety of damaging influences. (1)

What we register as coming from mother in our infancy are not just her conscious decisions: we are deeply attuned to her unconscious too. Our perception of her is not limited to verbal communication. Words don't have much meaning yet. We are living in an undivided sense of perception. In this reality, we perceive things of her that she might not be aware of. We are not wondering what are the reasons for her frustration, anxiety, anger, or sadness. We only experience the deep discomfort of these emotions as they touch us. Specially those emotions that are negative and chronic. On a deep symbiotic level, her emotions become our own emotions.

Francis L.'s complaint was that he had unexplainable blank moments in his daily activities. They, in fact, occurred many times during our series of sessions when feelings started to arise, especially when it came to his loneliness. He was an adopted child. During the session he became aware that the only feeling he had shared with his mother before adoption was her pain and guilt. They occupied his whole feeling world. When we asked him whether he was ready to give them back to her symbolically, he cried and refused. They were his only link to the woman that gave him life. We could go no further with him, except feeling touched by his difficult dilemma.

As adults, when we discover our deep symbiosis with mother's emotions, we need to learn to take distance and to develop the skills of mothering our own inner baby child ourselves. We need to communicate positivity to this child, embracing it with our love and support.

THE WORLD AND FATHER

After the first months, father becomes also important for the baby. The baby in its being, starts reaching out to him too. If it is allowed and acknowledged, the father's natural response to the baby is in many ways similar to that of the mother. He will touch and make sounds, and look at the newborn as often as she does. The earlier a father is involved in caring for a child, the sooner he can touch, hug, kiss his newborn, the stronger will be the bonding between father and child. Of course, his way of approaching the child might differ in its expression from the mother's. But it is good for the child to receive different forms of attention and approach. The baby's feelings for itself come through the contact it has with both parents. The baby needs the love and attention of both to become itself. As Thomas Verny remarks:

> A child's self-confidence and self-image are the result of *all* the messages he receives from his parents. Whether this occurs through the stroking, hugging and gentleness of his mother or the physical play of his father, or viceversa, does not really matter. The important thing is that he receives jointly from his parents the encouragement to be himself. (2)

THE SHAME AROUND OUR NEEDS

If at the beginning of our lives we have not been loved and acknowledged enough for who we really are, as adults we find it difficult to value ourselves for our own presence. We try to cover up the deep shame we feel about our own being by doing and producing. This can happen in different ways. We can try to fight for the attention, or manipulate, or beg for it. But none of this will fill up the hole of unworthiness.

GIVING AND RECEIVING

Everyone has needs.

As babies, we are totally dependent on the outside world to fulfill our needs. We need bonding, nourishment, love and care. We have no control over what comes or does not come. Our needs and their fulfillment are totally in the hands of others.

Just like a baby needs to bond with its mother through touching and hugging, as adults, we need to bond with others through love and intimacy. Merging, physical touch, and appreciation are nourishment for the soul and the body: they make us more vulnerable, softer, more open to life. It is part of our human nature to long for all this. This essential need does not come from a lack, but rather from an overflow: I pour out my being and make myself available to receive the other's being. It is a dance, a play, where joy is felt in being both on the giving and the receiving end. In that way, sharing and outpouring the richness of our being is as strong a need as receiving the love that comes back. But in doing this we open up our dependency to others, and with it our childhood wounds around this, might start resonating again.

When as adults we touch our childhood wound of negative emptiness, we start experiencing ourselves again as lacking and deficient. In these moments it is very hard to admit our real needs. In our adult world, we learn to be ashamed and afraid to ask. Reaching out, asking for love or appreciation, are synonymous with being needy. When we do it anyway, we might touch again the feeling of unworthiness and rejection of our being as we experienced it in infancy. In our identification with not being good enough, we become afraid to give. We start to hold back and what we have to share loses its value. When we start anticipating this rejection, and we dot share any longer, we become heavy and burdened with our unexpressed love.

To prevent ourselves from falling into the hole of negative emptiness, we develop different strategies. All of them are developed in our childhood and are based on the feeling that the needs we feel are not right.

THE DIFFERENT STRATEGIES THAT PREVENT US FROM EXPOSING OUR NEEDS:

The renouncer
"I don't need it anymore."
- We have given up.
- As children, our need to share meets no response. We feel abandoned, unloved, and unwanted. We learn to resign and disconnect from our desires, or to reject them.
- As adults, we believe that by not needing anything anymore we will return to our original space of being, of emptiness.
- Underneath the superficial renunciation lies a volcano of needs and desires. We judge ourselves for it.
- When others expose what they want, we condemn them, but we also secretly envy them.

The complainer
"It's never what I really need."
- We feel that we exist only when we need. We identify fully with our undernourished part, and keep it alive all the time.
- As children, we don't receive enough nourishment. We learn to protect ourselves by tightening up around our core. This tension becomes part of our identity. Only when we are hungry can we feel ourselves.
- As adults, we believe that in order to survive, we should never be fulfilled. We ask for more and more, but reject it when it comes. We feel it is never the right nourishment, and that we cannot trust it.
- On the surface, we present an image of being available and dependent, but underneath it, we have lost the capacity to relax and to receive.
- When others provide nourishment to themselves, we feel jealous, but when they offer it to us, we are not be able to accept it.

The giver
"I want you to need me."
- We focus our own needs on others.
- As children, we learn to disconnect from what spontaneously flows from us, and lose a natural exchange with others.

- As adults, we substitute this exchange with calculation and trade. We find out what others need, and often give it to them, even before they know what it is themselves. We believe that if we stop doing this, nothing will come back to us.
- On the surface, we create an unselfish picture of ourselves. But underneath, our own denied needs are boiling. We do not trust that who we are is the gift that we can share.
- In our giving to others, we feel cheated and unacknowledged by them. But when they offer us something back, we avoid the exchange.

The controller

"I don't need."

- We reject all needs. We fight against them by not needing anything.
- As children, we learn that to be dependent is infantile. We have to be strong very early.
- As adults, this gives us a feeling of independence. We feel self-reliant and free, but have to stay alert to conceal any other sides.
- On the surface, we show that we have everything under control. Underneath it, we are constantly struggling with the deeper belief of being needy. Although we will never give in to it, we are not free of it.
- We long for others to come close to us, but when it happens, the feelings that this intimacy brings up are too threatening. Our state of being, trust, is replaced by control and criticism of our own and other people's needs. Only when we are in power, do we believe we can just be.

As long as these strategies prevent us from feeling the natural needs we experienced in our childhood, we will be unable to be really intimate and to love. The moment we become aware of them, their hold on us releases itself, and we find ourselves able to respectfully share our needs of giving and receiving.

RELEASING UNEXPRESSED NEEDS

The strategies that we develop as infants to handle the rejection of our natural needs are also written in our bodies.

In our physical helplessness as infants, we have no other way than to adjust ourselves to the attitude of our surroundings. In this way, we learn to disconnect from what we experience as painful. When our needs are not met, we learn to detach, and withdraw our energy from our bodies. This develops into what is known in the Reichian body work as the "oral" body type.

As adults, when we suffer from this detachment, we experience a lot of weakness and collapse in our legs. Our body frame has grown thin and elongated, and our chest has become sunken and closed. We have difficulties to expand and receive nourishment. Opening up to it brings up again the unbearable sensation of deficiency that we felt as babies.

For some of us, the wound of deficiency becomes visible in our bodies. For others of us, it has gotten covered by layers of compensation and protection. But when we journey back to our infancy, and we uncover this wound, we all meet these sensations of undernourishment and lack of care locked and hidden inside our bodies.

The collapse that originates from this, is often accompanied by hate. As babies, when we withdrew, we pulled all our life energy together in a tight knot. There was nothing extra left for warmth and love. Sometimes the only way to survive this pain was through hate. In our adult life, this hate might be buried deeply, under layers of resignation and defeat. It's essential that we reach this cold spot inside of us, and bring the warmth of our expression there.

This involves the physical and emotional expression of our infant needs. We need to create a safe environment in which we can kick, rage, and scream. We have to reach out again with our arms, to ask and reclaim our needs and wants. In this vital expression, we own again our self respect, our natural fullness, and our yes to life. Janov says:

> I believe that the angry man is the unloved man—the man who could not be what he was.... But need is basic; anger is secondary—it is what happens when need is not fulfilled...it is more a case of "Love me, please. Why can't you love me? Love me you bastards!".... Once the need is felt, there is scarcely any anger left. (3)

Deva S., whose progress we have followed throughout this book, rediscovered in this experience, the deep sense of peace and oneness she was born with:

> When, during the session on need, she called out "Mama!" she tried for a long time to hold back all her pain by closing her mouth tight. There was a long silence, no voice was coming through her anymore.
>
> Then, she surrendered to her pain and only her crying could be heard; her grief, without beginning, without end, took over.
>
> At the end of the session, she held a soft pillow to her heart as

if she were embracing her infant self in her arms. She opened up to welcome her baby self and could cry for the isolation that she had to begin her life with.

At the end of this deep cry, Deva S. experienced how her baby self was finally giving in and merging with her adult self. A silence followed, but this time it was a stillness beyond words, and an opening back into a long-lost state of being.

The last two sessions of this process were for Deva S. a gentle and loving reentrance into the world of meditation, opening up again to what is possible once the essence of trust has been regained.

The need to share

The main need we all have as children is the need to share ourselves.

When, as adults, we regain this original state of sharing, we are able to relax and rest in our own being and self-worth. Out of that, our love will start flowing again, effortless and free.

When Premartha took sannyas, Osho told him:

> You will be surprised to know that the Sanskrit word for greed is "lobha," and the English word "love" has come from that word "lobha." It is a very strange coincidence that the word "lobha," greed, has become "love" in English. But there may be a certain significance hidden behind: in fact, it is greed that becomes love—if transformed; if it passes through understanding, awareness, it becomes love, it becomes sharing. (4)

REDISCOVERING TRUST AND BEING

The original dimension of union and trust that we were bathing in at the beginning of our lives is never lost. In a moment of merging with nature, the ocean, a beloved, a master, we return to that feeling of union, becoming deeply nourished by it. In those moments, we experience merging in its essential quality. As A. H. Almaas says:

> It is interesting to note here that the desire for merging is not really the desire for another person, it is rather a desire for the merged state, the golden and sweet fullness. Because in the undeveloped infantile condition it was experienced with the mothering person, it becomes associated with being with, or merging with, another person.

However, this golden fullness can be experienced alone, without the presence of another person. (5)

Through the longing for the merging with the other, we become aware of the essence of merging itself. This golden space is available to us all the time. It's an essential expression of existence itself. Now that we recognize the beauty and value of it, we can bring it in our life, and heal our infant selves with it.

THE ATISHA MEDITATION

Atisha, an ancient Buddhist master, contributed a very beautiful meditation technique that is the basis for one of the three main paths of Buddhism. This technique can be used as a doorway to embrace our original pain and transform it into light. Our adult hearts have the capacity and the strength to open up to the pain of the child in us.

Welcome and breathe into your heart the feelings of rejection, abandonment, and isolation that you felt as a baby. You can transform it by breathing out compassion, warmth, love toward that pure and helpless part of yourself.

This simple meditation is enough.. Let relaxation descend. Trust and receptivity are again available to us. Rejoice in the deep recognition that existence is full of gifts and nourishment. Life welcomes us exactly as we are.

Buddha says (6):

To have friends in need is sweet

And to share happiness.

And to have done something good

Before leaving this life is sweet.

And to let go of sorrow.

151

THE EVOCATION

S<small>VARUP</small>

Calling mother

I am part of a circle of life and light
I move back in time.
I am back in Genoa, the city where Manú was born. As I walk around the market close to her home, I am at ease in the ordinariness, the dailiness of these surroundings. I inhale the salt air from the sea mixed with the smells of the fish stalls and the perfumes of Mediterranean herbs. There is also a smell of fresh white focaccia just out of the oven. I can hear the shouts of the vendors, their accent full of Portuguese melody and French undertones. I see their carved faces, weather beaten and full of edges. I walk through a sea of simple mankind going about their jobs.

I come into view of Manú's first home. It is a large apartment building, square andmodern, a window into the new world.

I enter the building. It smells clean. The tunes on the radio intermingle with arguing voices.. As I go up the stairs, the world below becomes fainter and more distant.

I enter the apartment. There is a shadowy, hushed atmosphere inside it. The baby is sleeping.. The apartment is modest, very clean. Mother is in the kitchen. She wears a flowery dress: her body is voluptuous, and smells like milk and honey. She moves around the house very silently.

Her mother is there, on a visit from abroad. She joins in the housework, she whispers and chatters. She wears French perfume, and her nails are painted. There is an unspoken solidarity between mother ad daughter, the recent birth has bridged the gap between them, for now.

I tiptoe into the room where the little baby girl lies. I come close to her bed, and look down. She is sleeping, her little fists are clenched. She has a frown on her forehead.. I wonder at the fragility of this small being, so thin and yet so strong in her determination to be there.

I allow my consciousness to float out of my adult body, and enter into the body of the baby girl.

I feel myself lying here in the bed. The sheets are clean, fresh, comforting. I am lying in the shade, in a world without strong sounds. I rest in a vast space which embraces me.

I can feel mother next door: her silence is like a song to me, it has a sweet and soothing taste...the presence of grandmother is more removed, and yet I can sense it, refreshing and crystalline, like a mountain stream.

Suddenly, I feel a need for physical contact, a need for reassurance: the space feels too vast, too big...I call out for mother. Louder. I scream with my full voice, moving my fists up. I want my mother. She has to come, now.

I hear her footsteps. The door opens,and she comes in: lightly, almost no sound, a centerdness and presence that makes me feel safe. She takes me in her arms. She gently pats me on the back, she comforts me, she is here...

She takes me to the kitchen, where her mother is sitting, twirping away like a birdie, and cutting potatoes.

In my mummy's arms, I let go. I am surrounded by the cosiness of woman, the warmth of mother, the giggle of female...

I am part of a circle, a circle of life and light, of giving and receiving. From mother, flows a silent wisdom, and unshakable presence. Behind her, from grandmother comes lightness, spirit and beauty. Beyond them, I perceive existence as mother, a deep and soft humming that pervades my body and melts away the tensions.

Calling father

Connected in a space of wellbeing

It five years later. It is high summer. We are at the beach. The air is celebrative, an alive mix of donuts, sea-salt, suntan oil. It is golden hot.

Father is in his favorite place, lying on his belly on a towel in the sand, baking in the sun. Ease exudes from him. His is a world of sensuousness, and body...the worries and cares of his work and his responsibilities are now just a frame, a platform that makes it safe and possible to let go...

I am sitting close by, under the big umbrella, with my red bucket and my yellow spade, a small bandanna askew on my head, sweaty and delighted, just happy to be alive.

I want to share my happiness with Daddy...I call him, I come closer...I touch him, gently, on his face. I like the tickle on my hand of the stubble on his chin.

He turns around. This time he has all the space for me. A lazy, sweet, melodious space, with a tinge of seriousness which makes me feel safe and protected.

He smiles, squinting in the sun, childlike and yet so big and secure...

I relax, and continue playing. Now we are connected, in a space of wellbeing, defining each other's space, and sharing a smile of contentment.

MY PERSONAL EXPERIENCE WITH THE ISSUE OF NEED

PREMARTHA

Calling father

I feel like a little emperor

As the adult, I return back in time. I find myself walking down the road of my childhood. It is summer, and still early in the day. The fields look golden, with ripened wheat. The homesteads, spread out along the road, look well cared for. Around the red bricked houses there are orchards and gardens. Here and there there are colorful patches of flowers. The main road is paved with cobblestones, and from there spread out smaller lanes, bordered with wild roses.

As I come closer to my childhood home, I recognize the familiar tall elm trees, that give shade to the house. Everything feels very peaceful. The stillness of the countryside is emphasized by the songs of many birds. They inhabit the forest that surrounds the fields.

I look for my father. I find him in the big barn, with his favorite horse. He is preparing the horse to be taken out. In the shade of the barn he has almost become invisible. His colors match perfectly the colors of the surrounding. The raw wood and the yellow straw are one with the colors of his clothes, browns and greens. The light shines in the stable, making golden patches on the shadowy walls.

As I come closer I can feel his presence. He is with himself. His gestures have a natural grace, with the easiness of someone who knows how to move around. His body is filled with nature, with a strength that comes by itself. His smell is that of earth and animals. The expression on his face is full of attention. Through it, I can feel the presence of a smile. He is happy, in his own world.

As I look at him, I notice that close to him there is the little boy me. He feels shy. Almost as if he is in the presence of something very sacred. I can see he doesn't want to disturb his father. But he is happy to be around him, to be allowed in his world.

On the next deep inbreath, I focus on my adult consciousness

154

and with a long outbreath, I let my spirit move out of my adult body and descend into my child's body, becoming the child me.

I am about four years old. I am wearing pants with suspenders, and a soft shirt. I have golden curls, and a shy smile on my face. I feel very honored to be so close to my daddy. I try not to disturb him by asking too many questions. I know he likes to be silent. So, I just stay next to him. It's fascinating to see how he moves, graceful and natural. As I tune into his movements, I feel a deep belly connection to him. I belong to him, he is my hero.

My soul longs to spread out through my little arms, I want to reach out to him, call his name, come close to him. My whole little body longs for physical contact with him. It's almost painful, like a sweet pain. Will he hear me? I am afraid that he won't notice me. That he is so used to be in his own world, that there will be no space for me there. I touch the despair that rises when he forgets about my existence. The feeling of hopelessness. It will never happen...

But as he turns around, I hear his voice. It's a deep voice, carrying lots of silence in it. He says my name. As he turns to me, he reaches out with his big arms, and I jump without hesitation. He lifts me, and for a moment he holds me tight. I can feel his heartbeat, and I can smell his body through the shirt my face is pressed against. I am in bliss.

Then he lifts me on his horse, and I am holding on to him. I feel like a little emperor, tiny on the huge back of the horse. I know he is there for me.

Calling mother

Our worlds become one again
Deeply nourished by the essence of my father, I now return further back in time. I come back to the time shortly after my birth. It's the same home, just now it is the Autumn season. The Dutch sky is overcast with dark clouds. There is wind and rain. The trees behind the house are getting bare. Everywhere there are golden and red leaves that have fallen. It is cold.

Inside the house, it is cozy. I can feel that my father has put on the wood stove. The smell of the burning wood mixes with that of the wet earth outside, and with the smell of the animals int the stables surrounding my childhood home.

As the adult I am now, I experience the house of my childhood as small. But very protective and warm. There is the smell of home cooking, tasty food that my mother prepares. My sisters are playing in the kitchen. There is the sound of the radio. Nobody is really listening. It is cozy.

I am searching for my mother. I find her in bed. Her bed has been placed in the living room, and a fire has been lit in the fireplace to warm up the space. She looks delicate and pale. My birth has been a home birth. She is used to the birth process. I am her fifth child. She looks very sensitive, with a soft aura, her movements are very slow. It is clear that the birth has taken a toll from her body. But around her is an atmosphere of contentment,. She is happy, her last child is a boy. Not only for herself, but also for my father, who has been waiting for a male child.

Her being smiles. She is surrounded by a golden light.

Around her, my family is active. Her sisters are there, taking care of her. They create the space for her to relax. Everybody is concerned for her to handle well the aftermath of birth. My sisters come and go, sometimes they cuddle up with her for a while, and then they leave for their own space again.

As I feel my mother, I notice that close to her, in my crib, there is the little baby child me. I come closer. I observe the tiny little face and hands, that make soft squeezing movements. The baby is sleeping, and once in a while little tremors spread through its body.- Everything around it feels very delicate and sweet. I feel very attracted to this child.

With a deep inbreath, I release myself from my adult body, and on the outbreath my consciousness descends into the baby child's body. I become the baby child.

I feel very sensitive. I can still feel the incredible experience of birth around me. I need time to disgust it. I need silence and space. My being needs to spread out in this little body. At the same time, I need love and care. I long for being close to my mummy. There, it feels safe, cozy and familiar. Her vibration puts me at ease, making me sleepy and relaxed. Once in a while, I want to reach out to her. I need to drink from her breast, taste the honey milk that feeds me, smell her skin, listen to her friendly sounds.

My consciousness allows me to reach out. I start calling her: "Mammy, mammy...". It reflects what I couldn't express when I was really a baby. This time I allow it..."Hold me mammy...Touch me... Love me...". The sentences roll out of my mouth. They come with such an urgency, there is nothing I can do to stop it now. My crying becomes really loud. There are moments when panic enters, and I want to stop and resign, retreat inside myself. But I continue, giving space to all the withheld emotions that are there. My crying becomes anger, my anger becomes rage. The rage spreads all through my body. It takes over, it becomes a total scream.

Then, suddenly, I become aware that my mother is listening. She sits up in her bed and reaches out to me. Someone with big secure hands takes me and puts me in her arms. It's unbelievable, this sensation of homecoming. A river of tears releases itself. My tears and her tears. She has accepted me. She is bonding with me. I can feel the golden merging with her.

Our worlds become one again. We disappear into each other. When I reach out to her breast, I find her nipple, and I suck greedily. They are all mine. They provide a world of sensuous sensations all over my body.

Later she cuddles me, and sings songs to me. I don't do anything. I am simply in a state of bliss. I love her with all my little being.

When I return to my adult body, I can feel the healing sensations that this journey has created in me. I feel very grateful for the golden essence of life, that has been reborn in me. Now I trust deeply that I can take care of the baby child myself. I am ready to father and mother myself.

THE RECIPE

REACHING OUT

Visualize and feel the young child you. Become aware of what this child would have really needed from its father.

Observe the father of you childhood in a resourceful moment. Notice him at a moment of happiness or contentment, Notice the child-you close to him.

Now allow the child to reach out to him, opening its arms wide. Support the child to call him by his name: Father, Papà…Connect sentences to it.

Notice your father turning to the child-you.

Feel his embrace as he takes the child-you in his arms.

Visualize and feel the baby child-you. What would this child have really needed from its mother? Observe the mother of your early childhood, closely after birth, in a moment of golden merging. Notice her peacefulness, her delight.

Feel the baby child-you close to her. Allow the child to reach out to her, opening its arms wide. Support the child to call out her name: Mother, Mamma…Let other sentences come: "I need you, I love you…".

Observe your mother turning to the baby-you. Feel her embrace, as she surrounds the child-you with all her love and tenderness.

CHAPTER 9

WELCOMING THE CHILD (0 YEARS OLD)

The birth has to happen, it is a natural phenomenon. You cannot prevent it, but you can suffer it or you can enjoy it. That is your decision. Enjoyment will be a great experience for the mother; but that needs some consciousness, some awareness, some watchfulness of her own unconscious ways so that she can relax, and the unconscious cannot interfere in the process of relaxation.

If she relaxes there is every possibility that the child will also relax, because the child has learned in all these nine months only one thing, just to be with the mother. If the mother is sad, the child is sad. Now there are ways to find out whether the child is sad or not. If the mother is angry, the child is angry. If the mother is in suffering, anguish, that anguish penetrates to the child too because the child is not yet separate. Everything that vibrates the mother's being also vibrates the child; there is a synchronicity.

(Osho, From *Misery to Enlightenment*)

BIRTH MEMORIES INFLUENCE OUR LIFE

To be born is not something that happens only once in a lifetime. We are constantly dying to the past and being born to the moment. Each morning upon awakening, we are born to a new day. Each day, we move through situations in which we are confronted with the fact that we have to let go of what we know and feel safe with, into a new space of not knowing, and surrender.

In each one of these moments, we are touching the deep-seated memory of our birth. We are looking at the world through the eyes of the newborn baby we once were.

Inthis way, birth memories still influence how we approach life. Feelings of fear, anger, or depression that we might notice coloring our life force, can be directly related to our early life memories. Our experience before and during the birth process, and our first impression of life around us, determine to a great degree, our trust in life as adults. To regain that trust again, we need to go through a rebirth.

A GRADUAL JOURNEY BACK TO BIRTH

For the most part, we do not connect events in our daily life with those that happened long ago in our personal history. Most of our birth memories have disappeared from conscious recall.

And yet, it has been discovered that under hypnosis or guided trance, many birth memories can be retrieved. Clinical experiments have been conducted in which, under hypnosis, a number of people were guided back to their birth. The descriptions they gave of the circumstances of their birth and their positioning at the moment of delivery could be compared with the clinical records, the delivery notes. They were accurate in all cases.

In our personal experience with the Childhood Work, we have noticed that using a method of gradual return into childhood, allows people to open up to the unconscious content of their mind. They start to relive their prenatal period, their birth, and their entrance into the world.

WHAT HAPPENS TO US SHORTLY BEFORE BIRTH?

As we focus on our birth, we need to bring our attention how our mother felt cared for and protected around that time.

According to medical studies, the easiest deliveries happen with women who:
- Are at ease and relaxed with themselves,
- Have less ambivalence about becoming mothers,
- Have an emotionally and sexually satisfying relationship with their husbands,
- Have a supportive environment in which their own mothers are involved.

What was our mother's situation at the time of our birth? To find out, we have to journey back to our past, and from there, reenter our family home.

Tune into the atmosphere there. Was there a peaceful atmosphere, with little conflict and disagreement? Was our parents' life situation secure, and could they welcome us from a relaxed position? How was the connection between them at that time? Was our father involved in our birth? Did our parents receive support from the larger family, e.g., grandparents, uncles, aunts, or close friends?

Through what we know and feel about that time we can understand how our motherwas affected by it. We can feel how it affected us living in her womb, and how it influenced the atmosphere around our birth.

160

For the most part of our Western history, the belief has been that a child at its birth is completely unaware, and feels nothing of what is happening. The birth of the child was only seen through the eyes of its mother and father; there was no experience for the child itself. We were unaware that much of how we perceive the world as adults, is still through the eyes of the newborn child. We did not know that the events at birth left a deep imprint on our personality. We thought that the memories of the child were only born at the time of its early personality development, around age three.

> *In fact, children up to the age of three or four still have very precise and vivid memories of their birth. It is just that adults don't consider the possibility of asking them what it was like. As the personality structure gets more and more sophisticated, these memories recede into the unconscious. They become unasked for and forgotten, but they do not disappear. In her work with "problem" children in England, Svarup came across the case of a four-year-old boy, D., who was on his way to chronic anorexia, like his mother. As she directly asked him what his birth was like, the little boy proceeded to explain that he had knocked at the door, and his mother refused to open.*

WHEN THE MOMENT OF BIRTH COMES

At the end of our stay in the womb, close to nine months for most of us, we are still completely one with the world, and the world with us. The feelings, sounds, and sights we perceive in the uterus are as much part of us as the sensations in our own body. There is no distinction between our inner space and the space that surrounds us. Yes, we do receive news from our mother about her state and the way she responds to the world around her. When this input is friendly, it ripples through our peacefulness, but it lasts only for a moment. Afterward, we return to our original state of being.

During this time, we are floating in a warm protective pool of amniotic fluid. It surrounds us, creating a feeling of union and one-ness.

It is as yet not clear what triggers the birth process. Sheila Kitzinger, an expert on childbirth and midwifery, reports that the contractions in the womb are already happening before the beginning of labor, but at that stage they are not experienced as painful by the mother, and are felt as pleasurable by the fetus. (1)

Recent research conducted by Caroline McMillen (2) indicates that the impulse initiating the birth process is set off by the fetus.

Some inner spark triggers its hypothalamus, which sends a message that passes from the fetus to the mother.

What science has been unable to discover is the underlying mystery of what that inner really spark is. However, it seems to have become clear on a scientific level that it is the baby who initiates its process of entry into this world by sending to its mother the message: "I am ready!"

In this impulse lies the secret of our will to live, to come out, regardless of the difficulties and circumstances that lie ahead. To acknowledge that we actually initiated our own birth process, might support us in recovering the totality that we need for the challenges in our present lives. As Stanislav Grof says:

> In the context of the birth memory the individual experiences a condensed review of all his or later successes in life. The experience of birth thus functions psychologically as the prototype of all the future situations that represent a serious challenge for the individual. (3)

Once the process is triggered, the child, as well as the mother, have to surrender to the outer circumstances, which will either support and strengthen this core impulse, or will push it back or delay it.

When the moment of birth comes, we experience prolonged emotional and physical pressure. We have not been exposed to such strong physical tightening before. Now we are suddenly pushed into the birth canal. For many of us, this experience lasts several hours. We are exposed to the full force of our mother's contractions, squeezing and pushing us around. Our feelings alternate between sensations of pain, excitement and pleasure. There is:

• Great pain when the contractions start to exert pressure on our head, neck, and shoulders.

• Great excitement when the contractions push us, with our arms and legs being wildly thrown around.

• Great sensual pleasure at being washed by the warm maternal fluids streaming over us. Through the massage of her uterine muscles, our skin is stimulated for the first time, our body being squeezed and rubbed.

When we finally reach the last part of the journey, our delicate skull is pushed through the vaginal opening. then our whole little body slips out. At that ppint, many of us are separated from mother by a premature cut of the umbilical cord, before it has stopped pulsing and our normal breathing function would have taken over. Leboyer, the initiator of natural childbirth, describes:

To cut the cord, as soon as the child comes out of the mother's womb, is an act of great cruelty.... To keep it as long as it throbs, is to transform birth.... The child, oxygenated by the cord, takes its time.... In a short time, the breathing is full, wide, free, joyful. (4)

Or we are suddenly exposed to bright, harsh light, loud noises, cold air, and people we don't know, who pull at us, clutch us, and finally even slap us on our bottom, so we start screaming. Wilhelm Reich says:

When a child is born, it comes out of a warm uterus, 37 degrees centigrade, [98.6 degrees Fahrenheit] into about 18 or 20 degrees centigrade [65or 70 degrees Fahrenheit]. That's bad enough. The shock of birth...bad enough. But it could survive that if the following didn't happen: as it comes out, it is picked up by the legs and slapped on the buttocks. The first greeting is a slap. (5)

When we finally can relax in our brib or with mother, we have already experienced one of the most intense journeys of our life. Our sense of being welcomed has been challenged deeply, and we need all the time in the world, to integrate what happened, and to come back to ourselves.

TRAUMATIC BIRTH EXPERIENCES

What we have reported is a description of a normal birth in a hospital situation. Natural childbirth has only recently gained a strong foothold, and the awareness around childbirth is still very young.

When there are birth complications, the child is exposed to a more severe treatment of its body and soul. It's important to ask ourselves, how it feels:

•   When our mother is put under general anesthesia during delivery? Our movements become uncoordinated, drugged and sluggish. We don't have the natural strength anymore to make it through birth.

•   When we are pulled out by steel forceps? Our body is pulled forward, and our neck is stretched out in an unbearable tension. We have to fight with a force which is alien to ourselves. We lose our union.

•   When the natural labor that we share with our mother is replaced by an induced one, and our joint effort in giving birth is taken away? Our mother loses all harmony with her body, her birth rhythms. Although we are not ready to be born yet, we are pushed out by an artificial force. We are disconnected from our mother's natural contractions, and forced to move by induced and imposed ones.

• To be monitored through a tiny metal electrode inserted in our scalp? The results shown on the monitor, are often used to prematurely perform Cesarean section on us. We feel invaded and watched.

• To be delivered by Cesarean section? We are deprived of the essential mixture of pain and pleasure, which introduces us to the experience of life outside the womb. We lose our sense of natural ecstasy.

> *Robert S. was a brilliant young man who had a great deal of determination to achieve whatever he wanted, but through stress and overwork. We were doubtful about working with him because he approached therapy in the same way. When we confronted him with his way of pushing himself to the limits, he cried. We took him on, feeling that he had taken his first steps in acknowledging his child inside who was tired and undernourished by his overachieving.*
>
> *The series of sessions proceeded well until the stage of birth. Robert S. was born by Cesarean, under very traumatic circumstances. We guided him through a healing experience of rebirth, where we focused, as we had done many times in such cases, on time, space, and above all, sensuousness.*
>
> *The experience itself went very well. But, a few days after, Robert precipitated himself into a state of panic. His whole stress-based identity was shaken to the roots. He could not function in his work from a state of openness. We tried to be with him and give him the space to relax and recuperate like a newborn baby, but he closed off and tensed up, reproducing the stress he was familiar with. When he realized we would not support his stress addiction, he stopped coming to us.*

The wounds inflicted on us at birth leave an imprint. They become part of our perception of ourselves. Thomas Verny says:

> As we move through life, we continue to change and grow. But events such as birth and weaning, which until now have been viewed as "objective," physiological phenomena, produce definite and long-lasting effects on the personality of a child. We must learn how to make the

most of these opportunities. (6)

When after bvrith complications or traumatic birth, the parents are able and available to support their child in integrating the shock, miracles can happen. Specially at the beginning of our life, we have an incredibly strong inborn capacity to heal ourselves. Even the most wounding birth, can be healed by love.

This can happen at birth or even later in life, through rebirth.

BIRTH, SEXUALITY AND SENSUOUSNESS

Birth is like making love. In love, at the peak of merging, a letting-go, a disappearance happens. It is in that same let-go and disappearance, that birth takes place too. In the final moment, when all boundaries are swept away, nothing can be held back or controlled.

During labor, mother and baby are engaged in something which is wild, mysterious, and much larger than them. The experience can last longer than eternity, and it rides in waves running between pain and pleasure.

Engaged in the birth canal, which is pulsing, opening, and closing, the baby becomes one with the sense of urgency leading toward the peak of birth. From all sides, there is pushing and squeezing. The intensity alternates between agony and ecstasy. There is no goal, no sense of direction. In this wild stream of birth, the baby feels its body for the first time as it is separating.

The experience of pushing its head through the birth canal, its tiny body sliding out in a cascade of warm water, is orgasmic for the baby. As that moment of let-go sweeps over the mother, her mind stops and her body experiences being part of something as vast as the universe. This orgasmic experience is, for both mother and child, full of sensuous power and raw life-energy.

Unborn anger

When our birth is mainly painful, lacking any pleasureand sensuousness, we may feel betrayed. Our response to this betrayal might be in the form of a primal anger. Most of us, remaining unconscious of it, turn this anger either actively against ourselves, or keep it inside in the form of constant rage, a feeling of mistrust of and betrayal by life.

By realizing the longing and the natural feeling that we had, already at birth, for an ecstatic welcome, we learn to accept that anger and see it as an unavoidable response. We start to express its residues in safe and responsible ways. The compassion growing out of it will reach and heal the infant in us.

> *This insight can be of great help in cases like Maria G.'s. Her childhood had not been particularly violent or traumatic. As we journeyed backward with her, she could of course find reasons for some of her personality traits. But nothing could account for the repressed rage which erupted against herself at different times, often in the form of accidents. In the sessions, she put all her energy into the completion with father and mother. But we noticed that she was, to a certain extent, producing very intense emotions toward both her parents' drawings because she couldn't feel much. When we asked her, she agreed she was doing this in the hope of releasing something which she could not reach. When we came to her birth, which had been long and difficult, that rage found its release. Her life-energy had been suppressed and stopped for hours on end in the birth canal. The rage that finally found wild expression in her rebirth could turn into a more life-affirmative expression. When we saw her again after a few years, Maria told us that she had not lost her tendency to direct that rage against herself. But with the awareness of its origin, she could now detect this self-destructive pattern as it came up, and be compassionate with herself.*

Experiencing the fear and excitement of birth

Another element of unconscious birth memories is expressed in the unexplainable fear that grabs some of us at times when we enter new situations. We might have the tendency to anticipate the worst that can happen, even if there is no real reason for it.

Whenever we start something new, the memory of our original birth is awakened. If this birth was peaceful, we will remember the excitement that we felt facing the unknown. We will experience the trust with which we arrived. But if our birth was painful or traumatic, we will be afraid. With each new situation, the fear and confusion we felt at birth, will unconsciously get activated.

When we consciously bring our awareness and healing to the traumatized baby child in us, and we allow it to experience a rebirth, the old imprint can be erased and in its place comes a new feeling of excitement, trust, and surrender towards the unknown.

Birth traumas and the use of drugs

The abuse of repressive or mood altering drugs is often directly related to unresolved birth traumas. This is as well true in the case of prescription drugs, as well as in the case of recreational drugs.

166

On one hand, it can be the unconscious repetition of having been sedated along with our mother during the birth process. While working through their birth process, it happens that people become aware of the smell of chloroform still lingering around them. They can feel in this moment how the anesthetic had suppressed their vitality at birth. In this way, in their adult lives they might continue sedating their desires and impulses.

On the other hand, drugs can be abused to stop our traumatic sensations related to birth from coming to the surface. Repressive drugs, with their temporary soothing and diffusing effect, can temporarlity take away the pain and create an artificial experience of wellbeing. In times of emergency, their use can be very beneifical. As the emergency passes, we need to let go of them. By continuing using them, we won't have the possibility to transform through awareness the negative imprints we gathered at birth.

During the last thirty years, there has been a conscious and professionally monitored use of hallucinogenic drugs to support the reliving and healing of birth traumas. Experiments of this nature have been conducted by researchers like Albert Hoffman, Stanislav Grof, Timothy Leary, and several others. Their literature has contributed to a deeper understanding of the implications of the birth experience on the human psyche. Their research has also contributed to recognizing birth and prenatal encounters as spiritual experiences. Stanislav Grof says:

> A deep experiential encounter with birth and death is regularly associated with an existential crisis of extraordinary proportion.... This crisis can be resolved only by connecting with deep, intrinsic spiritual dimensions of the psyche...the resulting transformation seems to be comparable to the changes that have been described as to come about from participation in ancient temple mysteries, or aboriginal rites of passage. (7)

In the East, with its treasure of meditation techniques, it has been discovered that the same shifts of consciousness, synthetically produced by drugs, can be attained naturally through different breathing methods.

Reliving birth through breathing techniques

By consciously going through our birth process, the experience of the past, which was fragmented or distorted by a surplus of pain, or an absence of pleasure, is brought back into balance again. In all the methods in which we relive birth, we experience the old traumatic birth as well as the possibility of a new birth, with its relaxation and expansion. In this way, the old imbalanced imprint of our birth is transformed into a new one, in which pleasure and pain complement each other.

One, by now well-known, way of bringing birth memories to our consciousness is through "rebirthing," a method introduced by Leonard Orr. It uses deep breathing as a tool of transformation, often bringing people directly in touch with their birth experience. This method was passed on to L.Orr by his Indian guru. It is one of the many breathing techniques in the ancient Indian spiritual heritage that address issues around birth. Leonard Orr says:

> The purpose of rebirthing is to remember and re-experience one's birth; to relive psychologically, physiologically, and spiritually the moment of one's first breath and release the trauma of it. The process begins the transformation of the subconscious impression of birth from one of primal pain to one of pleasure. (8)
>
> *In this method, you breathe deeply, in and out, through the mouth. The breathing takes place in the chest area, drawing the air all the way up and filling the lungs. The inbreath is full, the outbreath is relaxed and letting go. The breathing takes place in a continuous rhythm, in and out, without stopping. During the breathing, as you enter deeper and deeper into an altered state of perception, your unconscious, through body, mind and emotions, will start to release memories of birth.*

During the breathing, our body might start to spontaneously take on the fetal position, curled up as it was shortly before birth. As we continue breathing, we start to experience the opening of the birth tunnel and our journey outward. Be aware that in this process many feelings which could not be expressed in that early time can be triggered. Allow them, but whenever possible, return to the breathing. The relief and joy of breathing ourselves into a new birth is incomparable. The expansion that follows, and the great sensitivity and pleasure that come with it, heal and transform our original wounds of birth.

What can happen to us after birth?

After birth, we arrive in a new and unknown world. To feel at home in it, we need to be welcomed by our mother. Physical bonding with her makes us feel safe and protected. Out of these first impressions we feel life is friendly, that we can slowly expand into our new world. We are all born with a trust in life. It is coming from the same source that brought us to our birth.

The journey through our birth process has been very intense for us as newborns. But we have an immense capacity to heal ourselves. For this, we need an atmosphere of peacefulness. If we are received in peaceful and loving surroundings, even the traumatic birth experiences described earlier in this chapter, can be digested and transformed by us as babies.

All that we need from our caretakers is silence and presence.

As Frederic Leboyer says, connecting with the newborn child is a great exercise in presence which can be immensely healing for the mother too:

> To meet the newborn, we have to come out of our time which runs furiously...we have to "be here"...as if there were no more future, no more "after." (9)

In the time shortly after birth, our whole system needs healing and rest. We are barely focused on the outside. Our attention is mostly turned inward. Our eyes are unfocused, the sounds we make are formless, and even though we love to be held, we do not reach out yet. We are in a state of inaction, the Buddha state. This state, allowed and supported without major interference, has immense value. It creates for our future, the knowing that it is possible to rest and relax inside oneself. This is the greatest source of healing.

> *In our groups on Childhood Deconditioning, we experiment a lot with these original states. In one meditation, we ask the participants to remain with unfocused eyes for a twenty minute period. Afterward, when there is the opportunity to share their experiences, many report that it was almost impossible to stay like that. It brought up feelings of panic, disorientation, and loss of control. Some, though, reported the opposite. They gave in and experienced a feeling of centering, of being focused inward, which, when they relaxed with it, gave them a feeling of spaciousness and peace. But everyone is equally surprised to learn, through this simple exercise, how we perceived ourselves and the world around us in our earliest childhood.*

> *Another valuable experiment is one of Osho's meditations called Devavani (10). During this meditation, the participants listen to soft music. After that, they make soft baby sounds: "la, la, la, etc.," first sitting, and later standing, allowing spontaneous movements to happen. Then they lie down and become silent. Usually, after this meditation, the main feedback from the participants is that they feel very relaxed, soft and open, and*

that their minds are much less active. Again, it is a surprise for all of them to realize that this was our state when we were very small.

GIVING BIRTH TO YOURSELF

Kabir says:
> Be strong, and enter into your own body, for there your foothold is firm. Consider it well, O my heart! Goo not elsewhere. Put all imagination away, and stand fast in that which you are." (11)

What happens during a natural birth can be used as a metaphor for the second birth that so many masters have spoken about: our rebirth into the state of innocence of a newborn child. And yet, there is a great difference: This time, we give birth to ourselves.

Being pregnant with yourself

Even before giving birth to ourselves, we need to learn the art of being pregnant with ourselves. We need to become aware of the longing that is growing inside us for a new life, and nurture it. We can't force the process, and no effort will speed it up. We can just acknowledge the waiting and be fully present in it. Just like a pregnant mother experiences deep moments of unity and magic while waiting for the child, so can we start to value the nurturing and enriching period of waiting for our second birth.

Giving birth to yourself

Like the baby growing inside the womb, we too have no control over the impulse that sparks off the process of our second birth. Once the impulse comes, and existence wills itself through us into a new form, we can only let it through, totally surrendering to its force.

Surrounding yourself with love and presence

In the way that biological mothers and babies, in pregnancy and birth, need to be supported through love and care, we, on our path toward our second birth, need to surround ourselves with people and situations who support us.

Whatever in our lives brings joy, helps our hearts expand, and dissolves the fear of the unknown, is significant.

In meditating with others, we share and create a nurturing womb of consciousness. Growing in this atmosphere of consciousness, we become more easily aware of the big smile that existence welcomes us with all the time.

The second birth
The second birth in itself remains a mystery. It carries a taste of infinity, the fragrance of love and more. Each master transmits his or her experience of it in a different way, just as each newborn child carries into this world the expression of its own individual flame.

Each moment can be a rebirth
Life provides us with infinite possibilities to exercise the courage and surrender that we need for a second birth. The mystery of each moment is always available. Each time an impulse arises in us to move beyond our known way of living, the mystery is there, waiting to be acknowledged and rediscovered.

Kalil Gibran says (12):

> Your children are not your children.

> They are the sons and daughters of life's longing for itself.

> They come through you but not from you.

THE EVOCATION

My personal experience with birth

Svarup

I am traveling all the way back to the time before Manú's birth. I breathe deeply and leave my adult body behind.

Welcome to this life of depth and transformation...
I am a fetus in the womb. I am swimming in a warm ocean. I am growing. Tides are coming, tides are going. My pulse quickens, slows down, and then becomes steady. I am dreaming, and in my dream I am lulled by the throbbing, squashing, soft rumbling all

around. The distant voice of my mother echoes inside and soothes me.

An infinite time passes. I grow larger, and the space around me is tightening. I am now sliding among narrow walls. In my dream, I hear a tone, a sound, from far away. Like an inner call. A change is taking place. A shift in time. I am thumping inside with an urge. An impulse arises, as fast as light. I am ready.

My message rushes out through my blood, and reaches the moist cave I inhabit. It responds. There are great waves and movements happening all around me. I am washed by the waves of the first contractions. I struggle to turn. The walls are closing in on me.

The contractions subside for a moment. The walls of the cave are warm again, enveloping. The sound of the heartbeat reassures me. I rest in this embrace.

And then it starts again, and stops, and starts again. The ocean around me has turned into a flood of gigantic waves.

And it stops. An eerie quiet. Some high frequency of control remains caught in the walls. The womb around me cannot release it. I am caught in this tension. I shrink into a core of steel. And wait. The contraction comes again. I am overtaken by panic. I want to get out.

I tumble and knock around inside her as she walks, fast, holding herself together, to the hospital. With a great rush, the waters break.

Inside, I feel overwhelmed by this tidal wave, I drown in it, I try to swim upstream. And it's gone. It's all dry now. Dry and hot, my skin is rubbing against the iron grip of a dry womb. I hear her screams of pain. But I won't give up

I enter a dark narrow tunnel..

For a blink of eternity, a sense of defeat, weakness comes over me. I am losing, I can't make it, I want to die. And then again I push, I push...

I am climbing on a landslide, running on a marsh. I push on and on.

Suddenly, some wondrous magic happens. Beyond her agony, mother remembers me. The synchronicity of our hearts returns. She pushes, falters, and pushes again. I feel glimpses of warm sensuousness running through the tunnel that starts giving way. The ecstasy of her surrender washes over me like a blessing. We have found each other for this eternal moment of let-go.

I come out...I scream. Then I breathe, one time, two times, eight times.

I am in the arms of my mother. I take refuge in her familiar smell and the safety of her heartbeat. We are both spent, exhausted.

Through the hospital window, The Scorpio full moon shines in a velvety balck sky, and it whispers:

"Welcome baby girl, welcome to this life of depth and transformation…"

I float out of the newborn baby's body, and take a moment to feel.

I hold the baby girl close to my heart and tell her:

Existence has heard your call

Beloved baby girl,

Welcome to this world. You can take your time to feel yourself, to feel all that is around you. We will spend time together at the ocean, a wide, peaceful ocean, a friendly sea, where you can bathe in golden light. And when the light feels too strong, I will give you the softness of twilight, the pale colors melting into each other, and the soothing darkness where the stars smile in silence.

I will give you time to come out of the waters slowly. You can float in them as long as you wish, and trust that they will carry you to a safe shore.

The sound of the wind in the trees, the songs of the birds, the voices of friends, the silence of the Master will surround you in peace, so that the seed inside you can flower in its own season.

And, when the moment comes for you to move, I will support your impulse. I will let your body test its strength against mine, so that it can feel the wonder and the magic of its aliveness. And I will also surrender to the life which wants to be born through you.

I will be with you to taste, smell, touch, hear, and see the beauty in each and every new experience. And I will be there to give you the rest and comfort that you need to integrate so many new sensations. I am so happy that you are here.

I can feel your courage and your strength that draw you toward the new. I honor that deep knowing in you, that every time, beyond what was and has been, there is so much more beauty and truth to discover.

Beloved baby girl, let the full moon soothe you with its silver rays. Existence was waiting for you. She has heard your call.

Svarup

MY PERSONAL EXPERIENCE WITH BIRTH

PREMARTHA

I belong to humanity

I am breathing. Deep and full inbreaths are followed by a letting-go on the outbreath. As more oxygen enters my lungs, spreading into my bloodstream, I feel an expansion happening. The world is becoming transparent, the gaps between its content are widening. Inside my body, a relaxation. A sense of floating is setting in. The separation between me and my surroundings becomes less clear. I start to feel like I'm under water. I am slowly reentering the womb of my mother.

I am entering into a dimension where colors are full of radiance, sounds are muffled, and movements carry no weight, where shapes are solid, yet continuously altering. The breath of life moves through them, its pulse beating in rhythm. A gentle dance of contracting and expanding, of breathing in and breathing out, is taking place everywhere.

I feel so utterly content, at home, in this world of senses. I do not have to divide myself, or even know who I am. Inside me, exists the same stuff miracles are made of. There is no confusion and no separation. There is just an overwhelming gratitude for being absorbed by life.

I am breathing and yet I am not breathing. The breath flows through me, like through a hollow bamboo. I make no effort. I am only silence inside.

What are these waves coming through the waters? The pulsations that speak of a world outside my safe cave. They sound like words without form, sentences made out of vibrations, whirling through my silent world. Their meaning enters my solitude, jolting me. Messaages start radiating all through my being. In its wake, I am left overwhelmed..

Until I can be alone again, and one with all.

As the world around me narrows, I adjust. I curl up. I am resting eternally.

Suddenly I wake up feeling suffocated. I panic. There is not enough oxygen. I know I have to move. Where am I going, what forces me to leave my paradise? Let go of of the present?

Why am I being thrown around?

I become aware of intense voices. From my underwater retreat I can hear them. Through the waters, through the cord that feeds me, I receive my mother's message. She is there, but she is struggling.

She is afraid she won't make it. I feel her fear entering me, and it takes on the form of a slow but lethal resignation.

I could stop breathing now. There is an emptiness that's calling. Inviting me into a place without movement, where there's no pain. I could turn around and renounce the struggle. Just stop here, until paradise returns.

But from the source of life, a strength takes over. It shakes my whole world. An earthquake destroying the safety of my warm and moist cave. Its tremors spread through everything, again and again. I feel its power reaching my being. My will wakes up to this force of nature. I am born to life's will to live. It enters me with all its strength. A great excitement surges through me. I want to move now, I am ready for the unknown.

I am drawn into a dark and narrow tunnel. What is this sensation that I feel so suddenly? Am I getting a form, am I becoming separate? I am engulfed by a passionate pressure which makes me tingle in pleasure and cringe in pain. I am physical, I am moving. Is it death or life that is waiting for me? I don't care anymore. I am moving, slipping, sliding and surrendering.

Out I move, wet and slippery, out of the safe world I lived in for eternity, out into this vast world, where I know nothing. It is colder here and the light is sharper. The sounds have lost their diffused, underwater quality, they are suddenly loud and penetrating .

I am separate; I have lost my oneness. I have arrived. I am surrounded by a whole new world.

Where is the warm inner cosmos of my mother's womb that I came from? I can still recognize its vibrations close to me. But I know I cannot and do not want to return. I long to be taken in her arms now, to drink passionately from her breast. I am part of the world now.

I belong to humanity.

THE RECIPE

HEALING BIRTH

Open up to a healing of your birth.

Lie down on your side and curl up in a fetal position. Focus on the rise and fall of your breath. Visualize and feel yourself surrounded by your mother's womb.

Allow yourself to enter into a deep relaxation. You can surrender to a positive feeling of waiting.

Trust when the moment of birth comes closer, you will feel an impulse to move and stretch out. When this moment arrives, take a deep breath, and slowly, spontaneously, allow your body to start moving, stretching out from the fetal position into your full body length.

You can visualize a golden light at the top of your head, the crown. Notice yourself moving towards this light.

Visualize leaving the womb behind. Now feel your whole body surrounded by golden light. Her the welcoming voice of existence.

Allow yourself to completely relax and let go, feeling the support of mother earth beneath you.

CHAPTER 10

BECOMING THE CHILD
(FROM BEFORE CONCEPTION TO 0 YEARS OLD)

Life is impossible without a center...You may not be
aware of it, that's another matter. It has not to be created
but only rediscovered. And remember, I am not saying
"discovered," I am saying "rediscovered."

The child in the mother's womb remains perfectly
aware of the center. The child in the mother's womb *is* at
the center, vibrates at the center, pulsates at the center.
The child is the center in the mother's womb, he has no
circumference yet. He is only essence, he has no personality yet.

Essence is the center, that which is your nature, that
which is God-given. Personality is the circumference, that
which is cultivated by society; it is not God-given. It is by
nurture, not by nature.

As the child comes out of the womb, he comes for the
first time in contact with something outside of himself.
And that contact creates the circumference. Slowly slowly,
the society initiates the child into its own way.

(Osho, *Unio Mystica, Vol. I*)

THE FIRST DEVELOPMENT OF THE EGO IN THE WOMB

The deepest buried memories can still touch us emotionally.
Since they come from a time of which we have no conscious recall,
their influence on us is often unexpected and confusing.

Even at a very early stage, the stage that Leboyer labels as "L'age
d'or," the unborn child is affected by feelings such as love or rejection (1). But they remain like events drifting by, leaving no trace
behind. As the child's brain grows, these sensations and feelings
turn into more developed feeling-thought states. At this point, the
child in the womb perceives a feeling, recognizes it, and responds
to it. As his memory and experience grow, he gradually learns to
differentiate and make more distinct connections.

At three months in the uterus, the child cannot yet distinguish
the differences in more subtle feelings, such as ambivalence or
indifference It may experience them as sensations which affect it,
but will not respond to them consciously.

At birth, however, the child responds to even the most subtle feelings of the mother with precision, and is able to mirror them with bodily and emotional feedback. How does this happen?

Between three and six months in the womb, the fetus's nervous system becomes capable of sending signals to the brain. When it receives the mother's feelings, her tiredness, or her worries, the unborn baby tries to make sense of them. It responds by becoming excited, upset, or confused. If these messages create discomfort, it tries to defend itself against this through kicking and moving. In this way, the first stage of ego development begins. The child starts to learn. The impressions that up to that point only affected its nervous system are now registered by its brain. Through this, the unborn baby realizes that the impressions occur again and again, and that they come from an outer source. It has its first primitive understanding that this outer source is the emotions of the mother. From its previous state of oneness, the unborn child enters the experience of being separate.

If the input from the mother comes not too intensely, it actually creates the unborn child's intelligence, enhancing the growth of its self-awareness. The normal state of a child in the womb is emptiness and serenity. Outside action pulls the child out of this emptiness, calls for its attention, and sets in motion an emotional response. In this way, it creates a memory trace. As these memory traces consolidate, they create form and content in the child's original emptiness. Its choiceless awareness changes into an awareness of itself. This illustrates how important a role the mother's emotions play in shaping the "I" of the fetus.

If the mother is warm, loving, and nurturing toward herself and the unborn child, the "I" of the fetus, its self-awareness, is created out of this experience. If the mother is frustrated, angry, depressed, or ambivalent, the early ego is developed out of these feelings. The more positive a mother feels about herself and her baby, about childbearing and giving birth, the greater chance there is that at the core of the ego lies an emotional stability and a surrender to life.

INTRAUTERINE BONDING

Unborn babies can adjust their rhythms to their mothers with great precision. Long before birth, mother's and child's rhythms have begun to merge with each other. The bonding that happens in the womb is as subtle and complex as the bonding that occurs after birth. In the uterus, the child is deeply familiar with the mother's feelings and mind. This prepares the ground for its later responses, after birth, to mother's hugs, cuddles, gazes, and voice.

The optimum time for intrauterine bonding is during the last three months of pregnancy. The child now has matured enough physically and intellectually to communicate with its mother. But it does not respond to her input automatically. If the mother's moves are contradictory, or careless, the child may ignore them.

For the bonding to develop, a deep love for the child and for herself is needed from the mother, and a real understanding of the feelings involved on both sides. The unborn child cannot bond alone. If its mother is emotionally absent, there is no way that the child can connect. Thomas Verny says:

> Occasional negative emotions or stressful events are not going to affect intrauterine bonding adversely. The unborn child is far too resilient to be put off by a few setbacks. The danger arises when he feels shut off from his mother or when his physical and psychological needs are consistently ignored. His demands are not unreasonable: All he wants is some love and attention and, when he gets them, everything else, including bonding, follows naturally. (2)

A strong intrauterine bond is for a child a protection against danger and insecurity. If the mother can keep her channel toward it open, difficult and painful moments included, the unborn child will continue to thrive.

When a six-month-old fetus feels the reassuring vibration of its mother gently stroking her belly, when it feels well-nourished by her, and understood in the messages it gives, it feels loved. This requires from the mother a love for her pregnancy and a willingness to listen and tune into what happens in her womb. There is a great deal that the child has to share with her.

THE SCHIZOID CHARACTER

The unborn child is very sensitive to distress. Already, when it feels its safety and security disturbed by its parents' conflicts or fights, it responds with furious kicking.

But, when its safety is seriously threatened, through violence, attempts to be aborted, or sever rejection, the only possibility it has is to split and disconnect from its bodily sensations. The only safe world available is the world of its spirit. This results in what is known in Reichian body work as "schizoid" character.

As adults, when we carry this wound, our body structure is fragmented. The split we felt in the womb between body and spirit is reflected in the shape of our body. We contract our muscles, intestines, and heart out of fear of annihilation. Often we keep feelings on an intellectual level, out of fear of experiencing them in our body. Schizoid is not a label of pathology, it does not mean schizophrenic. It signifies that we have a deep unconscious attitude that when something feels threatening to our survival, we disconnect from our body. Sometimes, this feeling is more related to our past memories in the womb than what is actually happening in the present. We all have experienced, to different degrees, this "splitting" from our bodies in situations of shock. For some of us, though, this can become a life attitude. R. D. Laing describes it:

> [In normal circumstances,] the individual may experience his own being as real, alive, whole...as especially co-extensive with the body.... He thus has a core of firm ontological security.... If a position of primal ontological security has been reached, the ordinary circumstances of life do not afford a perpetual threat to one's own existence. If such a basis for living has not been reached, the ordinary circumstances of everyday life constitute a continual and deadly threat. (3)

In our experience of working with people, when this condition is present in an individual, and is within the limits of what we understand as "sane" (no need for medication or psychiatric treatment), the greatest healing takes place through giving oneself the space and the time to realize that the threats we project on the present are the memories of the hostile environment we experienced in the womb. Meditation, soft body work, and love are the best "cures." Only when the person is centered inside, can the hate and terror provoked by the life threat of the past slowly be released.

For all of us, meditation can open the door to retrieving the sense of serenity and timelessness that the imprint of birth and our entrance into the world of space and time have overshadowed.

WHEN BONDING HAPPENS NATURALLY

When things are peaceful, unhurried, and harmonious between the parents, the child being very sensitive to that too, falls in tune with it. The child senses the relaxing atmosphere and responds to it with trust and surrender. Feelings like love and acceptance greatly affect the unborn child. Then all falls into place, and the bonding with its mother happens naturally and spontaneously.

> *Louise P. was in her fifties. She came to us at a very signifi-*
> *cant moment of transition in her life. She had a deep feeling of*
> *inadequacy about facing the new challenges that were coming to*
> *her both in her professional and emotional life. She told us repeat-*
> *edly that she did not know anymore who she was and what the*
> *purpose of it all was. Her parents had divorced before her birth,*
> *and she had spent time with one or the other alternately. She had*
> *never seen them together. When she realized that her parents*
> *actually had made love to each other in a way that was inviting*
> *for her to enter, she was speechless for quite a while. The whole*
> *foundation of her self-image was suddenly in question. First she*
> *was stunned, then she laughed, then cried, and finally looked at*
> *us. It took some time for her to give a meaning and find a place in*
> *her life for the implications of her realization: that she had been*
> *conceived through the combined energy of her parents. Through*
> *accepting them both, she began to love herself more.*

The "hole of holes"

More and more mothers, nowadays, have become aware of what factors affect the development of their unborn children. During pregnancy they tune into their unborn children, and according to what their natural wisdom dictates, create for them the best possible conditions. But even in the best possible circumstances, there are deeper layers in the unconscious of each human being which need awareness.

The exposure in the womb to our mother's unconscious, creates in all of us the seed of our conditioning. It influences the way we see the world, the way we anticipate what will be coming to us or not, and the image that we carry of ourselves. It does make a difference for us to be growing in the womb of a mother who is identified with a Jewish tradition which deep down carries the imprint of a Holocaust, or a mother who is identified with a Dutch landowners' line, with its emphasis on self-control and sacrifice.

Each mother carries the "hole" of her family, her culture, her credo. On the surface, it is demonstrated in her behavior; on a deeper level, it creates pathways of fixed responses in her nervous system. Certain emotions, drives, and impulses can be expressed and, through her system, discharged. Others have to be repressed and their charge withheld.

As unborn children, our nervous system vibrates with our mother's neurological input. Whatever she cannot discharge outwardly, is discharged inwardly. We become the receptacle of all our mother's unwanted drives.

This phenomenon charges our nervous system and alters its vibration. It affects our organs and creates imbalance in them. In this way, we absorb the family "hole" before birth. Our responses to anger, sex, love, etc. are deeply influenced by our mother's responses and the impact they have on her nervous system.

In essence we are all full of love and self-worth. Yet, through what has happened at this stage, we live our lives experiencing a chronic tension or imbalance in our body. Through the tension or imbalance we hold the belief that love is unattainable, or that only by attaining perfection are we worthy of living.

What makes this situation paradoxical is that we build up the foundation of our ego with input, received through our nervous system, which does not really belong to us, but to our mothers. Or, rather to the culture our mothers come from. We might spend the rest of our lives trying to solve this puzzle. How can we fill up this hole, which in the first place is not ours, and which can be dissolved only by returning to the state of wholeness and relaxation that was there before the ego started to develop? A great support in keeping the influence of the "family hole" to a minimum, is the mother's willingness and interest in meditation. In those moments of dis-identification, her nervous system relaxes, and in the peacefulness of being with herself, tensions discharge and dissolve. This benefits the child immensely. Its unborn body can relax and expand. Its natural state of emptiness remains uninvaded.

It has happened many times that while regressing our clients to the moment of entering the womb after conception, the first response has been one of dismay and disappointment.

> *Aruna, an artist, when journeying back to the moment following conception, found herself commenting, "Oh, no, what did I do!" She felt desperate and trapped in an overcharged atmosphere, with no way back to the experience of lightness she had felt before conception.*
>
> *We took a moment with Aruna to consider what had attracted her to incarnate through her mother into her present life. Aruna recognized that her mother's essence, as she had perceived it before entering her womb, had been different: it had had a lightness and a radiance. As Aruna described it, she relaxed.*
>
> *We could then explain to her that the shock she had experienced earlier was a result of her first encounter with the conditioning surrounding the very same essence which, in its purity,*

had looked so beautiful. Aruna had met the narrowness and ten-
sion of her mother's suppressed emotions; she had experienced it
from inside the womb as some gigantic force surrounding her.

    As we continued moving on through the womb, we reminded
Aruna at each stage of the process to reconnect with the original
longing that had inspired her to come to this life. And at each
step, an expansion and a tranquillity began to descend on her.
What seemed like an overpowering prison she had been trying
in vain to escape from all her life, became just the shadow of her
first experience in this life. The realization that her longing, her
search, had been intact throughout the whole process enabled her
to be more centered and disidentified.

THE SECRET OF THE BEGINNING

In the great ocean of the womb, we swam and dreamed, trans-
muting from cell to embryo to fetus, until our human form was
completed.

In this womb lies the secret of the beginning. This secret is at the
border between matter and spirit, and bears a great mystery: the
appearance of life in all its magnificence and potential.

The mind, whose primitive, unconscious layers developed only
after the first few months of life in the womb, cannot grasp this
mystery. By journeying back to the intrauterine period and further
into conception, we touch poetry and spirituality. We sound the
deeper chords of our participation in existence. We move toward
"remembrance." As R. D.

Laing says:

> *Only to remember to remember, or at least to remember that*
> *you have forgotten...*
> *Each forgetting is a dismembering.*
> *I must never forget again. All that searching and research-*
> *ing those false signposts, the terrible danger of forget-*
> *ting that one has forgotten. It's too awful. (4)*

Our search brings us back to these roots. After peeling all the
layers, we come to the threshold, the quantum leap: our entry into
this life and into this body.

All the spiritual traditions pointing to remembrance (Buddha's
sammasati, the Sufi zikhr, the Tibetan bardo), indicate that only
consciousness can fill in this gap of discontinuity. Beyond forms,

consciousness has no beginning and no end. Lao Tzu describes "it" as follows:

> There is a thing confusedly formed,
> Born before heaven and earth.
> Silent and void
> It stands alone and does not change.
> Goes round and does not weary.
> It is capable of being the mother of the world.
> I know not its name
> So I style it "the way." (5)

When we move into the pre-ego realm, into no-mind, we cannot hold on to any beliefs. The light and wisdom that the real master shares can help us on the way. But, the ultimate truth has to be experienced directly. The accounts of innumerable individuals who have walked down this path are encouragement to move along further. They are the "fingers pointing to the moon."

Kabir echoes in his own song:

> I laugh when I hear that the fish in the water is thirsty:
> You do not see that the Real is your home, and you wander from forest to forest listlessly!
> Here is the truth! Go where you will, to
> Banaras or to Mathura; if you do not find
> your soul, the world is unreal to you. (6)

Our exploration, a journey back beyond conception, is a metaphor for rediscovering our sense of participation in existence.

We didn't just happen to come here.

In some very essential place in us, we wanted to come. We wanted to discover or to complete things, to live or share. We were pulled to this planet to participate, to go through birth, life, and death with totality, burning the light of our individual flame. That is the gift which makes us really alive.

Our parents didn't just "happen" to us.

We were attracted to their color and their fragrance, to the rhythm and the song of their essence. Beyond our familiarity with them, they will remain a mystery to us. When we journey back to the essential state we were in before we entered the world of forms, we meet them there, in their essence and potential. We can acknowledge what affinity and attraction pulled us toward their qualities, and honor what those qualities initiated in us. We are with them partakers of a greater dance. Our deepest expression of love and gratitude toward them is to honor what they gave us, and to look beyond their forms at what life gave us through them. Then, we can let them go and wish them a good journey on their path.

The trust of a newborn baby, the strength of a toddler, the natural intelligence and creativity of a little boy or girl are essential expressions of our individuality. We can reown these qualities effortlessly now. All we need to do is embrace them inside ourselves, with love and thankfulness.

Rumi says (7):

> You were a drop of sperm,
> Became blood, then grew
> Into such a beauty.
> Oh human, come close to me
> So I can make you better than that.

THE EVOCATION

My personal experience with the womb, conception, and beyond

Svarup

I set off once more on the path that will lead me back in time. I am aware that this is a journey that will lead me further back than I have ever gone. Along the way, I will meet Manú at different ages. We will move all together to the very beginning of this life. And, at the end of our journey, we will merge and become one again.

Meeting the eight-year-old Manú

I am in Milan, where the eight-year-old Manú is waiting for me in her room. I can see her now. She is lying on her bed, reading an old book of fairy tales from Tuscany.

She looks up and sees me. A glimpse of recognition. I invite her to come with me on a magical journey. She reaches out for my extended hand. We giggle at each other as we softly walk through the apartment. Manú's little sister looks at us with her beautiful, large, innocent brown eyes, puzzled. We wave at her. We will meet again, maybe one day we will get to know each other. We reach the front door and slip through it.

Meeting the three-year-old Manú

And off we go, hand in hand, down the road of time. We are back in Padova, where we find the little three-year-old Manú in front of the wooden magic box. She is watching television. Her round little body is concentrated, responding to the action on the screen. She turns around, and her deep, intense dark eyes meet ours. I ask her, "Would you like to come with us for a journey?" She nods and jumps out of the couch, and after a questioning look realizes that she is not expected to straighten up her clothes or comb her hair. She trustingly gives me her chubby hand and the three of us move along.

We continue our walk. The eight-year-old is matching my stride and regaining suppleness, and the three-year-old is trotting along, singing fullheartedly her own made-up songs.

Meeting the baby Manú

We are now in Sampierdarena, Genoa, where the baby girl-me was born. As we climb up the stairs of the apartment block, I hold the hands of my two little girls. They are silent now, realizing that something very magical is about to happen.

We tiptoe through the very small apartment and reach the room where the baby girl lies in the crib.

We lean over to see her. She is lying there with open, unfocused, receptive eyes. At the core of them, there is a lake of being, unpolluted by personality, a clean window into her soul. I allow myself to float into those eyes, connecting with the essence, the spark of life that is at their center.

Floating into the baby's eyes

Rest. I experience a sense of deep rest. I shift in a dark luminous universe. There is no form, no space, no time. I am in full emptiness. I am drifting at the edge, in an eternal moment of gap, in between lives, in an opening of nothingness, peace, sleep.

Fragments of past lives float behind me like shards of forgotten pain, joy, birth, and death. I experience distant, remote flashbacks of other bodies and their struggles. In my dreamlike state, a thread of continuity starts to manifest itself. It is like a sense of purpose, a significance that links all of this into a search. An inner recognition awakens me. A longing that feels like a pure crystal beckons me forward. I remember the serenity experienced and lost again so many times.

Recognizing the essential energies of my parents

Something moves within and I look down. I see the energy of a man and the energy of a woman attracting each other.

I recognize the essence of my father. It has a red bronze core, whirling and expanding into fine rays of orange and gold. It vibrates with a gentle humming, a song of longing. It's light and shifting, and warm, like desert sand.

I look at the essence of my mother. It is a riverlike flow of turquoise, shimmering in tones of cobalt blue, indigo, sky blue, and pale green. The freshness of it is so inviting. It ripples in a playful way, then expands into silent lakes, and cascades with a tingling sound.

Conception

I witness the dance of these two energies, free from the layers of personality around them, free from the tangles of emotions. It's awesome beauty. I feel an invitation that pulls me to both of them. I reach out for the warmth as well as for the freshness, I long for both.

The dance between them becomes faster, in a whirlpool of surrender and passion. I turn, ripple, blow, fly into their energy field. Faster and faster. An explosion of white light.

In the womb

An eternal instant passes, and I am a living cell inside my mother's womb.

I am floating in a warm, endless ocean of pink and gold. I feel the urge of life in me straining to multiply, like a fire burning and stretching in all directions, pulsing. I am overtaken by this intensity, surrendered to matter. The journey has started. The longing moves me through.

One month, two months. My mother realizes she is pregnant. Currents of mixed feelings ripple on the ocean around me. The waves crash to the shore, bounce off, and come back to me. I am drifting amid a stormy sea. I treasure my longing inside.

Three months, four months. Life growing in me. My sensations become richer and more differentiated. I can hear sounds, I can feel the water on my skin. I suck my thumb and dream. Sometimes I am jarred by mother's dreams or by whirlpools of anxiety and fear. I am holding on for life.

Five months, six months. I can hear mother's heartbeat, the vibration of her thoughts. There are occasional flashes of yellow lightning on an overcast night sky. And then, no movement, drifting again in the vastness of a calm sea. And I dream of my longing.

Seven months, eight months. There is less space around me. My body grows larger. I often feel jarred, knocked about by sudden movements. Mother's breathing is like a fine drizzle for my thirsty body. And I nurture my longing inside.

Nine months. I want to get out. The struggle, the interminable struggle. Her control and her agony against my will to live. Deep down, at the very core, my longing moves me forward, like a lighthouse beckoning me through the storm. I swim, I crawl, I push, I climb for my life. I am out.

The same river moves us on

After birth, I am lying here in my tiny bed recovering. I am resting, allowing life to expand through me in its natural time and rhythm. I have a heart that feels, a belly that needs. And, deep within, a longing.

I see the shape, vibrant and alive, of three shadows over me: a larger one, two smaller ones. I feel a recognition. It is the same river that moves us on.

Coming back to my adult body

I allow my consciousness to float upward, savoring for an instant the weightlessness and the freedom from physical bondage. And then, I allow myself to descend, reentering my adult body, standing there at the edge of the bed.

I feel the gap between my breaths, the pulsating silence and the love in the room. I pick up the baby girl-me and hold her close to my heart, honoring the courage and endurance of her innocence. We will move in the same trust.

The three-year-old Manú and the eight-year-old Manú are looking in wonder. As I hold the baby girl, I beckon them to follow me.

Our essences become one

We slowly walk out of the room and move forward, all together, to a place we all recognize. It's the place where trees sing, where birds fly in freedom, where children can be themselves.

We stop and feel. I receive the trust and being of the little baby-me in my heart. Our essences become one in a soft outpouring of golden light.

Then I turn to the little three-year-old Manú. I see her sensuous little body vibrating with aliveness and adventurousness. I receive the essence of it in my belly. I become one with it in a gentle explosion of orange and gold.

Then I turn to the eight-year-old Manú. I love this girl who has been waiting and treasuring her dreams with such longing. My eyes merge with hers, eyes that can still see beyond the walls and reach out for beauty and wonder in all. Our essences become one in a subtle radiation of blue.

Gratefulness

I see the journey that still unfolds ahead of me. I move on with the treasures I have rediscovered inside. As I walk forward, I recognize so many moments where my longing shone through the texture of everyday life. As I pass those moments, I pause in each of them to acknowledge and remember, savor and inhale. This is such a beautiful life, I don't regret any of it.

Here and now, I sit in gratefulness, letting the sun that shines through the leaves heal the scars that make me who I am.

MY PERSONAL EXPERIENCE WITH THE WOMB, CONCEPTION, AND BEYOND

PREMARTHA

The sacred bond that holds us all together

I am returning to my childhood home. I am looking for the little boy-me. I don't want to look for him in his room. It feels too narrow now for him to be there.

I walk toward the open field bordered by a forest. From there, starts the gray-blue, misty land, and there is the promise of the river. Here, at its edge, stands an old tree. Its branches spread out wide, its leaves creating a royal crown.

I look into the tree and see in its crown, the little boy-me. He's sitting on a small seat he has built himself out of some scraps of wood. He is looking out all around him. I call him by his name, "Hey, Wim!"

He is about seven years old. He looks down at me. "What?"

He seems to be pretty much in his own world.

"It's me, Premartha."

He smiles at me and I feel protected by his certainty. He's grown stronger then I imagined he would. I ask him, "Do you want to come down and go on an adventure with me?"

I see his hesitation. But when I continue looking up at him, he suddenly climbs down. I like feeling him close to me. He's looking pretty much relaxed with himself as he says, "Where do you want to go?"

He has a nice, clear voice. A bit shy on the edges. Or is it reserved?

"I can't tell you yet! But if you can trust me, let's just start. I have a feeling of what we are looking for, but I'm not sure what will really come."

He likes my honest explanation. He nods and gives me his hand. It's warm. We walk together. We have to step over puddles and cross a narrow patch. So I let his hand go. He goes ahead. I follow him now, until we come to the side of the farm.

There's a heap of silver-white sand against the wall. The remains of some building work. It is close to the potato field, overlooking the road. It's quiet here and sunny. Nobody is around.

There, in the middle of the sand, sits the little boy-me, three years old. He is building things out of sand. He is chubby and sweet to look at. But what's remarkable is the silent atmosphere around him. This must be a place where he can be on his own.

I call to him, "Hey, Wimke!" He looks up at me. I am stunned by the blue of his eyes. It is very concentrated, and I can feel the strength of his presence.

"Come with us. We are going to discover something."

He looks at me, and at the seven-year-old-me. I can feel that he wants to come immediately. He drops his little sand forms and comes closer. I feel touched and full of affection. I smile at him. This brings a shy smile to his face. Then suddenly he steps toward me. I feel happy, bow down, and take him in my arms. He sits straight there and looks ahead. I know I shouldn't stare at him now. It's time to move.

"Let's go kids." Now we have to enter the house. I put my finger on my lip showing them to be quiet.

All three of us understand that we don't want to wake up anybody. We quietly step through the kitchen, entering our parents' bedroom.

In the corner stands an obviously much used crib. In it, I can see a pale-pink blanket, and an edge of the sheet.

Slowly we all gather around it. Then we look inside. I can see a little head with downy, damp hair. Round baby cheeks. A little curly mouth. It is the baby-me. He's sleeping, and around him is an atmosphere of healing quietness. The baby is resting. He is silently floating in the peaceful waters of his dream world. All three of us are in wonder. The two little ones look very intent, as if recognizing something in the newborn child. I can feel the sacred bond that holds us all together.

Then with a little yawn, my baby-child opens its eyes and I look into them. Beyond the form and shape of the little body, there is a vastness, a space without limits. It draws me in.

The original source

I am floating. I am the floating itself as much as the one who is floating. I am expanding and contracting. It is healing, refreshing. I am resting in my original source. Being one, being all. Being dark and fluid restfulness. In an endless, deep blue universe. Radiant, luminous. Full of truth, goodness, and beauty.

Behind me lies an endless journey. Being born, growing, getting old, dying. Birth and death as doorways into an endless space. Remembering the lives before. Recognizing. Realizing. Understanding.

Until a longing is stirred up again. A slow unfolding. Knowing the journey must continue. Energy moving outwards. Exploring. Expanding, Searching now. Moving onward.

Feeling attracted

Being attracted to a movement of energy far away. Coming closer and closer. Noticing the meeting of a male and a female energy. Feeling attracted.

Coming so close that I can observe the pure energy field of my father.

I experience a great rushing, like from a huge waterfall. The water is strong, full of power and desire. It thunders down and crashes on the rocks below. My father's energy is wild, uninhibited like Pan. It is gutsy, the color of free-flowing blood, and the deep red-brown of the fertile earth, with purple-blue crevices and caves full of shadows. There is yellow at the core. Fire.

The fragrance is of wet earth and a unashamed smell of lust. Of animal instincts and wild grass.

The sound is deep but slow, with a tone of longing. A calling out. An evoking. The movement of his energy is evolving, contracting, and holding. Then letting loose and letting go again.

It is the presence of his pure energy. Unconditioned, unjudged, unperverted.

Next to him I observe my mother's energy. First I notice a sound, long and seemingly endless. High and melodious, a sound that spreads out, and evokes images of blue skies and azure rivers.

I watch this dance of her essential energies. It's very subtle, organized in patterns, like a mandala. But a continuously changing mandala. Shades of lilac, blue, pink, purple, and violet, transparent, softly arranging itself in endlessly new and unique patterns. Circular but not round. Circular in a triangular way, sharp and soft at the same time.

The fragrance is very subtle. Almost absent. Yet, at its core, there is a warmth and a generosity.

The movement is inward-centered. Yet, at the same time, it supports the movement to expand outward.

Her essential energies. Beyond personality, opinion, hurt, and reaction.

I am one

Their energies are coming close to each other, and they are touching.

There is no question of melting. It doesn't seem possible in the nature of things. I can see my father's energy enveloping, entering, my mother's energy quivering and opening. Yet, both of them remain mysteriously defined in their own essences.

I get pulled in now. Into the fields of their energies. I first go through my father's energy field. It takes me in and I feel warmth, darkness, completeness entering me from all sides. I feel nourished by it and supported.

Then I enter my mother's field. There is an uplift, as if I am going to fly. For a moment, it is almost too much, too light, too fast. But her sound draws me through.

As their energies have come to their utter expansion, I enter into a tunnel filled with light. I move through it. I am pulled forward.

I have entered the inner cosmos of my mother's womb.

I am one.

I am contented. I am growing. Limitless, but with form.

Being in creation

One month in the womb. Floating. Being in creation. Wonder.

Two months in the womb. Close to the time my mother feels she's pregnant with me. Pregnant again. I can feel her shock. Her disbelief. She has been afraid it would happen, now it has become a fact. Her womb reflects her turmoil. The peacefulness is totally disturbed. I cannot let go now. I will hold on.

Three months, four months. I am growing. Inner organs are completing. I float in the warmth of the womb. Warm colors entering unborn eyes. An utter comfort of being. There is a sadness on the edges. I am growing now. I am a boy.

Five months, six months. The womb draws close around me now. There is a limit to this inner cosmos. I am sleeping, dreaming, dozing, floating. I am weightless.

Seven months, eight months. I feel the walls of the womb enclosing me. Slowly my safe and quiet world is becoming too narrow.

Nine months in the womb. I am more and more pressed together. But I am flexible, and so is the womb. Then I give the sign to go. It shudders all through my body and being. Around me everything is pressing and pushing, contracting. I don't know anything. I am scared.

I am out.

I am alive. I made it here. I don't know what is waiting for me. But I know I want it.

And later, much later, in the silence of the farm, I open my eyes. I look into the eyes of my grown-up self. I see his blue eyes focused on me. Intent, yet gentle.

I know he knows my journey now. I am tired, but strangely satisfied. It has not been for nothing.

I gently allow myself to float back into his body.

Home again

I become my adult self again. I stand at the baby bed in the farmhouse. I become aware again of my three-year-old and seven-year-old self being here with me. There is awe and wonder in their eyes, and also a silent recognition. We are here together, in this moment, all one.

Slowly, I take my infant self out of his crib. I bring him to my heart. He belongs there. I breathe his gentle presence in, an innocence and a knowing. I breathe the essence of this part back into myself. Courage.

Then I turn to the three-year-old-me. I love him so much. He's cuddly, but with his own strength. I take him onto my belly. We look at each other. We smile. We trust each other. And I breathe the essence of this part back into myself. Joy.

Now I embrace the seven-year-old-me. I hold him in my arms. Our heads are resting next to each other. I give him all my respect for what he managed to do. To his intelligence and his budding creativity, I bow down in gratitude.

Inside, I hear a song:

"I am sailing, I am sailing. Home again, across the sea…."

I feel complete and I know I have to go now, to leave the childhood home behind me and to return to this ever-changing life. It has been good.

THE RECIPE

WRITING A FAIRYTALE

Write a fairy tale in which the hero is the child-you.

It needs to be your own life story, but written as a fairy tale.

For example, your mother can be a fairy, or a dragon, a witch, or a princess. And your father, a king, an ogre, or a woodcutter. Write whatever comes up in your fantasy.

You need to start the story with, "Once upon a time, there was a little girl (or boy)...." Then specify what special gift or quality this child has brought with it into this life. Mention what happened to the child, that made it lose or forget its gift...

To complete it, describe how this gift returned to your adult life. Which magical person, or persons, supported you to retrieve it.

End the story with having regained this quality in your life. Let yourself visualize and feel what happens to your future, when this gift is allowed to flower in you.

Svarup's fairy tale

Once upon a time, a little girl was born. She had the gift of fire and wind, and truth was her nature. Her parents were both coming from the land of fire and wind, where they had spent their youth mastering wondrous skills in various arts. Her father had been a poet and a dancer, weaving colorful clouds and breezes around his enthralled audiences. Her mother had been a warrior who could set the hearts of large crowds aflame. But, alas, both her parents had lost the use of their gifts through a terrible misadventure.

After eloping from their native land, they had taken refuge in the land of earth, hoping to spread the wind and fire and create a new paradise for themselves.

Unfortunately, as soon as they had arrived, they realized their mistake. The alien audiences whose attention they had hoped to capture sneered at them and turned their backs away. It didn't take long for them to understand that the earth people did not at all appreciate anything too hot or too windy. No one wanted their crops, so painstakingly grown year after year, to be destroyed by anything so extreme.

As the two couldn't return to their homeland without facing the wrath of their families and the ache of their failure, they decided to adjust. So, when the little girl was born, both her parents had bent to the rules of the land of earth.

Only in private, within the solid four walls of their abode on the edge of the village, would they tell their wonderful tales of their glorious past to the little girl, always warning her not to repeat them to anyone, lest they could be discovered and sent away.

The little girl, with her own fire brewing and her own wind blowing, didn't know what to do. She learned to hide more and more, forgetting her true nature. As she grew among the earth people, she wanted badly to belong to them. She learned to speak the language of earth and made many friends among the people. Only occasionally, would she burn in shame when a flame slipped from her tongue.

As the years went by, the little girl grew into a restless young woman. By then, all had been forgotten. Her parents had become well-established earth citizens, and they lived in a large mansion with many, many walls. Nothing was changing anymore.

No longer able to conform, she followed her longing for the strong wind of change. This longing brought her to many lands, very hot and very colored.

One day, after so many years of wandering, she felt exhausted. That was the time for the Master to touch her. So far, she had been too busy searching to be available. As she looked into the Master's eyes, she could see the source of all that fire and wind shining through them. And she remembered.

She settled contentedly for many years at his feet, allowing his wind to blow her to all corners of the world and back, burning with his fire to a glowing incandescence.

Until, one day, a large Hurricane blew the Master higher and higher, back to the Universe that had always been his home.

Alone on earth the girl, now a woman, first looked around in sadness. But then, she found out that once more, the search had to be started, for she would never forget the bliss of being carried by the wind of change and the fire of love.

And, lo and behold, from a deep, faraway corner of the universe in her heart, she heard her Master's voice saying:

"Beloved, the search is the goal, enjoy your life!"

Ma Satyam Svarup
    Satyam: Truth
    Svarup: Self-nature

Premartha's fairy tale
    Once upon a time there lived a little boy in a faraway country by the sea. This country was rather small.

    Its larger neighbors were always thinking that small means inferior. As we know, this is similar to what big people think about small people, also called children. After listening for years to its neighbors' comments, the whole country began to believe that they were true.

But the little boy didn't know this yet. He still experienced everything around him as very large. He could see the trees just as enormously big as they were, and the fields around him as endless. He knew that there was no end to all he saw, and he considered that very normal.

Unfortunately, the little boy's father and mother had long ago forgotten all this. When they were small, they were forced to learn that it is very dangerous to be large, and that to be safe, they should start thinking of themselves as small.

They had done their best to learn this really well, that one has to say that, by now, they could not even remember anything else.

To learn from his parents that everything was small was such a shock, that the little boy didn't even dare to doubt it. And so it happened that he gradually lost his certainty in the largeness of life.

But the funny thing is, that even though after a while the little boy became very adapted in showing smallness, something deep inside stayed irreversibly large.

Maybe he had just been allowed to experience it a little too long, and now he couldn't forget about it anymore. Whatever it was, it made him promise to himself that one day, when he was old enough, he would prove to his parents and even to his country that the principle of smallness was a complete lie, that in reality everything is very large.

By the time he met the old wise man, the little boy had grown up. He had traveled all over the world, and had gathered voluminous proof of the true principle of largeness. He expected the old wise man to approve of all his efforts and the discoveries he had made. After all, he was known by many as the one and only Master of all that is large.

But to his consternation, the old wise man looked deep into his eyes, and said with a smile, "You have been discovering only half of the truth."

The little boy, who had grown into a young man, again felt the insecurity that once had changed his large world into something vague and unclear. But seeing the love that was radiating in the wise man's smile, he couldn't stop himself from asking, "What is the other half then?"

"The other half is true smallness," said the wise man. Together with true largeness it forms the truth."

At that, the young man fell on his knees. And bowed his head down to the feet of the Master.

He could feel the exhaustion that had grown in him. Searching for proof of largeness and fighting for its existence had worn him out. He had had no time for pleasure, laughter, joy, and love. All that had seemed so irrelevant compared to the task of proving largeness. This had made him lonely and often sad. With the acceptance of true smallness in his life, he now felt suddenly free to be whoever he was. All the contradictions of largeness and smallness had finally melted. He could feel his heart filling up with compassion for himself, his parents, his country, and the whole world. It started radiating love to all of them, and that was very significant.

Swami Anand Premartha
Anand: Bliss
Premartha: Significance of Love

EPILOGUE

PREMARTHA:

The urge to cut all ties took over

And how does the story continue from here? As I metamorphosed from a child into a teenager, life took a 180-degree turn. It has remained unexplainable in my family how a quiet child like me could turn into an angry and rebellious youth. As a boy of around ten to eleven years old, I was still praised for how easy I was to handle. You could leave me in front of the TV with some chips and coke, and I would sit there, silent and invisible.

Then, one Sunday, friends a bit older than me came and invited me to go to the performance of a local rock band. When I got there, I was confronted with all of what I saw. Everything expressed obvious rebellion. It was in the leather jackets, in the faces that had no nice smiles, and in the girls who knew what they wanted.

Out of this, my big "no" was born. At least, that's how it looked from the outside. Nobody knew the "no" that had grown silently but steadily underground, with its roots in my childhood anger and frustration.

War started in my family. I started to dress the way I wanted. Tight and colorful. Pink elephant trousers, net T-shirts, fake leather belts, long hair. Each item I secured was a victory.

I soon found the "wrong" friends. Gone were the friends my mother would have chosen. And here they arrived, the girls that worked in the factory or the launderette, the boys that had all a wild streak.

As my sexuality woke up, I became full of fantasies. I discovered masturbation and it bloomed overnight into a full obsession. I was horny all the time. All the things so carefully hidden in the family had accumulated in my body and mind. Now, as a teenager, they finally found a way out.

The whole family united in the effort to stop this from happening. My sisters joined in the fight with my mother; my father fought his battle alone. But the more he withrew and disappeared, the more my fascination with the forbidden blossomed. It started to wipe out everything that had felt safe up to then. An urge to cut all ties took over.

There was no time to feel lost, which was at the root of my rebellion. I didn't know there was a wounded child inside who didn't know how to ask for help or support. There was no adult I could trust.

At 13 years, drugs entered my life. They symbolized the bonding we had together. We were the bad kids, the misfits. They became the secret we all shared, an entry into a new and unknown world. They symbolized the broken bridge from where we came.

I smoked my first joints. Soon this grew into a habit. Often the only thing that had any impact on me was to go unconscious. It was admired and respected. We all drank whatever alcohol we could get our hands on. I stopped caring for myself. I wore dirty jeans. And kept my hair long and uncombed.

When LSD came into my life, it opened up my perception. I fell in love with it. While on it, everything became alive and vibrating, mysterious and unpredictable.

Yet, at the edge of all these experiences was a darkness: the constant threat of a bad trip. The world that could suddenly turn evil. I could feel and see the beast inside. And I was afraid that if I let it break loose, it would take over.

When I finished school, I faced a world that appeared vast and limitless. I didn't know where to start. I had no direction in which to go.

I drifted in and out of jobs until I had made enough money to travel. I set off alone.

I loved the freedom of wandering. But, moving through unknown countries, the drugs and the aloneness started to expose deeper parts of me. Insecurity and fear surfaced. I didn't know how to deal with them. So I just continued.

When I arrived in Turkey, I hit the hippie trail. From Istanbul I followed it until Kabul. It was a paradise for misfits, colorful and out of control. I stayed until my money ran out, then I had to turn around.

I arrived back home on a Sunday afternoon. Nobody was there. I sat at the back door. I was skinny, had dirty long hair, and wore hippie clothes. When my parents arrived, my mother screamed in terror at the emaciated stranger lurking in the shadow of her house.

A contract between us broke. This was not at all her shy child anymore, this was a dirty male who scared her. This was not the mother who could protect and shield me, this was a woman in disgust and fear.

I moved to the city. And as I had done in my travels, whenever the fear and insecurity became too much, I would walk aimlessly through its streets.

In this way I made a friend, a street musician. He was a strange and unpredictable man who gathered a following of seekers and lost souls around him. I qualified as both. At night, in the darkness of his house, with just a candle and some incense, I listened to him playing the sitar. I started coming home.

Slowly, color came into my life. I painted watercolors. Inside them, I made drawings of thin, fragile beings. Maybe they represented a part of me, who had started to accept nourishment and fill up again. My new friend advised me to go to the local art academy and show my drawings. A real longing surfaced. The longing to give expression to what was happening deep inside me, to find out more about myself, and what living was all about. So I went and was accepted. I entered into the world of art. But I wasn't prepared for the process of learning a skill. I was impatient and arrogant about it. Why should I learn rules about how to do things if my real urge is to find myself? Disappointed, I continued painting, but the soul and the magic were gone.

In the end, I decided to travel again. To fulfill my big dream, and this time visit India.

India was home from the first moment I set foot in it. I traveled all over. I was looking for something I couldn't describe. Drugs only gave a little taste of the unknown now. They still intensified the nights at the Taj Mahal where I sat on its red watchtower, watching the full moon rise and glow vibrantly on the white marble. Or in Goa, when I lay down in surrender on the windy beach, they changed my loneliness into emptiness. Trekking in the Himalayas, living remote in Manali, sitting at the burning ghats in Benares all brought mystery and meaning to my life. But, after a while, a deep feeling of separation started to pervade everything I did. I was disappointed by not finding an alive source of wisdom. I felt pushed back to face my life.

SVARUP:

Lost in Secret Wonder about the Meaning of Life

As a child, I had girlfriends but I never quite managed to belong. Study and fantasy had grown to become my favorite companions. Mother and father were my intimate surroundings, and I loved the stories they would tell me about the golden past and the incredible future. I proudly regarded them as above the other average parents. My sister, six years younger than me, was my playmate, accomplice, and rival for the attention of my parents. Conflicts happened, but they stayed within the walls of our home. I lived in an ivory tower.

When puberty hit, the dam broke loose. A well of anger started to rise in powerful waves inside me. I wasn't aware of this anger, rather it was riding me, as I dove through dark, brooding spaces and surfaced into spiteful explosions. I didn't want to talk to my parents anymore.

Sex woke up like a budding, hot flower, winding its way through romantic dreams of popstars and long kisses in dark corners. I became hard and inconsiderate at home, and very shy and embarrassed outside.

Study, painting, the fascination for God and the Devil and the Universe remained my secret link to my little girl's world. But the little girl was now a teenager, wearing thick layers of mascara around her eyes, defying her parents' tolerance through sex and mingling with the wrong company. I tried hard and rather unsuccessfully to become what my mother called "vulgar," and my father would silently frown at.

Sixty-eight arrived. All around me, I started hearing the growing roar of a new generation that wanted to break loose, to voice anger, to be outrageous. I wanted to be part of it.

At that time, my father gave me the book "Siddhartha" by Herman Hesse, and a pink minidress from Carnaby Street. My mother gave me the "Manifesto" by Karl Marx and a taste for traveling. I couldn't thank them, then; I was too busy finding ways to rebel, creating the friction that I needed to grow out of them.

Throughout my whole teenage years I journeyed through revolution, fashions, hitchhiking, and sex, drugs, and rock'n'roll. I dreamed, consumed, and more or less digested every new experience. At the pit of my stomach, though, a hidden sensation of emptiness was lurking. It was a slight anxiety that asked for more, and a feeling of never quite making it to belong. I hid and forgot in my shy heart, a wish for the love and support which I couldn't, and maybe wasn't meant to, voice.

Meanwhile, I kept on studying, lost in secret wonder about the meaning of life, wise or foolish enough not to share that with anyone, except a couple of very close study friends who kept changing over the years.

Traveling was like dipping my feet into the ocean. Every year for a month or two, I moved outward, abroad. Israel, Morocco, Turkey. The little girl inside me was in awe of the beauty and strangeness, scared and attracted by it. The teenager was pushing past her limits and playing cool. In places like old Jerusalem or the Blue Mosque in Istanbul, I would suddenly come in touch with something new and old inside me, like a golden feeling of homecoming.

And then, as autumn approached, I would go back to the safety and the comfort of a mother and father who welcomed me with relief and pride. I was bringing back tidbits of the dreams that they had never fully forgotten.

Death struck like lightning just as I turned twenty. My father was killed in a car accident. It was sudden and irrevocable. It ripped my reality apart, in a much deeper way than I could realize. My mother's grief turned her hair white overnight. My sister withdrew into silent shock. I wasn't capable of making sense of what I was feeling. None of us was able to share with the others the depth of the pain that we all felt. Alone in my room, I spun through tears, guilt, fear, hate, numbness.

I went through a spell of Jungian analysis, too early to expose any of my feelings, feeling intimidated and estranged by a man in suit who seemed to stare through me at the void.

I entered a period of meaninglessness. While I still held onto my studies as an anchor to a lost paradise, the pain of loss and separation, denied and buried, started haunting me and pushing me to the edge. My youthful anger turned into hate. I became attracted to heavier drugs and darker friends. I played with death for a short time, walking on a thin line.

I still don't know, and I will maybe never know, what kept me on this side of the line. Maybe it was that my heart never stopped beating. In my feeling lost and my longing, I traveled to South America. In San Blas, an island off the Atlantic coast of Colombia, I fell in love with the Kuna, a primitive, colorful tribe. They had no word in their language for "thank you," because sharing was simply their life style. They listened to what their dreams revealed to them, and danced every day at sunset. I started drawing and writing there, bathing in their peacefulness and simplicity. They reflected my deep wish for a more real life, and yet I knew I could not remain. I carried them back to Rome with me in my heart. It was the echo of this beautiful meeting that brought a hue of mystery into the meaninglessness that I still felt in my soul.

When I turned 22, just before ending my philosophy studies at the university, something started brewing inside. This time, it was life knocking at the door. I grew impatient with books, I began to feel the personalities behind them. Suddenly I started perceiving Immanuel Kant as a pedantic, obsessive little man, Hegel as a bombastic German, Aristotle as a tight person afraid of chaos. Just as I had idealized them, I had to dismiss them with arrogance. I felt imprisoned by all their concepts, and thirsty for my own experience.

On a Buddha full moon (in April) I had my first conscious taste of meditation. I sat with an Indian guru, Dr. K., and about fifty of his disciples in a carpeted living room in a middle-class area of Rome.

The instructions were to just watch and sit silently. The darkness of the night, the full moon, the fragrance of jasmine lingered in the silence. I closed my eyes, forgot all about the instructions, and found myself in a quiet pool of serenity. At that time, I couldn't fully appreciate what had happened. It just remained like a seed and a blessing to keep on searching.

PREMARTHA:

I NEEDED TO CONNECT AND I NEEDED TO BELONG

When I came back from India, I realized that I had to start living an ordinary life. And that this would mean opening up to other people again. And this time especially to women.

She was tall, wild, and went for what she wanted. She was ready to fight for my heart. I needed to connect and I needed to belong. Our lives turned to each other. We both dove into each other, and dove in deep. Our honeymoon was traveling back overland to India. This time no drugs; all the intensity came from facing each other. Sex came easily. We were both capable of great hate that could leave us exhausted and weary. But we stayed bonded together in an urge to meet that was equally as great. When we came back, I started to study psychology.

Life was full of adventure and things to explore together. A few years followed, full of journeys and experiments. But as my hidden need for security came to the surface, I slowly started to make the relationship less dangerous. Things felt safer when they were known.

Our life started to take a solid form. We studied, we lived ecologically. No more drugs, no more flashy clothes. Everything became normal. We cut our hair short, and dressed well. Things started to feel perfect. The last step was to have a baby. It felt so matter of fact that I didn't even think about it. But at this point sex began to fail. We started to replace what at one time came easily, with a lot of trying. Frustration was setting in with sudden outbursts of hostility, followed by long silent retreats. Without knowing, I was repeating the patterns that I rejected so much in my parents.

I was in my mid-twenties, and I didn't know what to do. I was disappointed by the failure of our love. Yet, I couldn't let go.

It is a mystery to me what brings the Master into our lives. In that phase of my life, I cannot remember any thought or feeling about it. I was just unable to move. But I must have been waiting. Maybe I was calling out as I had done in my childhood. But I certainly didn't make any sound. I must have prepared the ground somewhere, in a deep part of me.

Because, one day Osho entered my life and broke it open again. The longing that appeared left me breathless, as if the sun shone with full force into the shadow of my being.

We shared enough love and friendship that she understood. "You love him more now than you love me," she said. And so, I decided to follow my heart.

SVARUP:

HE IS THE MAN

I met him at a party, on another full-moon night. He had just come back from several years in India, where he had been living in a cave up in the Himalayas. He was different from anyone I had met before. He hardly spoke, had the laughter of a child, and a touch of the devil. I thought, "He is the man." We sat around the squares of Rome for a whole night, silently communing with each other, while the world around us became a colorful temple of downtrodden hippies and marble statues that gave sacredness to our meeting.

We moved in together, built a house in the countryside, and flew to India. Upon arrival in Bombay in the middle of the night, the familiar terror of my childhood sleepless nights crept in. All sense of safety was gone, in a land where death was open for all to live with. We moved to the mountains. The silence of the Himalayas had a deep, overwhelming sound, and I surrendered to the simple life. I learned to make fire, bread, to wear one cloth for all purposes, and to appreciate what is truly essential to everyday life. Sacredness was a well-cooked chapati or a cup of warm buffalo milk.

After a few months, we returned to the West. As we landed, I realized that I no longer knew who I was. Gone was the safety of my studies. Gone was my political rebelliousness. I felt empty and confused, like an alien. I tried to control myself. I could not listen to the little girl inside me, afraid of this familiar feeling, begging me to stop and take care. I decided to bury my fears into the dailiness of household chores and taking care of my man, just like my mother had done in her youth.

Our child was conceived. Pregnancy was like a homecoming. I felt the full permission to wait, dream, paint, and finish my studies. Next to the fireplace, in deep intimacy, while life was growing inside me, I was once more searching for its meaning in Sartre and R. D. Laing. I was painting angels and colorful, vast landscapes, doing Yoga, and preparing my body to nurture and open up to the life growing inside my womb. I finished my university thesis on the day labor started. Now experience truly gained the upper hand on theory.

Birth happened quickly in an overcrowded Roman hospital. The mystery happened anyway. I recall the sensuous explosion, the gratefulness, the baby in my arms. We were separated immediately after for a few days. When we finally came together, it took an incredible effort to reconnect. The bridge was never fully repaired. Breastfeeding, holding, caring, adoring happened. And yet, a part of me remained distracted, brewing inside. I could not be the mother I thought I should be. I could not be the wife. Sometimes, in the dark of the night, I would hold Ram, that's his name, close to my heart, and share with him a fleeting moment of merging.

PREMARTHA:

Entering into Sannyas

Soon after my arrival in India, this time in Pune, I took sannyas from Osho. At my initiation, he said:

> One part of your will is fighting with another part of your will. It is a kind of civil war that goes on inside. And that's what the so-called saints have been telling people to do. Fight with yourself, fight with anger, fight with greed, fight with sex. Sex has a part of your will, and then you fight with it—another part of your will. This way you become entangled in a civil war, and to be in a civil war is to be in misery. You dissipate energy. You can't live, you lose all vitality. You can't be fresh and young, and you can't be intelligent either. You become poorer and poorer every day. (1)

His words got through to me. They entered a place that I had kept closed for a lifetime. I had the experience of how it felt to build a house on quicksand, but I didn't have any understanding of it. Instead of stopping and looking at the foundation of my life, I had been busy adding and repairing, changing the constantly crumbling walls of my personality. Here he exposed my whole personality. It felt like death. It made me want to run and hide. To retreat as I had been doing so many times before.

Yet, the love that reached me when he talked about the child that lives inside me, deeply touched my heart. It brought back the remembrance of childhood. Of a child beyond conditioning, beyond the prison of a personality. It felt like a fresh sea breeze entering a long-closed room, cleaning out the dead air hanging there.

As he talked to me about sannyas, he said:

> A real sannyasin will become a child again, he will put his fragments together again; he will not fight with himself. That's the first rule of sannyas: not to fight with yourself. Rather, try to understand, and through understanding, greed disappears, anger disappears, and they don't leave a trace; they don't leave wounds and marks behind. (2)

And that's how I entered sannyas.

The work around Osho has always been multidimensional. Therapy goes alongside meditation, working alongside playing, dancing, and singing. Everything has its own importance. I jumped wholeheartedly into the commune around him. I moved from participating in therapy groups to working in the commune, from meditation to celebration.

A new love affair with a woman happened. It was a very sweet and nourishing meeting. Surrounded by the commune, we could be like children. Exploring sex, intimacy, and friendship in a non-isolated way.

When Osho moved from India to America, Rajneeshpuram was founded. It was a communal experiment in the Oregon desert. At that time, I was given the opportunity to learn to lead groups in Spiritual Therapy. I started with Rebirthing. From there, I moved to Encounter, and then I fell in love with Primal and Tantra.

It was a great gift of life. It gave me the chance to intimately experience the joy that comes when one's potential unfolds. That of myself, and that of others.

It gave me permission to look back at my own life, with understanding and compassion. It gave me the skills to support others to look back, to learn from their own lives, and to "give birth" to themselves again.

Everything around the Master keeps on changing. As soon as it felt like the American commune would be there forever, it came to an end. And, as it came to an end, so did my relationship. It was with love that we parted.

SVARUP:

TRUE HELPLESS LOVE

After eight months I left. My little son was bounced around quite a bit between me, his father, his grandmothers. We were all hurt, acting out of our wounds, outrage, concern, and fear. Finally, I took Ram with me to London. I was once more moving into unknown territory. Ram became my imperious and affectionate companion. In the innocent way of a child, he would constantly give voice to both the fears and the common sense I ignored in equal measure.

In London, I was introduced to R. D. Laing, the hero of my studies and a symbol for a whole generation that challenged the concept of normality. Over the years that followed, my relationship to him became a complex one. He was a new father, and a teacher for me. He kept everyone on edge, with sudden outbursts of genius, anger, sarcasm, tears, and poetry. He and the people around him had lots of kids, little wise-eyed beings in all degrees of wildness. Ram was welcomed and taken in as part of the tribe. I had found a new family. I met philosophers, therapists, writers who were all, in a thousand and one ways, constantly experimenting.

After a while, Laing gave me a community to run. I could choose among those people Laing sent as possible residents Ram's response to them determined my final decision about their participation. In my unresolved omnipotence, I thought this was great, without realizing that a little boy needs quiet and some rules in order to feel grounded and safe. But, Ram had the oddest and most loving collection of baby sitters and friends I have ever come across.

Laing continued teaching and supervising me. I loved our talks that would spread across and stretch the mind all the way from Bateson to Buddha, with sudden turns into very down-to-earth practical advice about specific events in the house. He would also come to the house for a crazy, often musical, Friday dinner every week. The community quickly filled up with poets, artists, musicians who had all lost their way home.

Day by day, Patricia the poetess, Aemon the guitar player, Nicky the pianist, David the actor, and all friends and acquaintances would spend time in waiting. No medication was ever used. Occasionally, one of them would burst into a psychotic episode, faraway from the shores of a broken heart. Because, looking back, that's what it was: an unendurable well of pain bursting through a psychic structure that wouldn't contain it. Through the tears of the psychosis, for as long as it's peak lasted, fragments of truth, moments of light would surface. They were discontinuous fragments of the bliss that comes with disidentification. But then, the darkness closed in again, and they would feel less than ordinary. The well-meaning and well-organized English suburban world of launderettes, supermarkets, and fish and chips became the measure of the normality they could not attain. Their pain remained unacknowledged, at the edges, unspeakable.

I gradually became aware that in that respect I could not consider myself different from my "crazy" friends. I was trying to help them partly because I was fascinated by the heights they could touch, but also in order to drown my own unacknowledged pain and loneliness. It took me some more years before I also realized how much sharing and heartfulness I had experienced with them. I came to recognize that while my helpfulness had failed on many occasions, in our little "commune" I had received and given true, helpless love for the first time.

Ram started asking for his father with whom he had kept in periodic contact. He was five, he was a boy, and I couldn't set boundaries for him or provide enough male support around him. I sent him to Italy, to live with his father, initiating a process of separation that took years of painful silences and powerful confrontations for both of us to heal. He is now a young man, on his way to measure his idealism with the reality of his heart.

Around the same time as Ram left, the community came to an end. I felt really alone for the first time in my life, wondering what I had learned so far. The pain of separation from my little son was touching the deeper chords of an earlier feeling that had accompanied me since my own birth. I decided to stop denying this pain, although only after many years of work on myself and with others, did I come to understand and embrace it.

I said good-bye to Laing with gratefulness, and a growing longing for a truly ordinary life.

TRUST INTO WHAT IS MOST ORDINARY AND OBVIOUS IN LIFE...SANNYAS

I met some new friends. Colorful meditators from the world of Osho. They came from all sorts of backgrounds and did a very energetic and alive meditation together. It was called Dynamic meditation. I joined in. During the cathartic stage of this meditation, before I knew it, the scream I had contained for so long burst out. In the silence of the fourth stage, something that had slept in me for so long started yawning out of its slumber. When the silence ended into the last dancing stage, the gate that my little girl had thought closed for so many years, opened. The angels and devils of her childhood had become one. And they were alive, rebellious, ecstatic friends.

I went to see Osho in Oregon. When I saw him, I cried and cried, and a deep healing, a sense of trust, returned. Trust into what is most ordinary and obvious in life, and the permission to explore further dimensions of the heart.

More than once, this trust has been shaken and challenged by all sorts of events around the Master. Each time, up to now, these challenges have evaporated into an unexplainable fragrance, and into the renewal of the mystery of what transpires between Master and disciple. Osho's body has been burned away. And yet, the flavor of love that dispersed into the wind with his ashes is still alive inside me and all my beloved fellow travelers.

I joined the Osho commune in Milan. Life in the commune of the Master was sometimes pure hell. You were moved around, you were suddenly given a new job, rules were created and dismissed within one day, and that was our meditation. At the same time, though, this whole circus created an enormous amount of energy and alertness in all of us. I learned to do things I would have never done, from waitressing to carpentry, from accounting to working in a discotheque, and I met people whom I would never have chosen to meet. Celebration was on at any excuse.

I was also given positions of power which stretched and expressed sides of me that I wouldn't have otherwise liked to see. I found myself first totally identified with being someone "special," only to later see my bubble of self-importance blow up into nothing.

I started participating in therapy groups. I learned that the things I was denying and rejecting about myself needed to be faced, and exposed to the sunlight. Many times I felt deeply touched by rediscovering an innocent little girl hiding at the core of what I had disowned and judged about myself. As I learned to appreciate and recognize this innocence, more and more energy and love became available.

These experiences rekindled my passion for working with people. This time, it would be people like me, not mad and not sane, just individuals on the search. I started assisting and then leading a wide range of groups, but my love guided me to Primal...and to a Primal Therapist.

PREMARTHA:

WE DANCE JOYOUSLY AND INTENSELY THE DANCE OF LIFE

That's when I met Svarup. It took a while to get used to each other. In many ways, we are polar opposites. But the friction that this produces is also a source of creativity. We share with each other many different sides, the lovers, the friends, the fellow travelers, the partners in the work. We had to learn to give space to all of them. Initially, always one part tended to suffer while another part was growing. Sex suffered under the expansion of the work, and then the work suffered under our need to be friends. But, as we have always been committed to the seemingly impossible, we have kept recreating opportunities for all of them to flower.

It's a process that brings a lot of friendliness and compassion. Through it, we are learning that it's more fun to support than to sabotage each other. For that, we really need to look back at our childhood wounds, to understand the ways we learned to protect ourselves and mistrust others. But, with her I have felt safe to do this, and the child in me has not felt betrayed.

Our love remains something private. Since it is open-ended, it is impossible to define. We share the joy of being on the path to freedom together. To have compassion with each other when we stumble and fall. To understand each other when our fears and insecurities come with traveling on an unknown road. To learn the art of loving and the magic of supporting each other without turning it into overprotection and consolation.

We also share the peace of moving into intimacy and sexuality slowly and naturally. To bring light and awareness into areas that have remained dark and closed for a long time. To face the skeletons locked up in the cupboards of our past. Our meeting is also a reminder of how temporary things are. We learn to enjoy the preciousness of this moment, its expression, before all fades back into the greater existence again.

We dance joyously and intensely the dance of life. Over the years we have been living and traveling together, our own style of work has grown. One specific expression of it is the "Twice Born - Childhood Deconditioning" process. Since we have deeply explored our own past, with its pain and beauty, it feels like this is the right thing to share with others. It is a blessing to see how this work has come to a flowering.

We have always lived in the context of the Master and his commune. Initially, we lived closely around Him in the different Communes in America, Europe and India. After Osho left the body, we remained living in the Pune Buddhafield in India. After years, we decided it was time to leave, and explore the world with new eyes and new senses.

It has been a blessing to experience the beauty of the world. A few years ago, we discovered Lesbos, an island in Greece. There, close to the Osho Afroz Center, we found what we had been looking for.

In the beautiful hills, covered with oreganon and thyme, we settled and built our own home. We are surrounded by olive trees, figs and almonds. We created a beautiful rose garden next to our safe stone house, and built a wooden Japanese retreat house in a grove of poplars, oaks, pomegranates and wild vines.

Part of the year, we reside there in peace and gratitude. The other part, we continue traveling, sharing the work with all those friends that come to explore themselves.

These days, we find ourselves rich with the experience of a life together.

Life is an incredible teaching, and to have met a living Master in one's lifetime has deepened the teaching in ways we could never have expected.

What else remains, than to bow in gratitude to life itself....

SVARUP:

LOOKING TOGETHER AT WHAT LAY BEYOND US

Around this time, I met Premartha who was traveling around Osho's communes in Europe as a spiritual therapist. Our friendship grew into love and intimacy through the hiccups of constantly moving.

We were among the first to arrive back in Pune, India, when Osho moved into his ashram again in 1986. It wasn't easy to grow together around a master who was constantly exposing jealousy, comparison, possessiveness, and all you didn't want to hear about relationship. I had to face the urge to deny, justify, feel different from others. I asked Osho about love, and in one masterful blow he exposed me and lifted me up till I could look at it from his eagle's viewpoint.

> Instead of your life being an oceanic love, it is suffering in a gutter of dirty jealousy. But unless you start looking inwards and finding the roots, you will not be able to transform it.

You are blessed, Svarup, that just without any effort my silence reaches to your heart. It will purify you, it will destroy all that is poisonous in you—jealousy, anger, greed, attachment, possessiveness. It will make you just a beautiful flower of love. (3)

Throughout our time together, Premartha and I have shared a love for sitting at the feet of the Master. From this, we learned that by sitting and looking together at what lies beyond us, we could grow more intimate and friendly than by only focusing on each other.

For some reason which needs to remain a mystery, perhaps to keep its aliveness and openness, we stayed together. Through conflict, merging, heaven and hell, we got to know each other deeply. And we have made a beautiful time out of it.

We both worked as Primal therapists in Pune, in a whirlpool of different nationalities and conditionings, and in Europe, on the road through different countries.

The childhood work around the Master has been constantly progressing and evolving. In the beginning it was raw. Pain, anger, hate had to be released and exposed, like pockets of hidden poison that threatened the basic life energy. Catharsis, losing control completely in the safe environment of a field of consciousness and meditation was, and still is, a liberation for me and the hundreds of people we have supported in this experiment.

To this necessary explosion, more and more understanding and compassion for our human condition, both as children and parents, has been added. It is an adventure to unravel the intricacies of conditioning, and to support the natural capacity of the child in us to be real and true, to unfold.

The greatest gift for me is to watch what flowers when the false is removed. It is beautiful to celebrate this flowering for a moment together, and then part again on our individual search.

Out of this love, grew our branch on the tree of childhood work, which includes knowledge and poetry in equal measure, some methods, and our longing to reconnect with the source.

The journey is not over. We are entering yet another stage of our exploration, this time moving closer to life and nature, living the teachings of the Master, as well as passing them on.

In the fragrant world of ordinariness, in the middle of our rose garden overlooking the blue blue sea, we relax and enjoy the tremendous luxury of just being. In the sharing with beloveds, we enjoy the great privilege to be part of a greater process of transformation...

Life should not mean, life should be. An end in itself. Going nowhere. Enjoying here and now. Celebrating. Only then you can be soft. If you are trying to be of use, you will become hard. If you are trying to achieve something, you will become hard. If you are trying to fight you will become hard. Surrender. Be soft and tender. And allow the flow of life to take you wherever it takes you. Let the goal of the whole be your goal. Don't seek any private goal. You just be a part, and an infinite beauty and grace happens.

Try to feel it...what I am saying; it's not a question of understanding, it's not a question of intellectual capacity. Feel it, what I am saying. Imbibe it, what I am saying. Let it be there with you. Allow it to settle deep in your being: Life should not mean, life should be.

And then suddenly you are soft. All hardness goes, disappears, melts. The baby is rediscovered, you have again become a child, those transparent eyes of childhood are available again.

You can look and then this greenery is totally different, and the songs of the birds are totally different. Then the whole has a totally different significance. It has no meaning, it has significance. Meaning is concerned with utility, significance with delight.

Delight in it and you will be soft. Flow with the river. Become the river.

(Osho, *Tao the Three Treasures*, Vol. IV)

QUOTES

PROLOGUE
(1)   Osho, the Great Pilgrimage from here to here, Poona, 1988
INTRODUCTION
(1) R.D.Laing, The politics of Experience, Penguin, England, 1967
(2) Lao Tzu, Tao Te Ching, Penguin, England,1963
CHAPTER 1
(1)   Robert Dilts, Time lines, Anchor point magazine, USA, 1997
(2)   Osho, The book of Wisdom
(3)   John Bradshaw, Homecoming, Bantam, New York, 1990
(4)   Kabir, Songs of Kabir, from Osho, the Fish in the Sea is not thirsty, India, 1980
CHAPTER 2
(1)   Frederic Leboyer, Pour une Naissance sans Violence, Seuil, 1974
(2)   Thomas Verny, The secret life of the unborn child, Dell Publishing, New York,
        1981
(3)Osho, The hidden Mysteries of the Eastern temples
(4)Rumi, Magnificent one, Larsen, USA, 1993
CHAPTER 3
(1)   R.D.Laing, The politics of Experience, Penguin, England, 1967
(2)   A.H. Almaas, The point of existence, Diamond books, Berkeley, 1996
(3)   John Bradshaw, Homecoming, Bantam, New York, 1990
(4)   Bert Hellinger, Touching love, Carl Auer-System publishing, Heidelberg, 1997
(5)   Basho, On Love and Barley, Penguin, UK, 1985
CHAPTER 4
(1)   Alexander Lowen, The Language of the body, Macmillan, new York, 1958
(2)   Jessica Benjamin, The Bonds of Love, Pantheon books, New York, 1988
(3)   W. Reich, the Function of the Orgasm, Orgone Institute Press, New York, 1942
(4)   W. Reich, the Function of the Orgasm, Orgone Institute Press, New York, 1942
(5)   Saraha, Royal Song, from Osho, Tantric Transformation, India, 1978
CHAPTER 5
(1)   Margaret Mahler, Fred Pine, and Anni Bergman, The Psychological Birth of the Human Infant, Basic books, New York, 1975
(2)   Jessica Benjamin, The Bonds of Love, Pantheon books, New York, 1988

(3)   John Bradshaw, Creating Love, Bantam, New York, 1994

(4)   A.H. Almaas, The Void, Diamond books, Berkeley, 1986

(5)   Soseki, from Osho, Isan, no footprints in the blue Sky, Poona 1988

CHAPTER 6

(1)   Jessica Benjamin, The Bonds of Love, Pantheon books, New York,1988

(2)   W. Reich, The function of the Orgasm, Orgone Institute Press, New York, 1942

(3)   Arthur Janov, The primal Scream, Abacus, London,1973

(4)   Bert Hellinger, Touching Love, Carl Auer-System publishing, Heidelberg, 1997

(5)   Osho, Yoga the Alpha and the Omega, vol. IV, Poona, 1976

(6)   Marion Woodman, Mother as a Patriarch, from Mothers and Fathers, Spring publications, Dallas, 1991

(7)   Robert Bly, The Sibling Society, Vintage Books, New York, 1977

(8)   Robert Bly, The Hunger for the King, from Mothers and Fathers, Spring publications, Dallas 1991

(9)   Robert Bly, The Hunger for the King, from Mothers and Fathers, Spring publications, Dallas 1991

(10)   from Osho, Dogen, the Zen Master, India, 1988

CHAPTER 7

(1)   H. Almaas, The Pearl beyond Price, Diamond books, Berkeley, 1988

(2)   Jessica Benjamin, The Bonds of Love, Pantheon books, New York, 1988

(3)   Joëlle de Gravelaine, La Déesse Sauvage, Dangles, France, 1993

(4)   Marion Woodman, Mother as a Patriarch, from Mothers and Fathers, Spring publications, Dallas, 1991

(5)   Bert Hellinger, Touching Love, Carl Auer-System publishing, Heidelberg, 1997

(6)   Basho, On Love and Barley, Penguin, UK, 1985

CHAPTER 8

(1)   W. Reich, Children of the future

(2)   Thomas Verny, The secret life of the unborn child, Dell Publishing, New York, 1981

(3)   Arthur Janov, The primal Scream, Abacus, London,1973

(4)   Osho, Don't let yourself be upset by the Sutra, rather upset the Sutra yourself,
        Osho International foundation, New York, 1979

(6)   H. Almaas, The Void, Diamond books, Berkeley, 1986

(7)   Buddha, from Osho, The Dhammapada Vol. IX, India, 1978

CHAPTER 9
(1)   Sheila Kitzinger, The experience of Childbirth, Penguin, London, 1962
(2)   Garry Hamilton, New Scientist, Reed Business information magazines, London, 1998
(3)   Stanislav Grof, beyond the Brain, State New York University Press, 1985
(4)   W. Reich, Children of the future
(5)   Frederic Leboyer, Pour une Naissance sans Violence, Seuil, 1974
(6)   Thomas Verny, The secret life of the unborn child, Dell Publishing, New York, 1981
(7)   Stanislav Grof, Beyond the Brain, State of New York University Press, 1985
(8)   Leonard Orr and Sondra Ray, Rebirthing in the New Age, celestial Arts, 1977
(9)   Frederic Leboyer, Pour une Naissance sans Violence, Seuil, 1974
(10) Osho, Meditation: the first and last freedom
(11) Kabir, translated by Rabindranath Tagore, One Hundred Poems of Kabir, Macmillan, India, 1973
(12) Kalil Gibran, the Prophet
CHAPTER 10
(1)   Frederic Leboyer, Pour une Naissance sans Violence, Seuil, 1974
(2)   Thomas Verny, The secret life of the unborn child, Dell Publishing, New York, 1981
(3)   R.D.Laing, The Divided Self, Tavistock publications, England, 1959
(4)   R.D.Laing, the Bird of Paradise, Penguin, London, 1967
(5)   Lao Tzu, Tao Te Ching, Penguin, London,1963
(6)   Kabir, translated by Rabindranath Tagore, One Hundred Poems of Kabir, Macmillan, India, 1973
(7)   Jalal Al-Din Rumi, Magnificent one, Larsen, USA, 1993
EPILOGUE
(1) Osho, Don't let yourself be upset by the Sutra, rather upset the Sutra yourself,
      Osho International foundation, New York, 1979
(2) Osho, Don't let yourself be upset by the Sutra, rather upset the Sutra yourself,
      Osho International foundation, New York, 1979
(3) Osho, Om Mani Padme Hum, The Sound of Silence, The Diamond in the Lotus, Osho International foundation, New York, 1988

CPSIA information can be obtained
at www.ICGtesting.com
Printed in the USA
BVHW08s0736121018
529914BV00001B/336/P

9 783833 466021